MARTHA'S VINEYARD

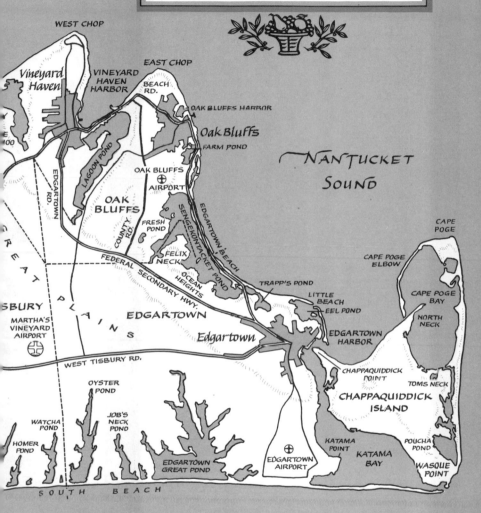

WEST CHOP

Vineyard Haven

VINEYARD HAVEN HARBOR

EAST CHOP

BEACH RD.

OAK BLUFFS HARBOR

Oak Bluffs

FARM POND

NANTUCKET SOUND

EE 100

EDGARTOWN RD.

LAGOON POND

OAK BLUFFS AIRPORT

OAK BLUFFS

COUNTY RD.

FRESH POND

FELIX NECK

SENGEKONTACKET POND

EDGARTOWN BEACH

FEDERAL SECONDARY HWY.

OCEAN HEIGHTS

CAPE POGE

CAPE POGE ELBOW

TRAPP'S POND

LITTLE BEACH

EEL POND

CAPE POGE BAY

NORTH NECK

GREAT PLAINS

SBURY

MARTHA'S VINEYARD AIRPORT

EDGARTOWN

Edgartown

EDGARTOWN HARBOR

CHAPPAQUIDDICK POINT

TOMS NECK

WEST TISBURY RD.

CHAPPAQUIDDICK ISLAND

OYSTER POND

JOB'S NECK POND

WATCHA POND

HOMER POND

EDGARTOWN GREAT POND

EDGARTOWN AIRPORT

KATAMA POINT

KATAMA BAY

POUCHA POND

WASQUE POINT

SOUTH BEACH

N
W E
S

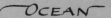
OCEAN

0   Miles   3

palacios

No Island Is An Island
by Anne W. Simon

There is acute distress across the country, a sense of outrage that the place where you live cannot be what it has always been. Crowds invade privacy and alter lives, subjecting most Americans to a change in their environment. It turns men against each other, challenges town governments, and is rapidly gaining the attention of the nation's lawmakers. We are quickly and painfully undergoing a land-use revolution.

The conflict is telescoped on the island of Martha's Vineyard where the life style of centuries has changed within a decade. Developers carve up old farms, the tourist business disrupts once-peaceful towns and the rural countryside. Despite the devotion of a prestigious assortment of influential people—college presidents, famous literary figures, noted political leaders—the Vineyard is seriously threatened. Its unique natural resources, widely

(continued on back flap)

No Island Is An Island

THE ORDEAL
OF MARTHA'S VINEYARD

No Island Is An Island

THE ORDEAL OF MARTHA'S VINEYARD

BY ANNE W. SIMON

GARDEN CITY, NEW YORK

DOUBLEDAY & COMPANY, INC.

1973

CREDITS

Pictures
M. Zide—1, 6, 21
Peter Simon—2, 3, 4, 5, 10, 12, 13, 14, 15, 17, 18, 23, 25, 26, 27, 28,
    29, 30, 31, 32, 33, 34, 40, 41, 42
Alfred O. Gross, from National Audubon Society—7
Photos by Edith Blake—8, 9, 19, 20, 22, 37
The Whaling Museum, New Bedford, Mass.—11, 16
Clara F. Dinsmore, Dukes County Historical Society—24
Vermont Development Agency, Montpelier, Vt.—35
Photo by Clerin W. Zumwalt—36
Sherburne Associates, Nantucket, Mass.—38
Wide World Photos—39

Maps
Drawn by Raphael Palacios
Original research for map entitled "Developments Under Way, June 1972"
    done by Susan Whiting

ISBN: 0-385-02574-2
Library of Congress Catalog Card Number 72–92242
Copyright © 1973 by Anne W. Simon, Trustee under Trust Agreement
    dated April 14, 1972
Printed in the United States of America
First Edition

To the memory of my parents
ALMA MORGENTHAU • MAURICE WERTHEIM
*who by their example gave me
an abiding devotion to
the land*

Foreword

The capacity of people to feel deeply about whatever part of the world they have become attached to is evident in today's massive struggle to protect the environment. It is the ability to be profoundly stirred by the sight of an ocean, a mountain, or an open field that urges us to apply ourselves to the question which has become one of the monumental dilemmas of our time—how best to make use of our land. Across the country, passions are aroused at the threat of loss of the land as we know it; people attack each other, despair, surrender, or are moved to put their minds to work toward a solution. Love of land, that fundamental feeling, touches off the use of many abilities among many people.

Love of Martha's Vineyard and the imminence of its destruction drove me to find out what had happened and what choices were still open for the island. It is not in spite of my emotions about this place (which are such that still, after more than twenty summers here, I greet it every morning with fresh delight) but indeed because of them that I embarked on the search for facts. I could not rest content with nostalgic memories of a now vanishing Vineyard because here as almost everywhere there is still hope, a slim but viable chance.

The Vineyard, small as it is and isolated from the mainland, is no monolith. Geologically, geographically, anthropologically, it has many aspects; it is socially, sociologically, and politically varied. Its history in itself could fill volumes; each of its six towns is worthy of detailed description; its winter people and its summer people have cultures within cultures, attitudes which cross every line, confound every rule. The island fairly bursts with pertinent information and has so many dimensions that no two people would describe it the same way, nor would they suffer the same threats, resent the same changes, endorse the same goals for the island's future. Vineyard people are likely to be as independent as the object of their affections.

To relate what has happened to this much-loved, highly personalized island, why it has happened, and what opportunities are still open to it required a selection from this abundant store. Rather than attempt an encyclopedic account, I decided to tell a few of its parts in some detail, and chose what seemed to me to be representative happenings.

Choice was arbitrary but not capricious. Events had to have made a dent, not only in my mind but on the island; their historical setting had to make them more understandable. The people I describe had to have assumed a meaningful place in the Vineyard spectrum, one way or another. Actions off-island, whether directed to the Vineyard from the State House in Boston or from the nation's capital, or indirectly related to what might happen here by their example, had to have the virtue of short-range impact and long-range implication. Anything that did not meet these standards was sternly, if often reluctantly, set aside.

This way of presenting the turmoil of the island as it confronts change has drawbacks. By necessity it omits some venerable island institutions, some pressing problems, some valiant efforts and important people; others are mentioned more briefly than I might have wished. Difficult as it was to exclude certain of my personal interests—places and people who particularly fascinate, infuriate, or enchant me—the importance of what is happening here to alter the Vineyard, possibly forever, asks for an objective view.

I have attempted to tell enough about certain parts of the

island's ordeal to present the whole. As it happens, the awful
dilemma of land use on this small island of Martha's Vineyard
in turn suggests, in minuscule, the outsized problem in the nation.

The situation changes all the time. As a nation, our ideas
about land use are still so unformed that last week's calamity
can be this week's victory and next week's trend. On the Vineyard, during the crucial months which are recounted here
against the background of the mounting crises of the 1960s,
there has been no certainty about what will happen to anything. Even the fish in the island waters are in a state of flux,
attendant on threatened exploration for oil off the Grand
Banks. A statement about fish, fishing, or fishing boats, accurate
as it is written today, may be hopelessly out of date when it is
read tomorrow, and this applies to almost everything except
what has been said and done, a record which is part of history.

This book does not presume to be the last word on what has
happened to the island. Because it is alive and moving fast, the
Vineyard will not stand still for a last word between hard
covers; even its weekly newspapers cannot keep up with its
news. But if what has been here recorded helps us know where
we are going by understanding where we have been, it will,
perhaps, add a measure of hope to the island's future. In this
sense it is a love letter to Martha's Vineyard.

My ever deepening interest in this island's crisis has long
been encouraged by John B. Oakes, whose unshakable dedication to the evolution of a land-use ethic in this country continues to make a significant national impact; and by Henry
Beetle Hough, Vineyard sage, inveterate walker, and generous
adviser, who gave time and thought to this undertaking. I am
fortunate in having the firm if gentle editorial guidance of Ken
McCormick in creating this book, and the efforts of my
agent Dorothy Olding in its behalf. Writing it was expedited by

the enthusiastic interest of Eunice S. Whiting, able research
assistant, and by the Washington-based research of Virginia W.
Langman. Several fellow Vineyarders took the time to read the
manuscript, criticize and discuss it, adding understanding. I am
deeply grateful to all these people; they are part of this book as
are my children and grandchildren who will, I trust, always
know a Vineyard worthy of their beloved selves.

Martha's Vineyard
July, 1972

Contents

A NOTE ON SOURCES

The contemporary history of Martha's Vineyard exists chiefly in the minds of the people who made it. Most of it has not been recorded before this undertaking. I asked some of the key figures in this account to tell me their views on the subject at hand, information which I believe was essential for accurate reporting of what happened. They were exceedingly generous and co-operative, taking time from busy schedules to contribute to this account. My appreciation for this consideration is acknowledged with the most sincere gratitude to each of the people I talked with, whose names are listed in the back of this volume. They made this book possible.

The Vineyard's two newspapers were important in several ways. The *Vineyard Gazette,* founded in 1846, contains in its files a record of Vineyard happenings, attitudes, and daily life, from mid-nineteenth century forward, a rich lode made available to me through the kindness of its editor. More recent issues provided me with a running account of island events; editorials reflect a view of the current scene which, since the *Gazette*'s circulation is close to 10,000, is an influence not to be overlooked in considering Vineyard happenings. The *Grapevine,* started in 1971, puts its circulation at 4,000, has a different approach to the news and a different editorial stance, giving its readers added information and opinion. Both papers were invaluable.

All written sources are listed chapter by chapter in the bibliography at the back of this volume. They too reflect the contemporary nature of the subject which, except for the historical background, has not had time to become the focus of a book before this. Information was culled chiefly from pamphlets, reports, research studies, and position papers, some of which have not been published. Space does not permit inclusion in the bibliography of the voluminous correspondence which is also part of the book's sources. Some of the letters explain or expand on an action or position, some are in answer to my endless queries on one abstruse detail or another; some letters are an exchange between other people, made available to me by one or another of the correspondents. They are frequently quoted, by permission, as their writers' opinions.

I have included a listing of the various forms which the proposal for national protection of the island—the so-called Kennedy Bill—has taken to date. In addition to its research value, this first published documentation of the beginnings of what may become a law is a suggestion of the size of the undertaking ahead for the island and, by inference, for the nation.

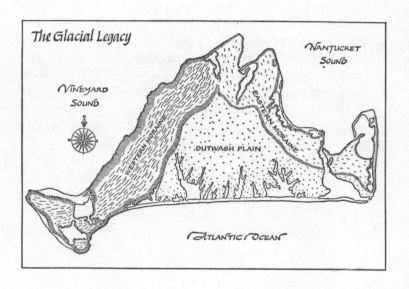

The Glacial Legacy

NANTUCKET SOUND

VINEYARD SOUND

WESTERN MORAINE

EASTERN MORAINE

OUTWASH PLAIN

ATLANTIC OCEAN

CHAPTER ONE

Island to Save

Martha's Vineyard is about to vanish . . . or be rescued. The choice can still be made and it matters more than one might suspect.

A pressing national dilemma—what use shall we make of our land—is particularized and highly visible on this rural island lying south of Cape Cod, one of the last warm-water islands of its size still relatively unspoiled on the eastern seaboard. An intelligent solution to the Vineyard's acute problems will hearten the nation, its extinction as an entity will lose us a chance that will not come again. Martha's Vineyard is not just another place, ripe for ravaging, but a unique national treasure, containing such a range of resources within its hundred square miles that it is of intense scientific, archaeological, geological, and historic interest. Aesthetically superb, it is as tempting to the destructive process as the apple in Eden.

Sudden change, the virulent American phenomenon peculiar to this era, which rages through rural places across the country, swift, planless, and devastating, has now jumped the seven miles of water from mainland to island and threatens to alter the Vineyard for all time. Change will homogenize it, grind its character to mediocrity, and make the place indistinguishable from the brutally overdeveloped mainland coast . . . vanished in all but name.

The pace of change steps up fast. Twenty years ago, even

ten, the Vineyard seemed indestructible, having been given its astounding variety by ancient glaciers, its history by human settlement dating back to at least 2270 B.C., and its remarkable character by harmonious interaction between man and land which has altered only imperceptibly over centuries. The nature of the island permeates its successive cultures; you find it in the whaling captains' white houses facing Edgartown harbor, in the rambling stone walls of Chilmark sheep farmers, in Gay Head wigwam holes and early Indian graves (burned over to keep the spirits from wandering), in artifacts from the Late Archaic people who hunted deer in what was then a great forest. It appeared improbable that the island identity could ever be destroyed.

No one wanted to destroy it, few believed it to be even seriously threatened. "We've kept the Vineyard this way for more than three hundred years," descendants of the first white settlers would say, "and there's no reason why we shouldn't continue to do so." The attitude was understandable. The Vineyard had, indeed, stayed more or less the same for three hundred years, and its residents—men who made their living fishing, farming, storekeeping, building, and, more recently, in real estate or the hotel business—traditionally took care of the affairs of the towns, voting on issues, making the rules, electing officials from among themselves.

Until the 1970s the Vineyard was peacefully immune to the modern stress that was about to attack it. The explosive pressures building up on the mainland for land development and tourist activity were too remote to threaten; there were, as yet, few visible reasons to cast off the old reliable ways, many reasons to believe that these were the best ways.

Waterlogged fingers in the dike managed to hold back offending change, defeating such proposals as a motel for the quiet fishing village of Menemsha, a portion of forest cut down to enlarge the airport, sewage dumped in the Vineyard Sound by

Falmouth, just across the water. Town meetings continued to discuss and postpone zoning, the Garden Club continued to keep advertising off the roadsides.

As the flood tide of change began to make itself known, such activity seemed like innocent child's play. With only the most subtle warnings, a dozen simultaneous pressures abruptly appeared: propositions for the island's first trailer park, first night club, first condominium on the beach, for more advertising ("Come to the unspoiled gentle islands!"), more commerce. Harbors and ponds became polluted, beaches overrun and littered, quarter-acre lot developments swept across old farms, and the lovely silhouette of rounded hills was punctured over and again by new houses.

On this island, in microcosm, the American dilemma is laid out. As a nation we have nowhere near the sophisticated land policy of the British or Scandinavians. To make optimum use of our land's many parts, we require an approach to the whole, a firm consensus, such as Britain's protective umbrella, from which we can direct change instead of being submerged by it. On the minicontinent of Martha's Vineyard—a political unit (with neighboring Elizabeth Islands it is grandly entitled the County of Dukes County) and a geographical unit, separated by water from the mainland—there is rich variety, fierce sectionalism and, until recently, hardly a whisper of island-wide planning. This has brought the Vineyard to the most critical time in all its history.

The story of its ordeal is that of the struggle to abandon habits of thought which had persisted for centuries. The Vineyard had to awake from its insularity, not gently but rudely shaken into consciousness of the new, terrifying era. People with an inbred devotion to this remarkable place had to learn to express it in unfamiliar ways, and many did, firmly putting into action the land ethic they had always held. There emerged Vineyarders with unassailable conviction that their island must survive. There were others who cared less and were unable to take a long-range view. The necessarily slow building of a vision of the future was overtaken by realities of the 1970s that would not wait. Thus, the island's crisis.

It is by no means simple to comprehend how the Vineyard arrived at its critical condition but it is vital to do so, not only because of the parallels which suggest the vast predicament of the U.S.A., but because of the island itself, this place of special grace. Understanding its past is the route to devising fast forceful action to protect its future, a not unimportant move in a society struggling to stay civilized.

There is not much time. A planning and engineering firm, having made a detailed study of the island, gives it only a few years to change its ways, putting doomsday at 1976, exactly when the rest of the United States will be celebrating the bicentennial of its independence. By then, the planners say, the Vineyard will no longer exist in its present state.

There has always been change on Martha's Vineyard. It is, in fact, the only place in all of New England where the ceaseless interaction between the land and sea can be demonstrated for the past one hundred million years. The island has been a lush primeval forest, a submerged ocean floor, rising from the sea in some ancient eras to support the dinosaurs of the time, or to become a great plain where small camels wandered, then covered again by waters. Each period leaves its mark in the materials of the Vineyard's clay beds.

Natural change is slow. Currently, the Vineyard is in a period of erosion, losing an average foot or two each year around its perimeter. As banks slip into the ocean, some shorefront owners plant bushes and beach grass on their exposed dunes and cliffs, hoping to preserve land which has now escalated in value to several hundred dollars per square foot. But there is no stopping the everlasting pressure of the sea.

"I'll have water-front property yet," a Chilmark farmer half a mile from the pounding surf says in partial jest as summer residents on the bluff gaze dismayed at the most recent slide of clay and boulders across the beach and into the water. And out at the magnificent Gay Head cliffs at the island's westernmost tip where the prehistoric clay beds—red, yellow, brown, white—rear some 150 feet above the waves, similar to England's Norfolk cliffs, and the only cliffs of such size on this continent, the U. S. Corps of Engineers makes an extensive, expensive study to determine how to prevent the gradual disappearance of all this grandeur, lately dignified as a National Landmark. Under consideration is a proposal for encasing the ancient clay in clear plastic to stop the interchange with the sea which, these very cliffs inform us, has continued since time immemorial.

In the early 1970s, just as man-made destruction of the Vineyard becomes apparent, the government's engineers propose to spend $155 million on the initial steps of erosion control for 120 miles of shore line on the Vineyard, Nantucket, and Cape Cod, transporting sand from the mainland, building groins and offshore breakwaters, and taking other remedial action. Some 20,500 miles of shore line in the United States, including the Great Lakes, Puerto Rico, and the Virgin Islands, were found to be eroding markedly, 2,700 miles (of which the Vineyard is a part) being in critical erosion condition. Even if our sophisticated technology can devise a way to stop what has been until now an everlasting land-sea flux, these cold engineering facts make us question whether we should spend our ingenuity and money to fight more or less benign natural changes or expend it on becoming respectable stewards of what is at hand.

Destruction of the Vineyard by sea and wind is not imminent. Although it is doubtful that there will be anything puny humans can do if the polar icecap melts, as some scientists anticipate, inundating Martha's Vineyard, Manhattan, and other low-lying islands in a rising sea, these changes are reassuringly slow, as past millennia demonstrate. The Vineyard, geologists predict, will be almost totally covered by water by the year 4000 (at which time, if my more pessimistic conclusions are correct, no one will miss it much), but barring some vast global accident, no man need absorb the stupendous event of an island's drowning in one lifetime.

We may have to experience something worse. What nature has done only in aeons, our society may do in the tiny space of a decade or two, and carelessly, almost unknowingly at that, without even applying the collective mind to the making of such an awesome decision, or using the planning tools now at hand which were invented in response to the mounting crises of the sixties. At stake are bountiful natural resources, rarely assembled in such wide variety within such a relatively small area.

This variety attracts an extraordinary mix of citizens to the Vineyard. One of Massachusetts' two Indian towns is at the west end of the island, one of America's first and most exclusive yacht clubs at the east, and in between, a community frequently cited as the only middle-class black seaside resort on the East Coast. There is as impressive a collection of powerful, important, and influential members of the Establishment here in the summer as can be found in any one place; there is a burgeoning enclave of its better-known young radical counterparts. There are descendants of Portuguese pioneers who came from the Azores and Cape Verde Islands on whale ships. There are new Vineyarders who have migrated to start a business or to retire in one of the three more urban down-island towns, there are New Englanders whose ancestors were the first white settlers here, whalers, fishermen, farmers, whose names still dominate up-island villages as well as the streets and stores of the towns.

This heterogeneous population has one passion in common. People who live on Martha's Vineyard, by their own frequent statements in the renowned, venerable *Vineyard Gazette*, the local paper recently acquired by James and Sally Reston, are in love with the island. They are now painfully discovering that love is not enough, in fact the outpouring of affection is a not inconsiderable factor in bringing the island to its present perilous moment of truth. Where the famous foregather, the near-famous come too and bring their friends. In ten years the summer population almost doubled to an approximate 42,000 at the start of the seventies, spiked by national coverage given to Frank Sinatra's yacht in a Vineyard harbor, the doings of James Taylor and his musical cohorts on a Vineyard pond, the late President Kennedy taking his wife water-skiing here, the Chappaquiddick tragedy.

Even without spectaculars, the island has become increasingly known as a summer resort. Between 1965, when prize-winning novelist Shirley Ann Grau wrote "The Vineyard Is the Place to Go," in the New York *Times*, and 1971 when Henry Hough, respected country editor and author of many sensitive books about the Vineyard, produced a star-studded memoir, "Escape in August to Martha's Vineyard," in *Town & Country*, dozens of articles, poetic pictures by such famed photographers as Alfred Eisenstaedt, gossip, recipe books, novels, and scandal about the island appeared in a wide spectrum of publications and have been a potent force in putting the Vineyard into the people business, as its Chamber of Commerce calls it. In 1972 the Eisenstaedt-Hough book, *Martha's Vineyard*, was still being advertised in the Quality of Life division of the Book of the Month Club; the *Gazette*'s new managing editor Phyllis Méras published a collection of Vineyard essays, *First Spring*.

The more advertising there is, the more publicity about the efforts of the island's literary luminaries—from Styron to Updike—to lead the simple life, the more telephoto-lens shots of a famous actress weeding her garden in blue jeans, or a senator sunning himself on the beach, the more the people business builds.

The weather helps too. Because water warms more slowly and holds heat longer than land, summer comes later to the island than to the mainland and lasts later. Lilacs and crocus bloom in May and Henry Hough happily reports the swimming to be fine at the end of October. Soon thereafter the prevailing wind switches from southwest to northwest and the winter, generally milder than on the mainland, sets in.

Although violent late-summer hurricanes tear into the Vineyard and nor'easters—those freezing three-day blows—are as expected as days of heavy fog, weeks of rain, there is, year round, the temperate influence of the Gulf Stream, that sixty-mile-wide river of warm water, moving at an ambling two and a half miles per hour, passing close to the island on its way east across the Atlantic. It warms the Vineyard Sound to an average 72° when Massachusetts Bay is 52°, it nearly meets the chilly Labrador Current flowing down the New England coast (and because each has a marine population suited to its own temperature, the waters around the island have an unusually varied populace), it has brought the Vineyard visits from the golden mullet, a delicate southern fish never known north of the Carolinas, and more permanent visitations of humans, longing to escape from urban miseries and looking for a place to settle. Visit the Vineyard on one of its irresistible sparkling summer days, when there is just enough offshore breeze to keep sails filled and bodies comfortably cooled, and less pleasing weather is forgotten; the people business develops at a formidable rate.

An explosive paradox is created. People who love the Vineyard love it because of its character, one facet of it or another, the very thing which their presence in ever increasing numbers, inevitably followed by rising taxes, callous developers, and the rest of the quick-change syndrome, must destroy.

Awareness of imminent disaster brings about a second paradox. The power to stop destruction of the island can best come from a consensus, some sort of all-island plan, as later described, or stronger still a regional plan for all the islands in the area (although no self-respecting Vineyarder willingly even acknowledges the existence of neighboring Nantucket) such as Senator Edward Kennedy proposed to Congress in the spring of 1972. But the character of the Vineyard, its very nature, depends on its variety—of terrain, towns, traditions, man-land-water relations—and this variety, which gloriously keeps the Vineyard from sameness, keeps its citizens from thinking of the island as a unit. It divides the six island towns from each other, the summer people from the year-round islanders, the man who lives on a pond's edge or inland farm from one whose view is the open ocean.

Everybody has his own Vineyard. Whether divided all must fall, or can unite, remains to be seen.

The Vineyard was divided even in its primordial formation, a fact colorfully underscored by the remarkable stone-walled garden of a Harvard Law School professor, its emerald lawn and full-blooming hybrid roses as perfect as an illustration in a seed catalogue. His friends call it his private slice of Edgartown; although it would be an expected sight in that county seat, what makes this small oasis remarkable is that its locus is instead some fifteen miles away in Chilmark, on the back of a dune which slopes down to the roaring Atlantic, in the hilly scrub country of the Western Moraine (moraine is the accumulation of earth and stones carried and deposited by a glacier) where the rugged landscape is less than hospitable to such horticultural delicacy. The professor patiently built a wall against the winds, hauled in topsoil to cover the sandy terrain, and regularly cultivates, fertilizes, and sprinkles the garden which could not survive where it is without such attention.

In the Ice Age, the Vineyard was molded to its present form, not by just one glacier but by two, which, with an outwash plain flattened by a lingering ice sheet, gives this small island three distinct topographies. The dramatic, boulder-strewn ridges and valleys of the Western Moraine where the glacier dumped huge hunks of rocks torn from mainland outcroppings (some thought to come from as far away as Maine) is known as up-island because it is uphill from the flatter contours of the Eastern Moraine, down-island; the Great Plains, almost at sea level, are indented only with gentle valleys of extinct glacial streams, rare sights which bear the indignity of the geologists' label, bottoms. Along with Nantucket, Cape Cod, and Long Island, the Vineyard marks the southernmost point of the glaciers' march; in its hills, a nineteenth-century geologist states, is "one of the most remarkable true terminal moraines anywhere to be found in the world."

From the air one can trace lines of boulders which mark the glaciers' scalloped edges up- and down-island. But only up-island, where the Vineyard's sole streams and small ponds are held by layers of preglacial clay, does the island become the spokesman for what happened to the whole northeast before the glaciers arrived.

This free-standing museum which lets us look back for a million centuries is relatively well protected from modern-day destruction, if for the wrong reasons. Developers eye the awesome assemblage with practical eyes, their engineers noting that the steep slopes of the up-island Western Moraine are generally unsuitable for development, eroding severely when vegetation is stripped off hillsides, that the complex folding of the ancient clay beds, held in such high regard by scientific explorers into our global past, makes well water hard to find and multiplies sewage problems. In their eyes, the imposing boulders are an expensive deterrent to rows of houses and the rocky land, which encouraged early settlers to sheep and cattle farming by providing material for pasture walls in abundance, detracts from easy profit because it requires clearing.

The glacial legacy to the Vineyard is manifold. The last glacial advance started about seventy-five thousand years ago, ended twelve thousand years ago; at the time of the ice sheet the sea level was three to four hundred feet lower than it is now and the bay and islands were inland areas. As the ice melted and the seas rose, some ten thousand years ago, the Vineyard's connection to the mainland was severed. Channels cut by the melting ice were filled by the ocean, making a series of fingerlike ponds along the island's southern shore, eventually to be dammed, by ocean action, with barrier beaches. These surprisingly sturdy sand spits (there are a hundred miles of them on Long Island, including Coney Island, Jones Beach, and Fire Island, a stretch on Nantucket and on the Cape) create unlikely neighbors—quiet pond and thundering ocean within a few hundred yards of each other.

The Great Ponds (ponds of at least ten or twenty acres, depending on which law you read) have been particularly prized places to live from earliest times. Wild fowl, fish attracted by the fresh water when it occasionally overflowed into the sea, shellfish, and the excellent fodder of surrounding marsh meadows made hunting, fishing, and grazing rights desirable . . . and still does. When it was discovered that man could engineer the change from fresh to brackish water by digging across the sand bar, the value of the land increased.

The Great Ponds, with their salinity controlled, are said to be among the best shellfish waters in the country. This is a rich but unimproved resource, the Vineyard shellfishermen stubbornly resisting the newfangled advance of shellfish farming, a technique first recorded by the Roman historian Pliny. Now, ironically enough, just as polluted coastal waters begin to cause a question about having any shellfish at all on the national menu and market, the importance of scientific means of growing and harvesting these delicacies becomes recognized as a top priority in the Vineyard's economy. The challenge to Vineyard shellfishermen, according to John Whiting, who is one of them as well as a noted anthropologist, is whether they can immediately make the move, traditionally requiring generations, from hunters-and-gatherers to farmers, a matter that is the focus of a later chapter.

Fringing the ponds are salt marshes which, an expert says, have required ten to twenty thousand years of geologic time to build to their present form and are, acre for acre, the most productive land there is—as a place producing microscopic vegetable organisms, food for fish, as spawning grounds and nurseries for many kinds of marine and aquatic animals and waterfowl, as feeding grounds for wading birds. They are also exceedingly tempting to developers, easy to fill in with a bull-dozer, attractive to purchasers.

So far, the Vineyard's marshes, along with those on the Cape and Nantucket, are said to be the most unspoiled in the entire eastern United States, but for how long? From the mid-fifties to the mid-sixties, more than 1,000 acres of Massachusetts' 45,000 acres of coastal wetlands were filled in and disappeared. Although it has long been known that the food supply of generations to come depends on how we defend our salt marshes, and although there has been legislation on the Commonwealth's books to guarantee their permanent protection since 1963, only slightly more than a third were under some kind of protection by 1971, a state official says, restrictions for the rest . . . "pending."

Quite different forces attack the island's upland ponds, kettle ponds formed by impacted hunks of ice from the retreating glacier, spring-fed ponds, ponds made from damming brooks, some of which race so vigorously toward the sea that they once supplied power to early island industries. These ponds, too, are likely to change; the accompanying swamp, under certain conditions, displaces the pond, nor is the swamp itself impermeable, being more than likely to eventually become a bog.

Just such a cycle was reversed by the intervention of a man who, vacationing on the Vineyard from massive urban responsibilities, is a passionate woods-walker. On a walk with knowledgeable companions he discovered a crude wooden dam embedded at the edge of a bog. Crumbling and dislodged, it had long since failed in its duty, which, the discoverers deduced, was to flood the bog to provide winter protection for the Vineyard's famed wild cranberries, which must have once flourished there as they do in other island bogs.

This bog lies in land which itself has a remarkable history, fully told in later pages, most recently having been purchased as a sanctuary by a ground-swell public subscription, to save it from development. The combination of circumstances of the morning walk, detection of the ancient dam, deduction of the land's history, resulted in an unsung, exceedingly sensitive marvel of restoration. Deep in a tall wood, a small serene pond now spills gently over a replica of that first simple dam, wild azaleas and sheep laurel sweeten the air, dragonflies buzz over the water lilies, and today's Vineyard, thanks to its imperiled but still viable man-land relationship, is the jewel of a pond richer.

Reading the land and reacting to it, as this man did, is the mark of a true Vineyard *aficionado* . . . and there are many, still, who pursue the never ending discovery, accumulating knowledge with combined awe and delight. For every man who knows the pond-swamp-bog cycle, or the marvel of oysters' sex life for which he will dig across a sandbar to provide the proper salinity for this mating in a brackish pond, there are those who understand the complex architecture of a dune, built by winds, anchored by grasses, wild roses, and strong-rooted poison ivy, or the slow growth of trees, kept down by wind and salt spray, which will nevertheless transform a meadow into a scrub oak forest. There are men who know that West Tisbury's rich soil propagates fine vegetables as well as every variety of wildflower growing in the entire state, others who have identified three pockets of rare plants, hidden in the up-island hills, others whose skin is ripped by brambles in the search for thickets of wild raspberries and blackberries. One specialist has catalogued seven hundred separate species of plants growing on the island, another knows what date it is by which migrating birds arrive at his feeder. There are books about the Vineyard's flora and its fauna; the local paper devotes a column to "Our Avian Visitors," a page to the fishing news from surrounding waters.

Fishermen, hunters, sailors, ornithologists, biologists, archaeologists, naturalists—each finds the Vineyard intriguing for his own reasons, each understands a part of the land and water which was not too different when the first white settlers arrived in the beginning of the seventeenth century. But one feels no certainty that the island will be allowed to continue to exert its natural leverage on man. Symbolic of trends that will make it into just another plastic place is that in 1971 the *Vineyard Gazette*, for the first time since I have perused its pages over more than two decades, carried an advertisement for swimming pools.

Swimming pools on the Vineyard . . . island of ponds, lakes, and beaches. Can we afford the artificiality, the loss of the island's natural environment? It is a complicated question since man has not yet found out what it does to him to be thus deprived. But there is a particularly potent Vineyard-centered insight. Like an arrow pointing us in the direction of wisdom is the startling fact that on this island, a species ended.

In the spring of 1932, somewhere alone in the underbrush of

the Vineyard's Great Plains, the very last heath hen on earth expired.

This was no ordinary bird, mostly because of the dramatic mating dance which men would wait for hours in the cold dawn to see. The male, as large as a pullet and colored like old grass, would inflate air sacs on either side of its neck to the size and color of oranges, raise long neck feathers and, in the posture of a fighting turkey, stamp its feet rapidly and make a booming noise that sounded like blowing across the neck of a bottle, an observer reports. Between boomings, the bird would half leap, half flutter two to three feet into the air, screaming with incredible enthusiasm. "Goblins cackled in weird laughter, whining and whimpering among scrub oaks. Strange hollow whistling noises grew in the air . . ." Shakespeare wrote in *The Tempest*, and some scholars believe that his description of the "strangely eerie and elflike noises" heard on an island by shipwrecked Antonio and Ferdinand was a report of the heath hen's mating ritual, observed on the Vineyard by the earliest English explorers, who took news of it home to England where it came to the Bard's attention.

The decline of the species *Tympanuchus cupido cupido*, the Pinnated Grouse, or heath hen, had been recognized since 1792 when the species, once "as common as drifting leaves in autumn from Maryland to Maine," according to one commentator, was reported rare in New Hampshire, and, in the next years, disappearing in Massachusetts and Connecticut. In 1836 the last recorded New York heath hen was killed on Long Island; by 1839 the species had vanished from everywhere except Martha's Vineyard; less than one hundred years later it was gone from the earth.

The end was a shock. "We are in touch with the reality of extinction," the *Gazette* commented, ". . . uttermost finality." A century of attention to this declining species, starting in 1831 with a closed season on hunting them from March to

September by vote of the Massachusetts legislature, extended to five years in 1844, and again in 1860, was too little and too late.

It was not enough to curb the hunting appetite, nor were well-meaning artificial measures effective. In 1907 two men raised $2,420 to acquire a reservation for the birds, the state contributed $2,000 and a warden, and trees were planted for shelter. But several bad fires swept the plain while the birds were sitting on their nests, and the females, instinctively motionless in fear, were destroyed with their eggs. In 1916 there were 2,000 birds; another bad fire at the nesting season reduced the population to 100 the following year. "Surely man could save the heath hen," an observer wrote at the time. "Man can do almost anything."

Man could not, however, manage this rescue. Emergency measures to protect the less than 30 birds observed in 1925 were useless. More acreage in the reservation, a special warden, a fire tower—nothing helped. Now the heath hen's picture hangs in the State House in Boston.

Somehow man so altered the environment of these once common birds as to cause their end forever. The species might have more significant immortality than a framed portrait if, by its extinction, it can cause us to stop and consider, while there is still time, how to use the island environment where *Tympanuchus* perished to the long-range advantage of *Homo sapiens*.

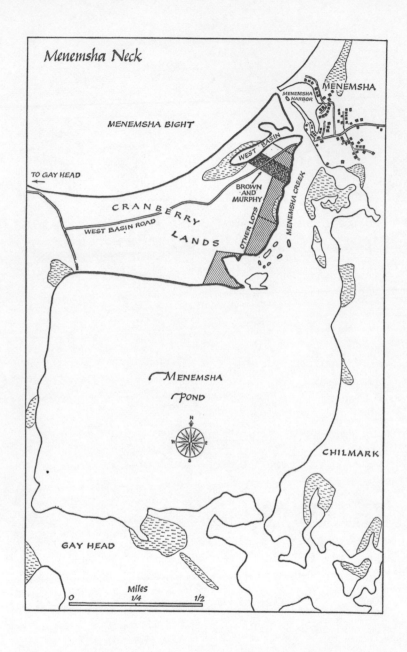

CHAPTER TWO

One Road to Ruin

Americans must decide whether they require such a place as Martha's Vineyard in which to survive as civilized human beings. Those who want its semiwildness—and many say the island's magnetism pulls them back from the ends of the earth—now have to fight for it. To fight effectively, they must identify the enemy . . . and here's the rub. There is no villain to tar and feather and ride off the island on the ferry's starboard rail. "Greed," it is said, "shows up more clearly on a landscape than on a man's face." I have scrutinized the doings of some favorite scapegoats: the Steamship Authority, Chamber of Commerce, big-shot summer people, small-town politicians, island real estate operators, off-island developers. I have found cupidity, even venality among them, in amounts large enough to justify the suspicion that their activities often do not benefit the island. I also discovered that, although many are irresponsible about the Vineyard, no one alone is responsible for its rapidly changing character.

Aptly enough in the present era, the primary force in the process of change is a conglomerate, a corporate villain not so easily done away with. It is made up of haphazard decisions and actions, arrived at without understanding of a fundamental goal for the island. Even the best of these, though widely applauded, fail the Vineyard because they keep the need for the hard labor of long-range planning at bay. In the small shortsighted decisions of the sixties is hidden the clue to options still open in the seventies.

One of the most notable of these decisions concerns a road which the little town of Gay Head (pop. 90) proposed to build across the sand dunes and cranberry bogs of Menemsha Neck, a narrow spit of land curving out into the placid waters of Menemsha Pond, and home to one of the Commonwealth's largest breeding colonies of gulls, black-crowned night herons (called quawks by old-time Vineyarders familiar with the birds' hoarse call), and rarer snowy egrets.

The dispute, starting in the summer of 1965, over construction of a road something less than a mile long and twenty feet wide, made headlines from Boston to New York ("Gay Head Threatens War," "The Right to Squawk about the Quawk") and involved U.S. cabinet members and congressmen, the governor of Massachusetts, a covey of lesser officials. There were months of wrangling, lengthy petitions, and angry words which we have not heard the last of yet. It appeared a David-and-Goliath battle from either side; birds vs. men was hardly an equal contest but neither was the small band of fishermen who wanted the road, in opposition to the newly formed Friends of the Island (later renamed the Vineyard Conservation Society), which summoned an impressive array of power against the road during its initial warring summer weeks.

Emotion ran high. "I'm fighting mad at all this outside interference," Gay Head Selectman Leonard Vanderhoop told a reporter at the time. "That road is going to be built no matter how much of a fuss they make. . . ." Residents, mostly Indians whose forefathers settled on the Vineyard before the first white man ever set foot on it, had been talking about building this road for forty years. In 1938 the first of four bad hurricanes intensified interest as the little scalloping boats were repeatedly scattered and damaged at their moorings, open to the southeast winds, while those in the West Basin were not disturbed. In 1959, the town dredged the Basin; in 1963, Gay Head voters appropriated the town's share of the estimated $8,000 cost of the road (a quarter of the total; under Chapter 90 legislation, another quarter is supplied by the county, half by the state) and the next year started to bulldoze into the dunes, having been promised the state's co-operation.

Speaking for the birds, the Friends of the Island put telling pressure on the then governor of Massachusetts, John Volpe, to "delay authorization" (which, translated, means to withhold state funds) pending further study. Besides protection for avian nesting grounds, the Friends cited the "extraordinary scenic complex" of the area around the pond, the possibility that the road would lead to construction of a marina and then to commercial development of the Neck, which would bring more pollution to the pond by attracting more and more boats to anchor within its protected harbors. "The list of charter members of 'The Friends' reads like the index of Who's Who," the Boston *Globe* commented, mentioning Katharine Cornell, Thomas Hart Benton, Michael Straight, novelist and former editor of the *New Republic*, John Oakes of the New York *Times*, M.I.T.'s Jerome Wiesner, Dr. Leona Baumgartner, Richard Pough of the Natural Area Council, a well-known conservationist, this writer, and others as founders.

The Friends, had been struggling with an amorphous mass of conservation-minded ideas since their initial meetings. Now, having raised some funds and hired a young professional, Bruce Blackwell (since vocationally relocated in the island's leading antique store), they plunged into their first finite problem. Meetings in Michael Straight's living room overlooking the serene pond evoked efforts to protect the quawks as well as what the *Gazette* called "one of the fairest spots in North America." As a result, protests piled up on the governor's desk from the then Secretary of Interior, Stewart Udall, Senator

Edward Kennedy, a "Dear John" letter from Congressman Hastings Keith, who represented the Vineyard's district in Congress, from such prestigious organizations as the National Audubon Society. The *Gazette* suggested that the Neck be made a wildlife preserve or added to the National Seashore, others backed the idea of further study. The governor, having put a stay on the funds, turned the matter over to his able young associate commissioner of public works, who he might not then have guessed would five years later be sitting in the State House in the governor's chair, still worrying about Martha's Vineyard.

Francis Sargent showed his statesmanlike qualities in his cool handling of this political hot potato. At the end of August he quietly called a meeting with representatives of Gay Head, the county, and the Friends, flew unheralded into the Vineyard with some staff associates, talked with the group he had convened in a steaming airport office, and in forty minutes flew off again with an agreement. The road would be built but the scenery and birds would be undisturbed; the compromise was for a "limited-access road," details to be worked out. Although there was some cynicism ("Road OK'd —Birds KO'd?") in the press and elsewhere, most parties felt that they had at least partially won their battle. "I want to commend you," Bruce Blackwell wrote Sargent; ". . . through diligence and perseverance [you] managed to pull the rabbit out of the hat."

It turned out to be an extraordinarily fertile rabbit.

Sargent had taken the fishermen's request at face value. To get from one end of the Neck to the other so that they could moor their fishing boats in the West Basin was what they said they wanted, and the road, as planned, made that possible. Since it ran through Indian common land, called Cranberry Lands, they were simply changing the use of that strip of land; the limited-access provision—no driveways, exits, entrances, or turnouts—could not be imagined as interfering with the fishermen's stated purpose in wanting the road in the first place. But this state protection meant state control: on completion, the little road was to become a state highway, taken by right of eminent domain.

This was anathema to the people of Gay Head, but it was not until the town meeting voted on the proposal in March 1966 that the reasons were acknowledged. The vote to reject the state road was 17 to 3; it is partially explained by historic resentment of the white man's land grab, which had been going on for the more than three centuries of white settlement on the Vineyard. Interestingly enough, the man whom the Indians asked to forward the Gay Head protest to the state was Massachusetts Representative Benjamin Mayhew, since deceased, descendant of Thomas Mayhew, who in the seventeenth century bought the islands from a British lord "and forthwith," he wrote, "I endeavoured to obtain the Indian right of them."

An even more significant reason was finally revealed. Enforced, the limited access rule would stop several property owners from reaching their lands on Menemsha Neck.

There were six of them, some Indian, some white, who owned individual parcels ranging from four to twelve acres on the perimeter of the Neck, the rest of which was indeed commonly held Indian land. Until the vote they had been less than talkative about these lands; one would not have suspected that the specter of future development was anything more than typical conservationists' hysteria. But now the new state road, which you could not drive off of or onto except at its ends, flushed the landowners—and a pair of real estate agents who knew all about these parcels—from cover. With this added dimension, Sargent's compromise made Menemsha Neck landowners resentful and the Friends alarmed anew.

Nevertheless, the road was built. In December 1966, when the Department of Public Works sent a messenger to Gay

Head with official notice of its new classification as a state highway, he was unable to contact the town clerk, Mrs. Maysel Vanderhoop, and so left the notice at the Gay Head Town Hall.

The inevitable result followed. First came the traffic, an occurrence which might have been foretold from the experience of Menemsha Basin Road just across the pond, built fifteen years earlier. "Already the drive is patronized daily by many sightseers," the *Gazette* reported at that time, "who have never before been able to drive so close to the Vineyard Sound on a surfaced way." Now Menemsha Neck became a favorite sight-seeing expedition; the gulls wheeled screaming in the air at the approach of cars although some nesting females stayed obligingly poised on their nests, delighting photographers. Soon the legal traffic was followed by jeeps and beach buggies which, disregarding the limited-access regulation, if it is even known to most Vineyarders any more, illegally careened over the dunes, crushing wild cranberries, beach plums, nests yellowed with the yolks of smashed eggs, and the dunes themselves.

In the summer of 1970 a New York widow who owns an old farmhouse in West Tisbury decided for personal reasons to sell her other Vineyard properties. She had heard that a new conservation-minded organization, the Vineyard Open Land Foundation (of which more later), was in the market for land important for preservation and so offered one of its leaders the approximately four acres her husband had bought on Menemsha Neck. "I would have sold it to them for half price," she said in a conversation the following summer, "just to see it preserved. I waited a year but got no reaction, so I sold it last week to Lynn Murphy for $28,000."

When the news got around there was consternation. Rumors flew. Lynn Murphy, a colorful, embattled boat mechanic whom Kennedy proposed for a Congressional Medal for his help to

stranded boats during hurricane Carol, and who is often em-
broiled in difficulties of one kind or another with local authorities, had most recently been deprived of the Menemsha
site he wanted for a boatyard. It was said that Murphy would
surely build the yard on Menemsha Neck, to be followed by
a marina, garage, hot dog stand, and other amenities of civilization. Gossips were mystified to discover that Murphy had sold
the land the same day he had bought it to a certain Richard
Brown. Interviewed, Brown talked facts, said that eventually
he and Murphy would each own half the lot, that Murphy
anticipated putting a boat dock on his half for repairs, that
Brown, who worked in a Boston bank, lived in Westport,
Massachusetts, vacationed on the Vineyard with his twenty-
two-foot Aqua sport fishing and cruising power boat, would
build a house on the Neck and anchor his boat off it.

Brown said that his lawyer assured him of "rights of egress
and regress" from his property, that he was unconcerned at
reports that the Cape and Vineyard Power Company would
not bring electricity down a limited-access way, that if he
couldn't get to his house by the road he'd "use a rubber raft.
I'm responsible, conservative and conservation-minded," Brown
said. "I know my character and what I want to do, and it's
lucky it was I who bought that land as I will do my best to
control my neighbors and myself."

Menemsha Neck had long been a favorite wild spot to
Brown, who said that if he could afford it he would give his
newly acquired acres to some conservation organization and
build elsewhere on the pond but, in lieu of that, offered to
trade his lot with any rich conservationist owning land on the
pond who would give him a house site in exchange. No one
came forward. Meanwhile Gay Head's fiery selectwoman
Thelma Weisberg insisted that she was "keeping alive the
battle of West Basin Road" and intends to get the road back
from the state, which never should have had it, she said, but

"took property that didn't belong to it, just because of a few summer conservationists." Apparently Brown or Murphy or any one of the other owners of the six lots will sooner or later take the next step in taming the wild lands of Menemsha Neck.

Whoever builds the first house or the first marina on the Neck may be tagged the villain, but in point of fact it will not be that builder, or Sargent, Blackwell, the Gay Head fishermen, the Friends of the Island, severally or together. Nor is it pond-front landowners who gaze past the Neck's low-rolling dunes to a luminous sunset and understandably would, like Brown, prefer to see the place stay as it is.

In the clarity of hindsight, one can see exactly what happened and what—barring a miracle of speedy action—will happen. Each person concerned had a perfectly valid position on the subject of the road, each sighted the future in light of his own interests, whether birds, boats, dollars, or an untrammeled view. With the road an isolated issue, whoever summons the most potent power will dictate.

But the road is not separate from the land and the pond. The villainy was corporate in that each party concerned aided the others in dealing with the road apart from its environment, although the disposition of the matter must affect (and already has affected) the nature of Menemsha Pond and its surrounding lands. The chance that was missed was to focus on the future of this part of the Vineyard, keeping in mind its innate dignity and cultural heritage, factors at least as telling as the requirements of fishermen, quawks, or gulls. Even a contemporary Solomon could not have meted out justice in forty minutes had this been the issue, for it concerns the record of many centuries.

Some of that record is provided by the writings of John Brereton, narrator or perhaps just a literarily-inclined passenger on the ship of the British explorer Bartholomew Gosnold, on a mission to bring home a boatload of sassafras root, which was much in demand at the time as a cure for syphilis. The Vineyard that Brereton saw from the deck of the ship was a high-canopied forest with many tall straight beeches, cedars, oaks, and a variety of other trees which happily included sassafras "in great abundance," as it still does. In 1602 Gosnold landed, perhaps the first white man to set foot on this island, although there are those who seek to prove that the Vineyard is the eleventh-century Vikings' Vinland, or was visited in 1524 by Verrazano, the Italian navigator exploring in the neighborhood.

In any event, Gosnold and his company did anchor, land, and explore, finding "such an incredible store of Vines . . . that we could not goe for treading on them," and Gosnold is generally credited with bestowing the name Marthaes Vineyard (the *e*, Henry Hough says, is the seventeenth-century equivalent of an apostrophe). Martha's identity has been pursued by a dozen scholars; it is said that she was Gosnold's infant daughter, his wife, mother, or perhaps his mother-in-law, a Martha Golding, who helped finance the voyage.

"In view of the existing customs . . . it is doubtful that the name of any woman other than the sovereign or some princess, would be selected for such purposes," Charles Banks says in his impressively detailed three-volume history of Martha's Vineyard. Banks believes that the name was given by Gosnold to the insignificant little Noman's Land, an island off the Vineyard's south shore where he first landed, and that our island was called Martin's Vineyard, probably for a Captain John Martin who accompanied Gosnold. In evidence that it was Martin's for much of the seventeenth century, Banks lists 51 documents of the period that so refer to the island, 9 that call it Marthaes; he believes that Martha eventually triumphed by phonetic accident.

Banks is alone among scholars to assert that the island was

named Martin's Vineyard or that there was a Captain Martin with Gosnold to name it for: "It is unfortunate to perpetuate his groundless theorizing," Henry Hough says with authority, having done a complete research on the subject, and having in his possession the ultimate proof—a photostatic copy of the Brereton narrative as first published in London. "The name 'Marthaes' is definite beyond any disputing," Hough says.

But the identity of Martha remains wound round with tenacious tentacles of grapevines, obscured by time, while her island becomes known to the entire nation.

The people living on the Vineyard when Gosnold arrived—some say there were 1,500, some say 3,000—were members of that now almost vanished family of Algonquin Indians who ranged the entire eastern half of North America. Most authorities believe that the Vineyard tribe were Wampanoags (meaning Easterners), groups of whom also lived on Nantucket, in eastern Rhode Island and southern Massachusetts. In 1617 their numbers were greatly reduced everywhere by a decimating epidemic, perhaps smallpox, introduced by European contact and regarded by the English King as God's sign that it was time to take over the territory, it being so depopulated by "that wonderful plague."

The Indians roamed all over the island, divided it into four governmental sections, each under a sachem, or chief. The sachemship was a hereditary position and the men who held it were landed aristocracy, a scholar says, heading "a genuinely aristocratic and almost feudal system which seems to have been unique with the coastal Alonquins." The yeomen under them had some rights and privileges but the common folk apparently had none. Their use of land, however, was democratic if not communistic; modern youngsters do well to look to America's early Indians for a land ethic. The Indians had their own language. They called Chappaquiddick Capawack, Gay Head Aquinuih, meaning land under the hill, which perhaps refers to the beaches below the cliffs, and the Vineyard itself Noepe or No-pe—amid the waters.

It had taken many centuries for the island's inhabitants to live as though they were, indeed, amid the waters. Recent excavations of six Vineyard sites, dating from 2270 B.C. to A.D. 1565, by archaeologist William Ritchie, looking for a coastal culture (an undertaking which, he says, is not possible anywhere on the East Coast except on the Vineyard because of the densely settled and disturbed condition of the land elsewhere), sheds considerable light on all of southern New England's prehistory. What Ritchie found was that the earliest Vineyard people were still mainly forest-adapted hunters of the white-tailed deer. Only very slowly did successive cultures begin to use the resources of the sea, starting with the most easily seen shellfish, the still sought-after quahog. Later diets included soft-shell clams and oysters, still later, mussels, scallops, fish, and finally marine mammals including seals and small whales.

The Indians made fishhooks from bones ingeniously bent into shape, nets from animal gut, flax, or woven grasses, spears for larger fish, Ritchie's digs reveal. Although they early ate wild roots and berries, mortar and pestles for grinding corn appear only in the later cultures, attesting to the relatively new undertaking of agriculture. Through the Northeast, according to Alvin Josephy, Indian expert, the time between 1000 and 1600 was marked by "an increase in the importance of agriculture, the growth of population, a rise in the number of settlements . . . and a general advance of cultural development." The Vineyard people lived in wigwam villages; one was on Chappaquiddick, others on Tisbury Great Pond and on Squibnocket Pond, in fact most were on the shores of ponds where there was a dependable supply of fresh water, shellfish, and small game. Like contemporary Vineyarders, some moved to the beach for the summer; the stretch of South Beach known as Zach's cliffs—hangout of today's hippies—was named for a Zachary Howwoswee who had his summer wigwam there.

"These people are exceeding courteous, gentle of disposition, and well-conditioned, excelling all others that we have seene," Brereton says, ". . . of colour much like a dark Olive; their eie-browes and haire black which they weare long tied up behind in a knott. . . ." Although some wore animal skins, Vineyard animals were too scarce and small to provide skin enough for wigwams, which the Indians made of woven flaggrass mats stretched over bent saplings. They enjoyed a varied menu, fished, farmed, hunted, traveled in dugout canoes made from majestic island trees, and worshiped thirty-seven principal gods, presided over by the great Moshup of whom they told many tales which, like myths and folk stories everywhere, reflect their tellers' own miseries, puzzlements, and hopes.

Mostly these were connected to the land. The Vineyard's existence was explained by the story of the giant Moshup, living on the mainland at the time, who had become annoyed at sand in his moccasins, kicked them off into the sea where one became the Vineyard, the other Nantucket. The Indians honored Moshup's marvels on the land, asked the sun and moon gods for rain, generous harvest, and fair sailing for their swift canoes. Stewart Udall, who himself has Indian ancestry, says the Indian understood long ago that "land was the ultimate home, a common possession of those who used it; he lavished on it the awe and love and respect we now seek to recapture as a land ethic for the future."

It is a belief not easily acquired. By the time the white newcomers on the Vineyard got around to returning some of the land which they "bought" from the Indians during the first colonization days, they were surprised to find that the Indians lived peaceably on the tract allotted them in Gay Head, in its original undivided state. "Each man cultivates as much

as he pleases," a visitor in 1800 notes, "and no one intrudes on
the spot which another has appropriated by his labor." A representative of the Honorable Society for Propagating the Gospel says that while one has half an acre, another has over a hundred acres but "there is no heart-burning, no feeling that the
latter has more than his share. 'I have all I want' says the
former and he is content. This state of things," the representative concludes, "is as happy as it is peculiar; how long it will
continue is a problem."

Established over centuries, it continued without pause while
the white man came, saw, and peacefully enough conquered
the Vineyard. Most accounts of the colonization sanctimoni-
ously note that the purchase of Indian land titles was accomplished not in one transaction but over a considerable period
of time, which presumably gave the Indians a chance to change
the object of their affection—the land.

This was an impossibility. The Indians' idea of land was
poles apart from the white man's. "To them, land and its produce, like the air and water, were free to the use of the group,"
Josephy says. "Generally, most Indians had respect, if not
reverence and awe, for the earth and for all of nature and,
living close to nature and its forces, strove to exist in balance
with them." Life and the land: one simply did not exist without the other, and their genuinely communal ethic penetrated
deep into this concept. It might have changed the colonists
into early ecologists, had they been able to learn from the Indians instead of imposing their own ideas on them.

What the white man could and did learn from the Indians
was their skill in whaling. Centuries of training developed
keen vision and dexterous handling of harpoons, made it possible for the Indians to capture whales from their canoes with
only the crudest implements. Indians were much valued by
Vineyard and Nantucket whaling captains, particularly as har-
poonists: Tashtego, the number two harpooner on the *Pequod*

in Melville's *Moby Dick,* is identified as a Gay Head Indian, and Joseph Belain, who died in 1927 at the age of seventy-nine, spent sixty of those years at sea, once earning a fabled $15,000, his share of a whaling voyage to the Arctic on which he was first mate.

In 1642 Thomas Mayhew, an Englishman who had settled in Watertown, Massachuetts, where he was having business troubles, bought the Vineyard from the Earl of Stirling and from a Sir Fernando Gorges who also seemed to hold a valid title to it. Mayhew's son, Thomas, Jr., preceded his father to the island and set out to establish a town at Great Harbour, now Edgartown.

At twenty-one or -two, Thomas, Jr., having been "tutored up" in New England according to a chronicler of the times, organized and became minister to what is said to be the first Congregational Church in America. But the small flock of parishioners, settlers enticed to the island from Watertown and vicinity by the elder Mayhew, did not satisfy Thomas, Jr.'s missionary zeal. "With great Compassion he beheld the wretched Natives, who then were several thousands on those Islands, perishing in utter ignorance of the true God, and eternal Life, labouring under strange delusions, Inchantments and panick Fears of Devils, whom they most passionately worshipped." Mayhew enthusiastically proceeded to Christianize these wretched souls, the first recorded instance of proselytism in New England. Hiacoomes, called the Forest Paul of his race by Whittier, also made history, a Vineyard historian tells us, as the first Indian convert in New England and the ordained pastor of the area's first regularly organized Indian church.

With Hiacoomes' help, Mayhew made considerable progress in spreading the gospel before being drowned at the age of thirty-seven on his way to England to report on the state of the heathens. His father, then his son Matthew, and many Mayhews following, continued the missionary calling among

the Indians and present-day Mayhews often pass the Place on
the Wayside, a Gay Head boulder and plaque which commemo-
rates Thomas, Jr.'s farewell to his loving flock. By 1705 the job
was more or less done; Experience Mayhew reports 104 score
families of Indians on the island, "of these there are no more
than two persons which now remain in their paganism."

The Indians did not join the white man's land ethic as easily
as his religion. In 1681 Mittark (or Mettack), sachem of Gay
Head, declared the tribes' ancient principles in writing: "Know
ye all People that I Mettack and my principal men my
children and people are owners of this; this our land forever.
They are ours, and our offspring forever shall enjoy them: I
Mettack and we principall men together with our children and
all our people are agreed that no person shall sell any Land.
. . . I Mettack sachem and my chief men speak this in the
presence of God it shall be thus forever." (Mittark had been a
"praying Indian," a Christian, for nearly twenty years when he
wrote this document if indeed he did write it; some believe it to
be a forgery.)

Two years later the old sachem died and his son sold the Gay
Head peninsula for thirty pounds, thus beginning the manorial
system in the Vineyard's Indian settlement whereby the Indians paid rent to one landlord or another for the land they
had once owned "forever." Dependent now on the state, they
were as aliens, paupers, idiots, and the insane in their relations
to the body politic, Charles Banks points out. "By an historical legal quirk," a representative of the Native American Rights
Fund says, "the Indians in the original thirteen colonies have no
Federal protection." The exact legal shenanigans which put the
Indians on a reservation, deprived them of their rights as citizens, and exacted fees from them is not clear from the casual
records of the times. It is generally only a matter of concern today when a purchaser tries to clear title to a house site in Gay

Head, the interminable convolutions of which procedure seem a silent rebuke for what has gone before.

Converted to Christianity, thinned out by disease, intermarrying with Negroes, South Sea Islanders, and Portuguese (which an eighteenth-century Mayhew says "has much improved their temperance and industry"), the Indians still built stone walls together for pastures in common, parts of which are visible today, still planted fields together, and together manned the canoes to pursue whales in offshore island waters. When the Massachusetts General Court changed the reservation into a district in 1862, enfranchised the Indians, and finally made Gay Head into an incorporated town in 1870, it took five years for officials to determine boundary lines of lands held separately and common lands, most Indians having hazy notions of their holdings; one woman entered a claim for land wide enough for four rows of corn.

When Gay Head became a town, each family was allotted its homestead and a homestead for each of its children. They drew lots for the remaining land in the reservation, according to Luther Madison, a leading Gay Head citizen whose grandfather, born before the reservation was disbanded, described this event to him some years ago. The common Cranberry Lands on Menemsha Neck, owned jointly by all the Indians, had six fishing shacks on it at the time, Madison says, and these, with the land they were on, each became the property of the fishermen who had put them up. Thus the common land was diminished by the now crucial six lots, some of which the original owners have subsequently sold although, Madison remarks, "It's hard to find the bounds down there."

Until now, nobody much bothered to try. Every year Cranberry Day was celebrated in Gay Head, the only town in the U.S.A. to have this holiday, on an autumn day selected by the cranberry agent, elected at the annual town meeting for this purpose. School was closed, business stopped, and the entire town turned out with their teams of oxen. Families rode the carts down to the Neck where the wild cranberries, hidden in the bogs there, flourished, planted, tended, and protected by the Great Spirit, according to Indian belief. The cranberries had no human maintenance but were efficiently flooded by winter rains, covered by fine sand blown over them by the high winter winds, seeded by nature's devices. While the women prepared picnics over fires built close to the dunes for shelter, men and children picked the crop with the long-fingered cranberry scoops which are now quaint items, bid on at auctions to add authenticity to Vineyard colonial décor. There were enough cranberries so that when the harvest was divided each family had eighteen to twenty bushels to sell, and in 1860 the berries brought eleven dollars a barrel in New York.

There was reverence as well as celebration in this holiday. No public relations man had yet invented the slogan, "New England's BIG Little Industry," now applied to the cranberry business, but Indian medicine men said that cranberries prevented the spread of disease, pounded them to a powder to make pemmican, which was mixed with meat, fish, or fat and had all the elements of a nutritious diet. In the eighteenth century sea captains used cranberries to prevent scurvy, and many of the Indians on the Vineyard attributed their excellent health to this native fruit.

People came from a long way off-island for Cranberry Day which, besides being a harvest time, was also a reunion, a time for conclaves and conference among the Indians. In 1950 the crowd was small, berries scarce, and only one pair of oxen was present; in 1956 the crop failed for the first time anyone could remember, due, it was thought, to late frosts and the interference of a WPA project which had attempted to transform the wild bogs to cultivation. In 1963, for the first time, there was no school holiday and the next year only a handful of people arrived in a truck. Cranberry Day became a memory.

Gay Head itself is changing fast. In a disturbing parallel to the heath hen, the Indian population declines steadily; there were 240 Indians in 1807, 227 in 1870, 173 in 1900, 103 in 1960, and in 1970 the provisional census figure for the town of Gay Head is 90 souls. Although an ethnologist says that some Gay Head families are the purest Indian stock remaining in the eastern United States, the Vineyard's last full-blooded Indian of royal descent, Tanson Weeks, died in 1870, and Bia Diamond, said to be the last who could speak the Indian language, in the early 1900s.

Dirt roads and footpaths were gradually replaced by hard-top ways, as were oxen by cars. The first paved road, an extension of the state highway, was built in 1870 and others appear at intervals, including, of course, the renowned West Basin Road. Electricity was brought to Gay Head in 1951, doing away with the necessity for a keeper for the famous Gay Head Light, originally installed at the order of President John Adams in 1798 and watched over by one lighthouse keeper after another ever since, until it was electrified. In 1955 the telephone, in 1970 the town's first selectwoman . . . and ever larger crowds of tourists, trudging to the cliffs to gaze, take a picture and buy a sandwich, coke, and souvenir at the cliffside gift shop.

Indians are having a difficult time holding onto their homestead lands. There are no longer any protective Indian laws whatsoever in the Commonwealth. Taxes were raised considerably when the late Ted Howell, a white real estate man and Gay Head's tax assessor, reappraised the land upward in 1959 to meet the town's budget. Many Indians, unable to pay inheritance taxes, must look forward to having their property sold when they die, or even sooner, instead of passing it on to their children. The industries—the Gay Head Clay Company, Gay Head Fire Brick Company—are shut down, unable to remove any more clay from the deteriorating cliffs. Scallops, tourists, and welfare provide the Indians with money today.

The Indians had the entire island of Martha's Vineyard, their No-pe, as common land for centuries, living off it, cherishing its special resources, celebrating its access to the forest, the sea, the cranberries. Gradually the commonly held land shrank, first to a reservation on the peninsula of Gay Head, then, when that was divided into individual ownership and could be sold on a drunken Saturday night for a cheap quart of whiskey and a few dollars, all that was left, safeguarded by common ownership, besides Herring Pond and the cliffs, was Menemsha Neck, minus the six privately held lots. Now that is threatened, by the Indians' need to use the West Basin, the building of the road, by the private owners' desire to build on their land. A recent legal opinion says that, although the Cranberry Lands are commonly held by the inhabitants of Gay Head, many of whom no longer live in the area, the town of Gay Head can, if it wants to, dispose of these lands.

Martha's Vineyard might still have the option to set part of its lands aside forever, as Sachem Mittark and his principal men pronounced. But as limited access becomes access maybe, or right of egress and regress, and lawyers and law-breakers invent ways around the stated intent of the celebrated mile of hard top, it becomes clear how badly we failed to grapple with the real issue the road raised. Today Menemsha Neck is recognized as a coastal wetland, vital to the survival of life in the oceans, a natural resource of extreme importance, protected by state law. But such is the eagerness to buy, sell, build, and make a profit, that even the laws appear unequal to the avidity.

We fought a battle over the West Basin Road and lost a war if it happens that we have forever destroyed this place, known as essential in its wild state by the Vineyard's oldest and newest ecologists.

CHAPTER THREE

Gatherers Yes, Farmers No

The abyss of the oceans, deepest part of the deep, is still out of reach of man. Slopes rising from the abyss toward the continents have just begun to be explored by research submarines, and the shallower continental shelf is somewhat better known. The shallowest part of the oceans of the world—the intertidal zone—we sail on, fish in, explore, and know the most about. A thousand times more food, by weight, is taken from here than from the open ocean. The coastal zone which borders the United States is fifteen per cent of the country's land area but one third of the population lives there, swarming toward the sea for its eternal comfort and for some less exalted reasons. What contemporary coastal dwellers will do with the land and waters is widely regarded as crucial to the future of man.

The question is no place more evident than on the island of Martha's Vineyard.

An annual meeting of the Quansoo Shellfish Farms, Inc., was held some years ago during the change of tide at the narrowest spot in the barrier beach which separates Tisbury Great Pond from the ocean. There were eight or nine shovels, twenty or more congenial stockholders, a barrel of beer, and an incredible sunset, all of which encouraged the gathering to accomplish its purpose. A channel had to be cut through the sand and completed precisely when the tide changed, a considerable miracle of engineering contrived by the blue-jean-attired presiding officer Professor John Whiting, anthropologist at Harvard and moving spirit of the company gathered on the beach. Strong tidal flow would widen and deepen the efforts of the shovelers; the opening to the ocean thus achieved would make the pond just enough colder and saltier to encourage the joining of oyster sperm and eggs, presently drifting unattached in the brackish pond waters. Within two days each minuscule new oyster would grow a complete bivalve shell which in two weeks would become so heavy that the larva would sink to the bottom of the pond. There it would attach itself to a convenient hard object and progress to succulent maturity, to be harvested and end its life under lemon juice on the half shell.

If this cycle was achieved in multiples of millions, or even thousands, the Quansoo company might make a profit. As it happened, the only dividends for stockholders were the annual shoveling bacchanalia. The corporation, formed in 1948, was out of business a decade later, having lost a total of some $30,-000, according to Whiting. The chief reason he gives for its failure was the reluctance of the town of West Tisbury to allow him and his several partners to pursue experimentation and research in raising oysters. "Some of us were absentee owners," Whiting recalls, "and the local fishermen thought we were making money. On the Vineyard . . . anathema."

This particular town's view of this particular undertaking only suggests the island's deeper problem. Its most valuable asset, possibly its salvation, lies in the shellfish gold of its ponds and bays. But just as the land must now be planned and managed in new ways if it is to give the Vineyard's special character a chance for survival, so, too, must its waters. New ways mean leaving entrenched tradition behind, and this does not come easily to the insular New Englander.

The passionate conviction that land can be owned by one man is matched by the belief that water cannot, that water is wild and free and what's in it grows wild and free for all to share. The law codifies man's belief, from international agreements about oceans between the countries of the world to Massachusetts law, which makes Commonwealth ponds of any sizable account the property of the towns in which they lie. The state legislates use of the ponds, the towns administer.

For centuries men of the Vineyard have shared the water's bounty, and it was plentiful. Whales which once disported themselves offshore inspired an era of prosperity and world renown for the island, told in the next pages. Today, swordfish and lesser species keep a fishing fleet chugging out of its home base in Menemsha, one of Massachusetts' two remaining old-fashioned fishing villages (the other is Rockport). The sturdy vessels, draped with nets and redolent of yesterday's catch, leave the harbor at dawn alongside the sleek boats of sportsmen whose idea of a vacation is to be where the striped bass and blue fish are before the sun comes up. In ponds and flats, islanders gather shellfish—scallops, soft-shell clams, quahogs, and oysters—using the right of law adopted in the seventeenth century which poetically provides that "every inhabitant who is a householder shall have free fishing and fowling . . . as far as the sea ebbs and flows within the precincts of the town where they dwell."

Vineyard fishermen have modern techniques but not a modern point of view. One man has a hydroplane to scout the position of giant swordfish which is radioed back to the sportsman taking his ease on the dock, but when he gets the news and sets out for the kill, he is still basically a hunter. Shell-fishermen remain gatherers, like their forefathers before them. The action not taken is to farm the sea. For the Vineyard, the choice, still open, is critical.

Historically, the rise of civilization is linked to the move from hunting and gathering to farming. It applies to the sea as well as to the land. If this civilizing process, which generally takes centuries, is to happen in time to rescue the Vineyard, it will have to hurry. For while it presented the island with a comparatively simple opportunity to solve some of its more pressing problems a decade ago, times have changed unbelievably fast. It is vastly more difficult of achievement today; tomorrow it may be impossible.

The prospects of shellfish farming were alluring in the 1960s. Vineyard waters—10,000 acres of them—were known to be among the best natural areas for shellfish in the world. With aquaculture (which an expert defines as some degree of interference with the natural environment of the waters in order to control and improve it), the crop could be vastly multiplied. Clearly, sea farming was an idea whose Vineyard time had come. It would give the island a solid economic base, the absence of which now forces it faster and deeper into the resort business with each passing month. By providing year-round, profitable employment, it would slow if not stop the exodus of young islanders and the annual tragicomic shift from summer employment to winter welfare which makes the Vineyard, surprisingly enough to those who know it only in its summer solstice, a "distressed area" on the state's books. It would supply a forceful motive to outlaw water pollution, which had progressed so far by the early 1970s that the state's Health Department found four Vineyard harbors polluted beyond safety levels and predicted a closing of shellfish grounds in the next year or so.

A solid opportunity for the civilizing step came when an energetic Harvard-trained young marine biologist, George Carey Matthiessen, and his assistant, R. C. Toner, proposed to establish a permanent shellfish facility in an Edgartown pond, the program to start with oyster culture, eventually to include scallops and quahogs. Although there has been a lobster hatchery on Lagoon Pond in Oak Bluffs since 1951, it is operated by the state for the benefit of all of Massachusetts. For the Vineyard's exclusive benefit, there had been only conversation and some unsuccessful attempts at aquaculture, such as the Quansoo effort, until Matthiessen came along.

The new proposal was significant and serious. Matthiessen had moved to the Vineyard with his wife and daughters, resigned from his job with the state's Division of Marine Fisheries (where he had been preceded a decade earlier by the Commonwealth's ubiquitous Francis Sargent), and had spent three years and $90,000 of public funds—all but an $8,000 county contribution coming from the U. S. Department of Commerce's Area Redevelopment Administration—to find out if it was biologically and economically feasible to mass-produce shellfish on the Vineyard under laboratory conditions. "Compared with other states, Massachusetts is way behind in shellfish culture and research," Sargent had said with foresight back in 1955. Now Matthiessen attempted to catch up.

The proposed hatchery was his answer. It was to be a privately owned, self-supporting public service, selling seed oysters to Vineyard towns at cost, and to people who might then start their own oyster farms. Matthiessen chose oysters over other shellfish for cogent scientific and economic reasons. Oysters have the highest nutrient value and are obliging bivalves when you know how to deal with them. They are easily reproduced artificially by a technique just perfected, can be raised in both kinds of Vineyard ponds—those occasionally opened to the ocean, and tidal ponds, generally of higher salinity. Once planted, oysters stay put (whereas scallops swim around, quahogs and clams dig), are self-feeding, and can be harvested without expensive gear, even in deep water. The crop is marketed in the "R" months when other Vineyard income is at a minimum, the price is stable, and the demand of an oyster-bar-oriented society far exceeds the supply.

Farming oysters, alone, would increase the value of the Vineyard's shellfish harvest by a staggering sixty-five per cent the biologists estimated. "Dukes County needs a good-size off-season industry," Matthiessen said at the time. "Shellfishing may continue indefinitely at its present level, but without management it will certainly never improve. If our program is successful, it should be a catalyst for similar developments of shellfish farming."

Since the island needed what the shellfish hatchery could provide, it appeared a foregone conclusion that the Vineyard would entertain Matthiessen's proposal with enthusiasm. Even the Matthiessen family was an asset; Mrs. Matthiessen included their four daughters in a popular 4H horsemanship program for thirty girls "who will all be better people for having come in contact with this family," the 4H director said. "I've never known a family to give so much of themselves. . . ." The Matthiessens had bought the barn and lands of Sweetened Water Farm a year before they could afford to buy the house; this they did in 1964. The entire family had become engrossed in and accepted by the Vineyard, no mean accomplishment. Now they were ready to make a lasting professional commitment.

In November 1965, some months before his contract with the government was due to run out, Matthiessen, making a routine application for use of a portion of a pond for his proposed hatchery, ran headlong into the age-old antagonism of gatherers against farmers.

Because pond waters are in the public domain, anyone who wants to try to grow his own shellfish must get a "bottom grant" from the town selectmen. A sign of the underlying attitude about these grants is their severe restrictions; they cannot be given in an area where any "substantial amounts of shellfish exist in a natural state." They are conferred for five years only, after which they can be renewed or not as the selectmen choose. The grant system has not been notably successful. Part of the opposition results from past leases, Henry Hough comments. "The herring fishery in Edgartown Great Pond was controlled for many, many years by the Mattakessett Creek Co. under a lease that also gave the company the right to seine striped bass in the pond. Other fishing companies had rights in Pocha and Trapp's Pond. Opposition to these special interests," Hough concludes, "sometimes led to violence, and the tradition of the old days is still lively."

Shellfishermen did not put enough time, effort, or cash into raising shellfish in what must, by definition, be a substandard part of the pond. "They didn't really farm it," John Hughes, nationally known director of the Lobster Hatchery, comments, "they mined it; just took and took and took."

Matthiessen needed the use of about twenty acres of pond adjacent to a site for his laboratory. He was planning for suspension culture whereby the tiny oysters, artificially reproduced in the laboratory, are planted on shelves vertically suspended in the water, a system more economical than beds on the bottom of the pond, protecting the oysters from bottom predators, mud, and other natural enemies. The water had to be deep enough for suspension, of reasonably high salinity, and in a spot protected from storms and moving ice. This he had found in a cove near Felix Neck on Edgartown's Sengakontacket Pond, an Indian name which means, appropriately enough, salty waters. "It's a small fraction of Edgartown's 3,000 available shellfishing acres," Matthiessen said, making his application. "It is we who are taking the risk. It seems to us that Edgartown has very little to lose and possibly a great deal to gain."

The Vineyard bristled with excitement. At a public hearing on the Matthiessen request in the Edgartown Town Hall, two of the town's three selectmen were for the grant, the other against. When it was approved, ten Edgartown fishermen and taxpayers filed a suit to block it, accusing the selectmen of exceeding their authority. Angry letters in the *Gazette* attacked the oyster hatchery idea as "a ravage attempt of our beautiful island," "not a grant for research but for personal gain." "Commercialism triggers the cancer which blights God's green natural areas. . . ." "Huge piles of half-clean oyster shells festering and smelling. . . ." From Indianapolis, a pond-front owner raised the ever present summer-winter conflict: "What happens to the desirability of the pond for summer residents when it becomes chock-a-block with shellfish grants?"

There were encouraging voices as well. The supporting selectmen said the project could have "a tremendous impact on the entire eastern seaboard." Robert Nevin, an Edgartown doctor, called the attack on the proposal "shortsighted." Everett Poole, entrepreneur of two island fish markets, took a long view. "The dream of a year-round economy for the Vineyard is nearly a reality," Poole wrote to the *Gazette*; ". . . we can develop a prosperity unknown here since the great whaling days." The *Gazette* itself urged approval of the grant; "The best chance for the future of the oyster fishery and for the economy of the whole island . . . [is to] establish the success of oyster farming as a fact."

The opposing selectman, an Edgartown mason named Cyprian Dube, dealt the still hopeful Matthiessen a crushing blow. The grant would hinder navigation, reduce real estate values, and curb freedom of the water, he said, and then accused Matthiessen of proceeding to use the results of his research before anyone else had had a chance to read the report of his three years' work and find pond areas to act on it themselves.

It was a cruel attack. Although Matthiessen and Toner had submitted regular quarterly reports to the state and federal agencies involved, they were not allowed to publish them themselves but by fiat had to wait on the U. S. Department of Commerce's promise that the information would be made public. "The state of island opinion would be far different from what it is if the government had released the report step by step," the *Gazette* commented. An informed guess of why this had not been done puts it at the feet of bureaucratic inefficiency. Nevertheless, on Christmas Eve, Matthiessen said that the government's "reluctance to permit us to publish our progress reports has cast a shadow over the project," and he withdrew his request for the Sengakontacket grant.

"We are not assuming the natural leadership suggested by our natural resources," a *Gazette* editorial comments in masterful understatement. Early in January, Matthiessen, spurred on by considerable emotional rhetoric from fellow Vineyarders, evolved a plan tailored to meet at least some of the Edgartown criticisms. He would demonstrate that shellfish farming could be a steadily productive industry, then proceed to the formation of a producers' co-operative wherein all shellfishermen in town would have an equal voice. And none of this would begin until the reports of the three-year research had been published by the government.

Again he applied for a bottom grant, this time up-island in the relatively small Stonewall Pond, which was yielding negligible amounts of shellfish. He cut the request from twenty to ten acres, would suspend oysters from floats at the edge of the pond, promised no shucking or water pollution. The late Benjamin Mayhew, then chairman of the selectmen in Chilmark, where the pond is, thought the project valuable. "I hope that this can be done somewhere on Martha's Vineyard," he had said during the Edgartown fracas. Now he presided at a Chilmark public hearing at which fifty people turned up on a cold evening in late January. Arguments were less virulent; the fishermen appeared to be for the project since they made little use of Stonewall Pond themselves. Again there were objections from property owners, one, a Chatham, New Jersey, boating enthusiast, wanted to start junior sailfish races in the pond:

". . . oyster floats around the entire shore line would make it impossible to conduct this most important recreational activity."

"Why not start it in Lobsterville Cove in Menemsha Pond—somebody else's back yard?" a candid voter asked.

The Stonewall problems encountered were pinpointed by Matthiessen: one was legal (he couldn't work out a way to be a Chilmark voter for one year prior to his application, a requirement for the grant), the other aesthetic, as he might interfere with the attractions of a small pond. In August 1966 the government finally released the report of the Matthiessen-Toner study and Matthiessen announced his departure from Martha's Vineyard at the end of the month.

The gatherers were victorious. "It was the stupid, selfish people on this island, the attitude of the so-called fishermen," John Hughes of the Lobster Hatchery tells a visitor. "There are only four or five true shellfishermen; the rest are carpenters and plumbers who take two weeks off to go scalloping and scrape the bottom clean. People who know better are afflicted with apathy and don't go to meetings," Hughes continues. "It's the little red hen and apple pie. When it's time to bake, nobody wants to bake; when it's time to eat, everybody wants to eat. Matthiessen wouldn't come back to the Vineyard for a million dollars," Hughes said reflectively. "And this is where he should be working."

The state shellfish commissioner, discouraged by Matthiessen's defeat, predicted that there would be no native oyster crop by the end of the sixties. Nineteen sixty-five, he said, was the worst oyster year since 1881 because of polluted waters, drought, change in coastal environment. "I just cannot understand why people resist progress on general principles alone."

General principles in this instance are neither general nor principles. The Vineyard people resisted progress for specific reasons; to wit, there is still easy money to be made from a few weeks' shellfishing. Even now, between fifty and a hundred people are employed just to shuck scallops on the island and part-time scallopers can make twenty to fifty dollars per day from October through March, the scallop-harvesting season. About 350 people are licensed to collect shellfish; most do it part time. Nevertheless, as the resort business increases, the fish business declines. The only way to reverse this trend and bring shellfishing up to its potential as a major island industry is, Matthiessen and Toner demonstrated, to base it on artificial reproduction and suspension—aquaculture.

Vineyarders needed a spirit of adventure to support Matthiessen's proposal and its implication, a new use of Vineyard waters. It was not forthcoming. Instead, islanders stood stolidly by the ways of their ancestors, or what they thought were those ways. Actually, the ancestral tradition was extraordinarily adventurous. Because colonial Vineyarders could and did respond to new possibilities, they brought about the island's most prosperous days, its great whaling era.

Whalers generally went to sea as boys, leaving home at twelve or fourteen for the long sea voyages. It was a young man's career; by thirty-five or forty, most whaling captains retired, historians tell us, to buy farms up-island, invest in fast horses, and although often temperamentally unsuited to it, practice the latest farming methods. Some of the remarkable dry stone walls in Chilmark and West Tisbury—a later vintage than those of the sheep farmers—attest to their skill and ingenuity, and in Edgartown their great white houses, complete with widow's walks, still stand. If farming was distasteful, the captains, who were men of repute in the community, often went into what was called the hotel business, which meant taking in boarders in those days, sometimes bought a store on the water front where they could keep an eye on the harbor and gossip with customers, or became town or county officials.

They were not fishermen by nature or divine right. Most

came from British yeoman stock and had migrated to the new colony with the intention of carrying forward their accustomed landbound occupations. It was the barren island soil, unresponsive to their labor, which first turned their attention to the sea. Whaling started with the then numerous drift whales, carried lifeless to the shore by the tide. Rights to these drift whales were part of land sales; Banks's history says that in 1658 an Indian chief sold Chickemmoo (the Indian name for Lambert's Cove) to the elder Mayhew, including in the transaction "four spans round in the middle of every whale that comes upon the shore of this quarter part and no more."

Soon Vineyarders, Indian and white alike, were not content to wait for the drift whale but chased whales they could spot offshore. As the use of oil in lamps increased in the country, whaling became more and more important to islanders; inventories of the period list "Half a Barrell of Oyl" [sic], "great Kittells," iron pots, and whaling irons to mark the monster with the huntsman's initials. Whales were tame then, and relatively easy to kill. Captain John Smith, exploring the coast in 1614, found them so "neighborly" that he spent some of his spare time catching them.

This idyllic state of things did not last. As man became greedier for the whale's yield, whales became wary. Less neighborly, they moved out into deeper waters. Bigger boats were built to go after them and soon Edgartown and Vineyard Haven bustled with boat builders and those in allied trades—riggers, caulkers, sailmakers, coopers (who made hogsheads and barrels to transport the oil for marketing). Now whaling voyages of two to three weeks were possible in sloops and schooners of twenty to thirty tons. By the time of the Revolution, whalers from the Vineyard and Nantucket had been from Greenland and the Gulf of St. Lawrence to Barbados and Brazil, and Thomas Jefferson reported to Congress that the Vineyard had a dozen sixty-ton whalers voyaging northward.

Whaling was one of the first co-operatives. Men were engaged to share the proceeds upon certain percentages, Banks says, according to their duties and responsibilities. The voyage of the *Lion* in 1807, for example, took oil valued at $37,661, of which one eighteenth, or $2,072, went to the captain as his share, in lieu of regular pay. The first mate got one twenty-seventh.

The bigger the boats got, the more islanders were in demand. Mainland capitalists financed ships and voyages, islanders manned them. New Bedford became the new whaling center as Vineyard shipyards were out of timber and Nantucket captains could no longer tow ships with a deeper draft across the sand bar at the entrance to their harbor. By 1791 whaling had reached its high plateau, which was to last for a happily profitable century or more, for in this year the whalers rounded Cape Horn and sailed into the unexplored Pacific seas.

In these strange waters, among the archipelago often peopled by cannibals and fierce native tribes, Vineyarders pursued the hitherto unknown sperm whale which lived only in the warm southern seas. Coral and exotic shells soon decorated Edgartown houses; in today's antique stores and at an occasional auction, Chinese vases, lacquered cabinets with mother-of-pearl inlay, and other treasures from the Pacific remind us of the adventuring whalers, and scrimshaw—whalebone carved by sailors to pass the time on long trips—is a much-prized island item. By 1822, thirty American ships were hunting the spermaceti as far north as Japan; a decade later the first baleen or "right" whale was hauled aboard the ship *Ganges*, starting whalemen on a new adventure in the northwest Pacific.

Through the Bering Strait and into the frozen Pacific waters, whalers from New Bedford, Nantucket, and Edgartown sailed their ships in the mid-nineteenth century. They stopped off in San Francisco for a go at the gold rush in '49, discovered and

explored new territories as far north as the Siberian Okhotsk
Sea, found yet another right whale species, the bowhead, which
was easy to capture, being peaceful by nature, not having been
frightened by hunters before.

No one knows for sure whether it was a Captain Royce of
Sag Harbor, New York, who first drifted through the Aleutian
Islands after the bowhead, or Captain Fred Manter of West
Tisbury on his ship the *Ockmulgee*. But in the season of 1848
both ships captured the largest whales man had ever seen. The
average bowhead is sixty to seventy feet long, Captain Ellsworth West recalls, takes its name from the head, which is one
third the length of its body, its ten-foot lips weighing two tons
each. Royce energetically circulated his story, Manter kept the
tale for his friends at home, but the Vineyard loyally has always credited him with inspiring interest in arctic whaling.

Again, new whaling grounds gave the industry a fresh boost.
The enormous bowheads had some four hundred narrow
slabs of bone, called baleen, on each side of the upper jaw instead of teeth—more baleen than any other species—and this
bone was of great value in those pre-plastic days, being light,
pliable, and durable. It was used for corset stays, umbrella ribs,
and horsewhips, brought up to $6.00 a pound. The Arctic
Ocean was rich hunting; a single bowhead's bone and oil together could bring $11,000 to $12,000; a century earlier, annual
profit from the total whaling industry had been $150,000. The
Arctic was also the locus of the greatest disaster in whaling
history. In 1871 the weather suddenly changed its expected pattern and more than thirty whaling ships were caught and splin-
tered like matchsticks by the crushing ice.

Through whaling, Henry Hough remarks, "the globe was
sprinkled with salt from one small New England shaker."
On these long, sometimes boring, often dangerous and lonely
voyages, men whose home was a tiny dot on the globe called
Martha's Vineyard took island ways with them; they also some-

times took a wife. One whaling man recalls a stint in 1895 as
chief officer under a certain Captain Joseph Whiteside who
"expected me to take complete charge of navigating the ship
north. The captain had his bride aboard, an eighteen-year-
old salesgirl from a New Bedford department store, and this
cruise was more or less in the nature of a honeymoon," the
narrator concludes laconically. "He was fifty-six."

Aboard a whaleship, about three times the length of a Vineyard house, the captain's wife made her husband's quarters her
home as comfortably as she could, using the galley at off hours
for her own concoctions. There is a collection of records con-
cerning these remarkable ladies. "Light winds from the SSE,"
a mate's entry reads, "a steering NNW under short sail until
9 A.M. Capt's wife got sick and so we made all sail for home. I
wish she would have a sick time every day if that would only
hurry us."

Separation had its own exigencies. Families were spaced according to length of voyages, or spiced by the appearance of a
baby when a husband had been away more than a year or two.
Vineyard society learned to accept such irregularities as well as
tales of little natives encountered in the South Seas with
familiar names of Vineyard captains. But ties were apparently
solid and trusting; one letter preserved by descendants is addressed, with the absolute assurance of a Vineyarder, to Capt.
Nathan M. Jernegan, Ship *Splendid*, Pacific Ocean.

Great numbers of whaling ships were commandeered and
destroyed during the Civil War; later, electricity, corsetless
women, and the discovery of oil underground sent the market
for whale products plummeting. Whaling just about ended
with the nineteenth century. "I was pretty certain that the
[whaling] industry was on its last legs," Captain West noted
in 1899 and prepared himself to haul coal to Nome, Alaska,
where there was a gold rush. Other captains enjoyed the
nineteenth-century rise in coastal shipping which made the

Vineyard Sound one of the world's busiest waterways, second only to the English Channel according to one report. The captains commanded coastal vessels, passenger ships, freighters; some settled down on the Vineyard to fish and farm, although profits to be had were a considerable comedown from even a mate's share of a year's whaling. In a typical year in the 1900s, one man's record shows, his income from fishing was $3,025, the potato and turnip crop yielded him $190, cranberries $95, and hay $35. Compensations often noted were the familiar vistas of meadow and ocean seen with a new perspective.

Whaling had intrigued the people of the Vineyard from its inception to its extinction, exciting the imagination of many of the ablest islanders of one generation after another for almost three hundred years. There was more to the enticement of "Thar' she blows!" than the profitable share of the take, more than the sporting challenge known even to the lowly fisherman waiting for a nibble at the worm on his hook. Whaling had the powerful pull of invention. Mobile not static, flexible not fixed, it was changed by the men who undertook it. Each could make whaling contemporary to his time.

From the first drift whale carved up on an island beach to the last bowhead killed in the Aleutian Sea, whaling was responsive to man's capacity to expand his vision for his own benefit. Thus did the ancestors of today's Vineyarders conduct their business with the sea.

Shellfishermen of the 1970s have a like opportunity but on a speeded-up schedule. Whether enough of the old-time courage and response to excitement which spurred the rounding of Cape Horn and the penetration of the Arctic Ocean survives in the descendants of whaling men who now control the island's shellfishing is a crucial question for Martha's Vineyard.

Mostly, they are prone to ancestor worship but the worship is literal, the spirit of whaling men being evidently not transferable to shellfishing. Gathering scallops, oysters, and clams on the Vineyard is still basically regulated by colonial ordinances, devised in mid-seventeenth century.

Early settlers knew the technique invented by ancient Romans of making an artificial hard bottom for larva to cling to. Perhaps they knew that the Romans had brought their primitive sea farming with them when they occupied England, where it was such a success that by medieval times oysters were a poor man's food, being so plentiful. Colonists gave town selectmen power to make bottom grants and to "control, regulate or prohibit the taking of . . . any or all kinds of shellfish." The law and the practice, hardly changed in the intervening centuries, says in effect that there is a way to encourage more shellfish to grow and residents can borrow part of ponds to do it, but cannot depend on long-term use of such privilege. The public right to collect what's in the public waters comes first.

Colonial shellfishing and its laws suited its time, based on the premise that nature, with the help of an occasional added hard bottom, would provide what the Vineyard needed. Still to come was the dramatic collapse in the 1850s of the great British oyster fisheries, such as those at the Kentish cliffs, due, an expert says, to greedy fishermen dragging dredges through the deeper beds, destroying the natural reproductive cycle. Greed and oysters appear to go together; the Roman Sergius Orata, described by Pliny as the first person to make artificial oyster beds, did so "not for the gratification of gluttony," Pliny says, "but of avarice, as he contrived to make a large income by this exercise of his ingenuity."

The revolutionary twentieth-century discovery of artificial reproduction of shellfish and twentieth-century Vineyard needs do not match the mores of colonial times. The scientific breakthrough enables man to plant shellfish in the proper environment for whatever size harvest he wishes, just as he learned to plant peas and corn in his garden at a much earlier stage of civilization. The new possibility for aquaculture came exactly when the Vineyard desperately needed a solid economic alternative to the people business in order to survive. But voters could not or would not seize the opportunity when it was made viable in the proposal of George Matthiessen. The old adventurous spirit of their forefathers languished.

In the next few years the people business turned out to be not as benign for the Vineyard as it might have seemed back in the first fine flush. Almost immediately it collided head on with shellfishing.

Islanders turned to building for the summer trade—houses, stores, motels, hamburger joints—and spent less time shellfishing. In Edgartown, for example, the number of people in construction increased fifty-seven per cent in a decade while those shellfishing decreased twenty-seven per cent. The less time shellfishing, the more likely a grab-and-run approach and the smaller the chance to start time-consuming aquaculture. As the people pressure increased, so did agitation for access to the Great Ponds provided for by state law, the old fishing and fowling statute having been amended to include recreation. Riparian owners on the ponds looked in the other direction, hoping the issue would go away if they paid no attention. Instead, in the case of Tisbury Great Pond, for example, Concerned Citizens' President Carleton Parker forced the issue by threatening to call in the State Access Board. Complying with regulations for access means more people using the ponds with more boats . . . and more disturbance to shellfish waters.

Then came pollution. More people on an unprepared, planless, sewerless island resulted in more homes, boats, and businesses discharging sewage directly into island harbors and ponds. "Without stringent [sewage] regulations," the Gazette said in late 1971, "the Island may be reduced to a state of crisis."

Crisis hovered that summer when U. S. Food and Drug Administration officials confiscated four huge swordfish which were over the safe mercury level and ordered them buried; when a doctor, testing hair samples of islanders, found a large level of mercury in those eating tuna, bluefish, and striped bass, advised, "If you must eat high-mercury-level fish, eat small ones"; when the shellfish yield of Long Island Sound was reported to be a quarter of what it had been seven years before as a result of pollution; when the State Division of Water Pollution announced in 1971 that there would be at least a year's delay in enforcing harbor regulations for boats, pending pollution studies.

"How many more studies do we need to tell us what we already know?" an irate citizen storms. Various government bureaus had made a steady stream of studies over the decade, examining scallops (scarce), harbors (polluted), oysters and lobsters (diminishing), clams (being imported by Poole to fill his export orders). But no study insisted, even after the Matthiessen report, that times had changed for shellfishing or suggested a radically new approach.

Shellfishing could still become a major island industry as these words are written, could still move from gathering to farming, but it would require an immediate giant step ahead. Every study would have to be based on the use of and requirements for artificial reproduction and scientific sea farming. Every applicable law would have to be promptly scrutinized and changed to make aquaculture on a grand scale achievable. Every place where shellfish might be cultivated would have to be protected against use—public or private—which might interfere with the sucess of the shellfish farms. Men would have to be assured that they could harvest what they planted, adjusting the colonists' bottom-grant system to aquaculture realities of the 1970s. Pollution would have to be stringently controlled. So would greed and self-interest; the junior sailfish races might have to be sacrificed to what would have to be an earnest, determined, all-island goal.

Possible? There's a chance. Men on the Vineyard are beginning to be afraid of the people business. They cannot tell where its rampant ravaging will lead them. They are turning again toward the waters.

A start has been made, not a grand-scale adventure in the manner of whaling voyages, but a tentative, toe-in-the-water start toward aquaculture. The Marine Research Foundation, which sponsored Matthiessen's Vineyard effort, has been reactivated by Thomas Flynn, son of its originator, although Matthiessen is now successfully established on the mainland where he has a commercial shellfish company, "precisely the type of operation we had hoped might develop on the Vineyard. Our operation," he says, "is in Wareham where there has been a long history of private oyster leases and where the co-operation has been outstanding." The Foundation aims to pick up where Matthiessen left off. "There are indications that the climate is more favorable now for such a move," the Vineyard *Grapevine* comments, and Flynn estimates that the island could produce a laboratory-initiated crop "roughly equivalent to the total annual oyster production in the northeastern United States."

For the first time in Vineyard history, a formal fishermen's co-operative has been established. The whalers' practice is now impressively institutionalized into the Martha's Vineyard Fishery Resources Committee, a non-profit corporation owned by the fishermen. The idea, first considered in 1940 but abandoned because of World War II, reconsidered by Matthiessen, was brought into being in 1972. It was proposed by John Waller, an Edgartown fisherman, and surprisingly quickly taken up by fishermen from all the island towns, meeting together to discuss what Waller calls "the low state of Vineyard fishing." In island fashion, Waller was immediately accused by his peers of trying to fix himself up with a job as the co-op's manager, but in a swift (for the Vineyard) two months, the co-op was agreed upon.

Its aims are to build a profitable industry. In Provincetown, the fishermen were told, a co-op started out with $25 and five men, now grosses $1.5 million a year, helps the financially depressed area by bolstering other industries. On the island, shellfishing, with proper cultivation and marketing, could support fifty full-time fishermen at $10,000 a year and another fifty part-time at $2,500, Walter figures. The co-op will be its own middleman, will have access to an existing northeast area fishermen's lobby in Washington, to federal funds for special projects and, most significant, to taking some waters out of the public domain for shellfish culture.

At long last the fishermen have begun to move toward farming the sea. It is painfully little and painfully late. The youthful generation of islanders, who might have given the move the vigor and adventurousness of their forefathers, had streamed off the island in the late 1960s and early '70s to settle, work, or just cop out elsewhere. Jobs on the Vineyard were scarce, the booming building business importing off-island labor, and, as land costs spiraled, it was hard to find housing which the young could afford. A recent high school class had just one graduate left on the island; eighty per cent of all graduates leave. This, combined with the influx of people retiring to the island, makes the population top-heavy with elders and missing the spirit that once sent the young whaling.

Island waters—the peaceful inlets, ponds gently ruffled by a passing summer breeze or turbulent in winter storms, harbors narrow-necked and protected, or generously open to ferries from the mainland—are sometimes dark blue, cerulean, pale green, or violet in the sunset, lying innocent and clear . . . and crowded with microscopic fecal coliform. Pollution of the waters is the most difficult barrier to the Vineyard's pursuit of aquaculture, an irony of timing.

If the will to farm the sea had been there in the forties or the fifties, or when Matthiessen made his proposal in the sixties, there would have been the motive, aggressive and insistent, to stop pollution before it got anywhere near its present level. "It is a curious and disheartening fact," Morton Hunt writes about Long Island Sound, "that although nearly everyone today is aware of pollution and is concerned about it, the awareness and concern have not yet affected inner feelings enough to make restraint and self-discipline automatic." The same is true on the Vineyard. Tools have been devised on local, state and federal levels to control pollution but the ability to put them to use is still not in evidence on the island.

The threat of the virulent people business was what finally bestirred Vineyarders to contemplate aquaculture. This same people business, if it continues to advance at the present unchecked speed, may make the civilizing step impossible. The trace of the old whaling eagerness surviving in Vineyard family genes is not enough to surmount the problems alone. But there is, now, an added dimension—the encouragement and wisdom which come from off-island, from the government hierarchy, from the minds of people who care about Martha's Vineyard but are not of it, from the new nationwide environmental awareness. The combination might be enough to turn the island, once more, toward the riches of the sea.

CHAPTER FOUR

The Wish to Protect

Off-islanders, as non-natives are known locally, are becoming a force in the Vineyard's future. They almost have to. There is no such thing any more as a carefree island vacation, no place to hide from what's happening. Valued vistas vanish before your eyes. Streets, stores, and roads are newly crowded as are the beaches; harbors and bays are polluted. Some people sell their houses and search for a less troubled place, some succumb to the temptation of subdividing their land, parting with an acre or two at a succulent profit, some try one way or another to keep the island's surviving virtues intact. Whatever they do, they are changing the definition of off-islanders.

The old concept of Vineyard visitors lasted through the 1960s. Just as islanders perpetuated traditions long beyond their time, off-islanders kept to archaic patterns in their relations to the Vineyard. When they needed to be boldly inventive in planning for the island, they were on vacation. Some of the nation's keenest intellects, with talents desperately needed in the mounting dilemma—land planners, scientists, economists, jurists, highly placed government officials, to name a few—continued the name and the game of being old-time off-islanders.

The very term suggests the Vineyard's view of the world as bordered by its own parameters, an attitude communicated to visitors sometimes subtly (try getting your roof patched or car fixed in an urban hurry), sometimes with a broadside attack;

"We don't want people coming down here to tell us how to run our island." In the Vineyard visitor pecking order, summer people are a cut above tourists, whose average stay is thirteen days and average amount spent $600 (longer and more than in Palm Beach or Bermuda, a Chamber of Commerce executive states with consummate pride), and several notches higher than the hated day trippers, who will break anything on the island, Vineyarders say, except a five-dollar bill. But lack of native ancestry keeps summer people a part of the off-island monolith. The Vineyard expects them to pay taxes, spend money, and not meddle.

In return the island opens itself to their enjoyment. It is a point of pride with Vineyard storekeepers, fishermen, farmers, and the rest to stay impassively unaffected at the appearance of a renowned off-islander on the premises. The resulting semi-anonymity, the absence of responsibility imposed by local insistence on local autonomy, and the dependable balm of land and water, are a welcome respite after a hard-working winter. Year after year, driving off the ferry evokes the same familiar sense of home revisited where, miraculously, nothing changes. For this, off-islanders accept the opprobrium of not completely belonging, joke about love-hate relations with the natives, complain of the minor miseries of Vineyard housekeeping, and generally play the classic summer-people role.

The quid pro quo of this arrangement exploded when the greater world in some of its uglier aspects penetrated the Vineyard. Off-islanders were forced to notice what was happening under the stewardship of the native population combined with their own passivity. Whether they were mild-mannered conservationists, occasionally roused to protective action by one issue or another, or goodhearted philanthropists, willing to pay for a settlement with their conscience, or those who would relax and let well enough alone, never bothering to think that the island needed their protection, they suddenly saw their actions boomerang. What they had done, by prolonging the tradition of off-islanders, was to indulge the Vineyard's limited vision almost to a point of no return.

The wish to protect the island had a dozen rudimentary starts. The late Elizabeth Hough, copublisher and editor of the *Vineyard Gazette* with her husband Henry, loved the look of the old icehouse and pond where salt and fresh water meet in a meadow near her Edgartown home on Sheriff's Lane. "When ice became extinct," Henry Hough recalls, "Betty worried about what would happen. She bought the ten acres for $7,500." Because this was too small a sanctuary to interest the august Massachusetts Audubon Society (with some 17,000 members, a $500,000 annual budget, and over 7,000 acres, the largest conservation organization in the Northeast and, it claims, one of the oldest in the world) or the Trustees of Reservations (founded in 1890 to encourage open space and preservation in Massachusetts, now with 44 reservations of some 10,000 acres), the Houghs started their own foundation in the 1950s, named it after the Sheriff's Meadow which they gave it, and spent $40 a year to keep it going.

Like its king-size models, Sheriff's Meadow Foundation was dedicated to "preserve natural habitats for wildlife . . . as living museums," among other high-minded conservation aims. The Houghs and their many friends and admirers added bits and pieces to it through the sixties. Nothing was too inconspicuous: an acre or two of marsh near the meadow, lots on Chappaquiddick, West Chop, Middle Road, a sector of a small pond known as John Butler's Mud Hole, and such, brought the holdings to fifteen by the early seventies.

Sheriff's Meadow—and old-fashioned land-saving—came of age on the Vineyard when Miss Emma Daggett, Robert and John Daggett, owners of Cedar Tree Neck, the farthest extension of the island into the Vineyard Sound, decided to sell the remarkable headland and some hundred surrounding acres of moors, pond, and woods, which had been in their family for more than a century. There had been long discussions between the Daggetts and the Houghs about preserving this land, sometimes joined by Allen Morgan, executive of the Massachusetts Audubon, sometimes by David Lilienthal, former chairman of the Atomic Energy Commission, whose summer home is on nearby Indian Hill, close to Fish Hook, the Houghs' family holdings. "The Daggetts had the same interest as Sheriff's Meadow," Hough says, "being completely opposed to exploiting the place for resort purposes. They wanted to keep it as it was for oncoming generations."

Cedars must have been growing on the striking headland and around the pond below it for centuries, Cedar Tree Neck being the recorded name in 1718, although the Indians called it Squemmechchue, meaning red fruit land and probably referring to the cranberry bog on the dunes, destroyed in the 1938 hurricane. The compact white homestead, which the Daggetts proposed to keep in the family, sits securely on a bluff looking across the sound at the Elizabeth Islands. It was built in mid-eighteenth century by Mayhew Norton, a ship's pilot, fifth-generation descendant of an English immigrant, who walked from his house to work, a fact only remarkable because the records show his usual destination to be New Bedford or Boston. The Daggetts' grandparents bought the Norton property in 1846 for $1,800, intending to farm it, but the grandfather, a skilled whaler, had disastrous results on the land and soon returned to sea, while his children walked up the hill and across the fields to the schoolhouse at Seven Gates Farm and later to work at the tannery in Lambert's Cove, three miles distant.

Now people drive their cars to Cedar Tree Neck to take a walk. In 1967, when land on the Vineyard's north shore was selling for $8,000 an acre (in 1972, $15,000 is not unexpected) the Daggetts agreed to sell the curving beach, towering head-land, and woodland on the steep slope which rises sharply behind it—a total of about 200 acres—to Sheriff's Meadow Foundation for $165,000, a fraction of what was being offered for it by developers. If it could be purchased, Henry Hough and his brother George would donate 60 adjoining Fish Hook acres, which contain a deep amber brook winding down the hillside in a ravine and additional beach, bringing the shore front to almost three quarters of a mile. Next to it is the 50-acre Alexander Reed Bird Refuge. The entire venture, Hough wrote in the *Gazette*, would be "one of the most significant steps yet taken in meeting the challenge of a future which threatens the Island in many ways. . . ."

With *Gazette* leadership, contributions poured in for the purchase, mostly accompanied by fervent statements of Vineyard-worship: "Roaming over Cedar Tree Neck has been one of the most rewarding aspects of my life . . ."; "The Amalfi Drive and Grossglochner Pass play an inadequate supporting role to the north shore of the Vineyard"; "As I walk along, I get Wordsworth's sense of something far more deeply interfused"; "We love the dear old island. . . ." Love letters and cash mounted up; the "land of our hearts' desire" collected $180,000 in seventeen weeks, ended with a total of $195,000 from over a thousand contributors, providing a fund for maintaining as well as buying the property. The cost of this achievement was a minuscule $1,000. "Could it have happened anywhere else?" Hough asks and answers, "I doubt it."

Cedar Tree Neck, the first fund-raising of its kind on the Vineyard, was a blazing success. A large white sign at the entrance explains its purposes and strict regulations (no swimming, picnicking, camping) to keep it a sanctuary. On a summer day, half a dozen people stroll through the narrow paths, enjoy the forest quiet, the re-created pond described in earlier pages, the empty, stone-scattered beach where gulls convene in peaceful conclave.

The land-acquisition impulse spread from Cedar Tree Neck to another headland, Wasque, on the northern tip of Chappaquiddick. Swept by winds from all quarters, its low dunes protect only scattered bayberry and blueberry bushes, the great Atlantic surf crashes against its stands. When 200 acres of this early Indian land was put up for sale in 1968, the first piece of 80 acres was promptly subscribed for, bought, and transferred to the Trustees of Reservations, which had a substantial foothold in the Vineyard, established by gifts from a few individuals: in 1959, the Cape Poge Wildlife Preserve, 391 acres in a long narrow spit of land stretching into Nantucket Sound at the other side of Chappaquiddick; in 1966, Menemsha Hills, some 60 acres in the Western Moraine on the island's north shore, gift of the Harris family, increased to more than 100 acres in the 1970s.

The remaining Wasque land could be bought for $170,000 and Edgartown enthusiasts followed Hough's lead, launching a public campaign. "A pledge to the future . . ." the *Gazette* said, encouraging gifts to "help transfer a Vineyard heritage to the custody of the Trustees of Reservations for all the years remaining to the human race." Again, money and love in generous quantities were forthcoming, and by the summer of 1969 Wasque Reservation was secure for fishermen, beachcombers, birds, and seaside wilderness.

Meanwhile, a remarkable example of what the naturalists call a "biotic community," where many single communities are interdependent—upland, salt marsh, woodland, wetland, meadow, swamp, bog, and beach—suffered the fate of many old Vineyard farms. On Sengakontacket Pond, the 200 acres of Felix Neck, named for its last Indian resident, had been farmed by the Smith family since the white settlers divided the land in the seventeenth century. Close to the cove where Matthiessen had proposed the hatchery, the old farm slopes down to the pond from verdant fields. But with the general island decline in farming, it was no longer a profitable enterprise, and taxes were high. It was purchased by conservation-minded George Moffett, Jr., given to the Massachusetts Audubon, to be managed by the Felix Neck Wildlife Trust as an educational center with classes for school children, bird and animal sanctuaries, self-guiding nature trails ("Turn left at the next marker and hear the yellow-throat warbler that nests in the pond-side underbrush . . ."; "Turn right at the next marker and find five kinds of ferns in the bog community").

When Felix Neck needed money for a headquarters building to serve as the conservation center of the island, a museum, and a director's residence for a full-time overseer (the very summer of expressing this need, a dog got into the wildlife enclosure at night and murdered a pet fawn), it followed the public appeal pattern which had been so successful for Cedar Tree Neck and Wasque. The reaction was less than enthusiastic. Enough money was garnered to build the director's house and enlarge ponds and bird-feeding areas. Expansion as envisioned had to await more cash.

There is a continuing dribble of individual gifts of land. The Nature Conservancy, a national organization which has collected 150,000 acres in forty-two states in just five years, and has a $6-million credit line with the Ford Foundation for quick action, made its debut on the Vineyard with a gift from Franklin Q. Brown of 83 Tisbury acres "to offset the intensive real estate development now in progress . . . by protecting wild bird, animal and arboreal life." (Following what is known as the "watchdog plan," it immediately conveyed this land to Sheriff's Meadow, subject to conditions which would mean a reverting of the land to it, should the conditions be violated.) Sheriff's Meadow resumed its modest progress, receiving a minuscule island in Lake Tashmoo from Gertrude Macy, who has looked at it in its natural state all her life and wants to continue to do so, the 2-acre Dodger Hole which, Hough says, is "a wonderful example of glacial pothole and marsh" donated by one of the Vineyard's first and largest developers, Alvin Strock (about whom more later). From the late Henry Cronig, who foresaw the Vineyard land boom before most others, particularly in Gay Head where he bought considerable acreage from the Indians, came a gift of 9 acres in Tisbury for a park.

Of the Vineyard's 64,000 acres, between 1,200 and 1,500 were in semipublic conservation areas at the start of the seventies, 4,500 in state forest (planted to protect the heath hen), and 240 in watershed land, "a fraction of the total island," Robert Woodruff, director of the Vineyard Conservation Society, says, "Since giving land has been completely haphazard, its diversity is amazing."

Amazing, too, is its effect. No one has tried another public campaign to buy land for conservation since the three efforts of the sixties, although family estates like the Daggetts' and old Vineyard farms like the Smiths' have flooded the market. Money and love appear to have dwindled, as far as the Vineyard is concerned. Further, the dramatic public outpouring apparently had a sedative effect on public responsibility. The government-owned summit of Peaked Hill, highest hill on the Vineyard (311 feet above sea level), which housed a radar research station, was put on the market early in 1970. Preference for such a purchase must go, the law says, to local government agencies and eligible educational or public health institutions. The government offered it to the town of Chilmark for $8,000, about half its estimated value. "The price is terrifically high," Herbert Hancock, Chilmark builder and selectman, said, "and the town needs a beach a lot more than it needs a view."

Nothing happened. From February to September, Chilmark sat on its hands. Although it was said that it had filed for purchase, "no eligible agency or institution submitted an application for it," the General Services Administration in Boston said. In October this most conspicuous hilltop, a checkpoint from land and sea, was opened for public bids and sold for $28,010 to a developer from the Cape. The Vineyard, which only a few years before had poured forth its generosity by saving and conserving the two headlands, could not come up with a way to preserve for itself the summit of its highest hill. The fundamental wish to protect, expressed in a manner appropriate to conservation as it had been in an earlier, simpler era, now set up the idea of dependence of public on private structure, a sense of "Let George do it," and the conviction that some George or other would. It penetrated far and deep.

"If you people down on the Vineyard are so interested in the island's future, why is it that you haven't come forward and bought more of the critical land for conservation the way they have in Nantucket?" a staff member in the governor's State House office asked me in response to a request for information on what was being done to protect a particularly vulnerable island spot. Coincidentally, the thought was impatiently echoed by Charles Haar, professor of law at Harvard, former assistant secretary of the U. S. Department of Housing and Urban Development, who was advising Senator Kennedy in the preparation of protective island legislation. "Why don't the rich summer people buy the damn island?"

Private funds instead of public protection? The results of the 1960s on the Vineyard show the weakness of this nonplanning. It cannot do the job that needs doing. Sources are finite; after two successful campaigns, the philanthropic urge weakened, and as development progressed, giving—money or land—declined. Even if an individual, or the general public, spurred by sibling rivalry with Nantucket, could be urged to preserve another few hundred acres for its flora and fauna, will yellow-throated warblers and five kinds of ferns survive in a polluted, overcrowded place? Will there be people who care to wander through a biotic community wilderness next to a hot dog stand?

The results of old-fashioned land-saving are individually valued—a walk through Cedar Tree Neck Sanctuary or a day in the remote sun-drenched salty glories of Wasque restores the soul—but collectively, these positive acts have a strong negative, serving as a red herring. They distract attention from the basic dilemma, both on the grass-roots level of the average man and on the heights of advisers to government leaders. It is easier to give an acre or two, send a check, and write a love letter to the Vineyard than to transform the gentle wish to protect into hardheaded political knowhow, which is, in this fast-changing time, becoming the only way to accomplish lasting land conservation. It is easier to call on the rich to buy up the land that needs preserving than to wade through the endless complexities of existing legislation which might be applicable or, even more difficult (and more necessary), to devise new laws and a new land ethic.

The ultimate in red-herringsmanship was the proposal of the Open Land Foundation, a conservation organization with a real estate twist, formed at the start of the seventies by some nationally known land planners who vacationed on the Vineyard, and a blue-chip collection of off-islanders. It would buy large parcels, protect their roadsides, and hide development behind them. Prime mover Edward Logue, planning wizard for New York state, formerly of Boston and New Haven repute, says, "At least you'll still be able to drive along island roads as though nothing has happened."

There could be no more pointed comment on what is happening. Island roads are innocent of advertising billboards and signs, cared for, and green, because they express the Vineyard's total character. It is no accident that they allow the solitude of dark-shaded canopies, the lift of spirit at a glimpse of rolling surf beyond glinting gray stone walls, the pleasure of neat hedgerows, redolent in summer with wild roses and meadowsweet. The roads are an integral part of the island, cherished as the island is cherished.

The Chairman of Trees and Roadsides of the Martha's Vineyard Garden Club, a vigorous, well-informed lady named Juliet Kraetzer, who has held the post for some years, has had some fractious dealings with the district engineer, Raymond Kelliher of Middleboro, Massachusetts ("He is always courteous, though," she says, "always answers my letters and sometimes comes up with some solution"), and with his subordinate Henry Sutton, superintendent of road maintenance on the island. One of the club's vice-presidents (there is one for each Vineyard town) told her of a "massacre" planned for the big oaks on the roadside near the North Tisbury dump. "I was there at 8 A.M.," Mrs. Kraetzer tells a visitor, "trying to stop them from cutting down a magnificent tree. They said it was diseased; I picked up a piece of bark and it looked fine to me. Then they said it was diseased at the top. I told them, 'You better cut off the top branches and fill in with cement or you'll have 350 mad girls on your back.'"

The 350 girls (about two thirds are off-islanders, according to President Mrs. Anthony Silva) are members of the Garden Club, which has had surprising clout in matters Vineyard since it was formed by ten Edgartown ladies in 1924, adopting the motto "The Island is Our Garden." The very next year it started its campaign against billboards on the island, which it has continued with notable success ever since. Thanks to the vigilance of members, almost no signs scar island roads. To keep the view unpolluted, the Garden Club members have used various persuasive tactics: letters to national advertisers, informing them of the club's wishes, withdrawal of patronage from continuing offenders, visits to persuade local firms or individuals or both who put up signs to cease and desist.

One stubborn businessman, newly arrived on the island, put an enormous billboard near his plant and resisted all standard Garden Club persuasions to take it down. Some weeks later his wife implored him to quit his job and leave the island. Her generally friendly nature had been everywhere thwarted, she said, by cool Vineyard shoulders. "Sunday after Sunday," she wept, "no one except the minister will even speak to me after church." The sign came down. Some years ago, none less than the Pacific Oil Company came a cropper *en face* the girls, who strenuously objected to the two large billboards it put up on Beach Road in Vineyard Haven. The president, treasurer, and advertising manager of the oil company had "not been aware of the sentiment at the Vineyard regarding billboards," they wrote, and removed the offending giants.

Up-island, the roads are not only sign-free but have had a special character, running between tall straight-sided hedgerows, clipped vertically in the old English manner, a style suggested by the Garden Club's first president, Mrs. T. M. R. Meikleham. It was faithfully carried out for many years by Vineyard highway engineers, the Amos, father and son, who used hedge shears with the delight of artists at work. Neglected in World War II, the trimming was reinstated thereafter with a $50,000 appropriation from the state. "A unique adornment of the island . . ." the *Gazette* says. "No one foresaw that within a generation many of them would be cut down."

In the 1960s the Department of Public Works declined to continue hand-clipping the hedgerows, although it agreed to try to keep them, and the character of the roads, by merely topping hedges four feet on curves and clearing in front of speed signs, said to be undertaken in the interests of safety for fast-traveling cars. A further economy followed. Trimming had been required five times a year; now, use of Diuron, a virulent spray, on the surface of the ground controls undesirable growth when it works into the root zone of plants by moisture. It need only be sprayed on every two years, according to Anthony Di Natale, commissioner of public works, and is used since the department no longer has the equipment, time, or money for hand-clipping. "We are no longer living in a hedgerow economy," the commissioner says.

Keeping trees planted and growing along roadsides, and billboards and signs away from them, has become increasingly difficult. Old sandy curving county roads, many of which followed ancient Indian trails, have slipped under the aegis of what is known as Chapter 90, legislation which allots a percentage of state road money to each county. The state pays half the cost of construction, the town and county divide the other half, and maintenance of Chapter 90 roads is split evenly three ways. The package is so tempting, particularly to poor counties like Dukes, that the string it is tied with is likely to be overlooked by local officials. On the Vineyard, the strings soon become evident; Chapter 90 roads have to be a certain width, surface, and straightness, and state engineers are notably unaffected by aesthetics.

"Of course we can't expect the state to go along with cowpaths any more," Mrs. Kraetzer says. "They have to resurface to take care of the added traffic the Vineyard is getting." The Trees and Roadsides Committee was monitoring work on the South Road, the island's first "hicway," which opened in 1738, following the course of an Indian trail and known as the Mill Path because it led to the mills on up-island streams. "Henry Sutton promises they're not going to widen or relocate as they repave," the chairman says. "Guess they're sick and tired of hearing us complain."

Loudest complaints were in 1967 when state engineers decided to cut down a large part of a renowned grove of beetlebung trees to straighten a slight curve in the road passing them. Chilmark Selectman Albert (Ozzie to his friends and the neighborhood) Fischer, whose nearby farm and cutting garden are the delight of urban visitors, together with Garden Club representatives, convinced the engineers to leave the trees, which name the corner they stand on, and the curve in the road, an unusual and celebrated victory. In West Tisbury, a like story had a less happy ending. To improve its narrow Indian Hill Road, winding through the trees and fields to the Houghs' and Lilienthals', overlooking Cedar Tree Neck, the town asked for state funds and got what the *Gazette* describes as "the sort of desecration increasingly associated with highway engineering everywhere." Across the Vineyard Sound, realistic Truro on the Cape says, "When we accept Chapter 90 money for repairing surface, we must accept the formula of widening and straightening," and firmly turns down state aid to fix two curving country roads.

But the Vineyard, beset with more and more traffic, fast cars, and a people-business economy, has added new roads and modernized old ones steadily through the last two decades. In the fifties, Moshup Trail, the oldest known way on the island, passing the old Gay Head village, the old Indian cemetery, and Toad Rock, which the Indians once used as an informal post office, caught the attention of road builders. "This great area of land is useful only to birds, deer, and rabbits," the town moderator said, and many property owners were persuaded that even with a modern road "the mighty riches of the countryside will remain unspoiled through the centuries." Old oxcart trails through it were once used to haul seaweed to high dry land where it was left in stacks so that the rain could wash out the salt and it could then be used for fertilizer. These trails, thickly overgrown, can still be detected winding in and around the black-top roads which now encircle the Gay Head peninsula. More evident is the development which has resulted from investment of public moneys in the roads.

Busy with "The Island is Our Garden" programs and Chapter 90 monitoring, the Garden Club committee did not pay much notice to what was about to happen to a back road down-island. Known as Ferry Road in 1700, it ran between Great Harbor (Edgartown) and Holmes Hole (Vineyard Haven). "It is in a good state of forwardness," the *Gazette* remarked in 1851, when the way was made a county road. "We passed over this road and are free to confess that we consider this the greatest improvement in locomotion ever made on this island. When the road is completed, we may look for an earlier arrival of the mail and more extended intercourse, both social and commercial, with our sister town."

In the twentieth century the road has made history for a different reason. It has become the Vineyard's first federal highway. In the 1960s it was transformed to meet the conditions of a secondary U.S. road, sixty-six feet wide, contoured with ten-foot shoulders twelve feet from the nearest tree. To construct it required cutting great swaths of trees and bulldozing land: no amount of protests changed engineering schedules. A few years back, Vineyarders had not really understood what the commitment of federal funds to this project meant; they were, in fact, pleased at the appropriation arranged by their then representative to the state legislature, the late Joseph Sylvia, and at the public hearing on the matter in Edgartown, all present were in favor.

Now cars whiz along the short, improbable federal highway from one sister town to the other, speeding on its smooth wide surface, skidding around its shoulders (grass instead of the usual crushed rock, as a concession to the Vineyard), and people begin to forget what a quiet island road looks like.

The more big smooth swift roads, the more cars, and the more signs to sell products to drivers en route. The Outdoor Advertising Association of America, founded in 1931, attributes its rapid growth to the popularity of driving (number one American leisure-time activity) coupled with a national network of good roads. The estimated investment in this business, it says, is half a billion dollars, and this does not include amounts spent in contortions to avoid government regulations, a thriving business in itself. Under Lady Bird Johnson's patronage, the federal effort to regulate billboards was stepped up with the Highway Beautification Act of 1965. Six years later, despite high-level interest in and support of the legislation, there are 250,000 more billboards on the nation's highways than when the act was passed, the New York *Times* says, a total of more than a million.

What the Vineyard's share will be, nobody knows. But it is certain that the pleasant unspoken agreement between the ladies of the Garden Club and would-be advertisers will not survive the new hard sell of a populous island crisscrossed with secondary federal highways. More to the point will be use of energies such as those of California's Monterey County, first in the nation to prohibit signs along rural roads, and the state of Vermont, where, after some twenty years of tough political organizing, all billboards are now prohibited and penalties for not taking signs down, or putting new ones up, are stiff.

It is an entirely different proposition to keep signs off Vineyard roads today than it was when Edgartown ladies first banded together back in the 1920s. If regarded as a cosmetic, as suggested by Logue's Open Land Foundation, or as a gentlemen's agreement, as was the custom in gentler times, it will be a memory within the decade. This relatively small aspect of change is symbolic of how the relation between people and the Vineyard must change, if the island's character is to remain.

A quick look at outdoor advertising, its regulations and regulators, boggles the mind. There are two kinds of signs; on-premise signs advertise the business taking place on that land —gas station, restaurant, motel—off-premise signs, chiefly billboards put up on land leased or owned by an outdoor advertising company which, in turn, rents its standard billboard (12 by 25 feet) or standard painted sign (14 by 48 feet) to the advertiser. According to Philip Tocker, president of the Outdoor Advertising Association, his business is "an active voice and energetic servant of the American system of free enterprise." Tocker says the off-premise sign (solemnly called a "display") gives the highest frequency of exposure to upper socioeconomic groups and is "an integral part of the business and marketing function." Signs are put in urban areas where the business exists and in rural areas where other businesses exist.

Massachusetts was the first state to control advertising on its own state highways. It started regulating in 1918, requiring the governor to appoint an Outdoor Advertising Board for this purpose. "Like many regulating boards, the O.A.B. has become the 'friend' of the business it is supposedly regulating," says Margaret Welch, legislative chairman of the Massachusetts Roadside Council, a voluntary watchdog organization whose list of sponsors is headed by Governor Francis Sargent. Several letters from Mrs. Welch are informative; the O.A.B. must approve billboard sites and almost always does. The industry, Mrs. Welch says, keeps a full-time lobbyist in the State House to see that any restrictive measures are defeated. To the chagrin of the advertising business, the governor made some headway in 1969, directing the O.A.B. to comply with local zoning in deciding on permits, and the Roadside Council has followed up by suggesting that this be made a law so that no future governors are persuaded to rescind it. Further, the Council has circulated a model zoning bylaw to all Massachusetts cities and towns; it strictly and straightforwardly keeps signs regulated. By 1971, thirty-three towns had adopted it, sixty more had asked for further information.

Federal, interstate, and limited-access highways have an even more strangulated tangle of regulations, not the least fantastic of which is a government gift, which President Kennedy dubbed "the billboard bonus," granted the state which will remove billboards, the bonus being added to the highway system to build more roads for more billboards to be built on and removed from for more money. One outdoor advertising company voluntarily removed over a hundred billboards on Cape Cod during the 1930s, its president says, when state officials indicated that they wanted the Cape to be "a particularly attractive scenic area. None of the . . . companies have constructed any billboards on Cape Cod since," he continues, "but unfortunately there are many odd-sized indiscriminate signs on the roadsides of the Cape, many of which are illegal." Nothing has yet been done about on-premise advertising on the Cape, Mrs. Welch reports. "Hyannis and Falmouth," she comments, "are a nightmare of competing signs."

The island can make use of the experience of its nightmarish neighbors, and of legislation which has evolved over decades. The science of projection and exponentialism will tell the pragmatist that there will be more federal highways and arrow-straight Chapter 90 byways on the Vineyard, that on them there will be more places of business for odd-sized signs, legal or not, and more and more upper socioeconomic traffic for which to build more standard painted displays. Unless . . .

. . . unless islanders and off-islanders alike drop their blinders and their antique relations to each other and to the island and get to work.

In the mere matter of signs on roads, a protective bylaw could be proposed, studied, adopted, and enforced in a matter of weeks, now that every town has a zoning commission. But John Schilling, selectman of Vineyard Haven, or Luther Madison in the same position in Gay Head, or any of the other towns' officials cannot do it alone and many would not if they could. It needs the expertise of lawyers and lawmakers, the backing of businessmen, the interpretation of sophisticated hard-working journalists, the wisdom of philosophers, to get a ruling that will stick, into the laws, fast. Not every place which has accomplished such an aim has at its command top men in these very fields. On the Vineyard at one time or another during the year are just such, loving the island, wanting to keep it from destruction.

If they apply themselves to roadside signs, they will then logically think about the roads themselves. Before deciding whether federal secondary highways should connect two sister towns, or whether Diuron is the answer for hedgerows, scientists, ecologists, engineers, and planners equipped with modern tools would want to consider island transportation as a whole. If the goal for the future is a pristine Vineyard, what kind of transportation will suit it best? Shall all transportation be in public mini-buses or on monorails, barring cars and tourist buses completely? Shall cars, buses, be limited in number? Size? Or should everybody walk, as Mayhew Norton did two centuries ago?

What happens to roadsides is part of what happens to roads. What happens to roads is part of what happens to Martha's Vineyard. Answers are indivisible from the whole, if they are worth considering at all, and so locomotion will dictate what to build and how to build it without unwanted strings attached. And locomotion, as will be seen, is causing a furor on the Vineyard in wider and wider circles; buses, ferries and airplanes, as well as cars, beach buggies, and motor bikes are all sources of increasing difficulty.

From road signs to roads to the land itself, there are myriad options, details, devices, choices to be made. The sincere wish to protect is a prerequisite but not an answer. The Vineyard can no longer plead innocence or trust in its insularity for protection. It must stop pretending that the unshaven lounger in worn blue jeans is not to be noticed because he is, indeed, a distinguished member of the bar, editor of a world-famous newspaper, prize-winning scientist, or renowned economist but must, instead, harness every skill, power, and influence to harden the protective impulse into law. There is room for philanthropy and generous gestures, maybe even for vacations, but the off-islander is no longer licensed to stop using his mind in behalf of Martha's Vineyard.

Natives and off-islanders are discovering that, to keep the Vineyard's identity intact, there must be a joint venture, jointly conceived and carried out, or it has not the slightest chance against the power which today opposes the preservation of such a place. Without a working partnership, even the wish to protect will not survive.

CHAPTER FIVE

The Secret County Plan

Dukes County stirred uneasily in its island cocoon when problems which come with development began to disturb the status quo. The Vineyard's six towns are proudly self-contained, each making its own decisions and, surprisingly in such a small area, each with a character so distinctive that the summer visitor instantly feels at home in one town and not in another, a few miles away. But problems do not stay contained within town borders. The water table under the island is as placidly unaware of town lines as the stream of traffic above it. When one town allows misuse of water or roads or any other island connective tissue, effects are widely felt.

Safety is threatened. Together, Vineyarders need to protect their water supply so that it will stay sufficient for their requirements and pure, just as together they need to regulate land use, sewage disposal, traffic in the air, water, and on the ground, to say nothing of the over-all need for consensus on the island's future, which because of the Vineyard's unique nature is becoming a national concern. With the structure at hand, it is increasingly difficult for the 6,000 or more island residents to cope with the staggering problems attendant on the death struggle of a renowned rural place.

In the late 1960s there was an effort to move toward all-island planning. It was instigated by a few energetic citizens, each with his own separate motive, and encouraged by federal programs which made money and technique available here as elsewhere in the nation. This was a new, unaccustomed activity on Martha's Vineyard; the island had been studied before but it had never studied itself or even thought of itself as a unit for planning in the whole. The very act of undertaking to plan was a beginning, agonizingly slow, given the urgency of the times, and less than successful, but a beginning nevertheless, of facing the facts of the future, of leaving tradition behind. Although the plan failed, the effort did not. It led to unexpected progress.

The necessary giant step ahead is harder in the Vineyard than in many larger regions. Barricades, centuries old, block the way; temptations, new as tomorrow's dawn, for unusual island commodities of money and power, subvert progress in the desired direction. The Vineyard, its citizens discover, is a recalcitrant and more complicated subject to plan for than anyone might have guessed, a mixed bag.

The reigning sentiment is local control. The towns would not consider an all-island Board of Health, recommended some years ago by the district health officer, or an all-island police department suggested by the district attorney. "Everything here is multiplied by six," Manuel Maciel, a busy Vineyard plumber who recently finished a stint of eight years as chairman of the Selectmen's Association, says. "We have more fire-fighting equipment than the city of Boston." There are twenty-seven fire-fighting vehicles including—on this island where the highest structure is a church steeple—three hook-and-ladder trucks, one in each town which could afford the $60,000 cost; all are within five minutes of each other. There is a regional high school and hospital, but police cars stop at town limits, garbage trucks, where they exist at all, stay within town bounds. "We don't really need five police chiefs," Maciel says. When the

1. Great boulders brought to the
Vineyard by the glacier

2. Gay Head cliffs—"prehistoric
clay beds rear 150 feet above the
waves"

3. Pine grove near the sea 4. Bright meadows

5. Inviting harbor

8. Birds vs. cars—an unequal battle

6. Beetlebung trees saved

7. The last heath hen on earth

9. Black-crowned night herons, sea gull, and snowy egret at home on Menemsha Neck

10. Menemsha fishing shacks, nesting grounds, and West Basin in background

11. As it was—crossing Gay Head moors in an oxcart

12. Menemsha Light guards the entrance to the pond

13. Lobster Hatchery

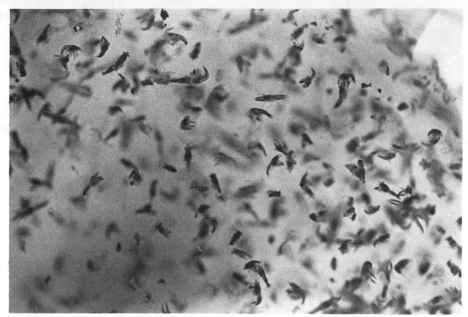

14. Aquaculture—infant lobsters

15. Old-style fishing

16. Whaling bark *Swallow* bound out

17. Clean water offshore

18. "The Wish to Protect"

19. Wasque Point

20. Hedgerows on sign-free Vineyard road

21. Once a cranberry bog, now a pond

22. "The island's oldest known way"—Moshup Trail today

selectmen considered regionalizing police and fire departments, leaving one fire truck and one police cruiser in each town for emergencies, "they were split on the idea. They would have to give up some control."

The price of control is either to keep pace with rapidly developing sophisticated techniques or to make decisions in ignorance. Leadership in the towns is sparse, burdens increasingly heavy. In one town, selectmen's weekly meetings, which used to take two hours or so, now run for five or six hours and often have to be supplemented by special meetings in between. A particularly well-liked and trusted citizen who has been in one public office or another for most of his adult life, works all day at his own job, spends every weekday evening at meetings, and on Sundays attempts to absorb the literature piled on his desk from various government bureaus, then goes fishing for a couple of hours "to air out my brain."

Most people's public-minded energy stays within town limits too. Although the usual explanation for lack of interest in island-wide affairs is apathy, the present crisis adds an extra dimension. Problems seem so big and so invincible that the people renew their dedication to keeping towns intact because it appears that in that arena they can run things as they would wish to. "They're scared to death of what will happen next," Maciel says, "and want to feel as though they can have a part in it."

Town structure, built at a time when fish wardens and fenceviewers were important officials (in some places, the jobs still exist), creaks under the weight of multiplying responsibilities and cannot meet present regional needs. But islanders apparently prefer town government to the terrors of unknown authority. Despite three stern editorial scoldings in one year in the *Gazette* on the lack of an all-island Board of Health, towns continue to try to handle complex sewage disposal and water supply problems by themselves, and in most instances add this function to the selectmen's responsibilities, having a Board of Selectmen which is synonymous with the Board of Health. No member of any town's Board of Health had any formal health training until 1972, when a nurse from the hospital joined the Tisbury Board of Health; the lone pioneer was appalled at what she found.

Strong town government combined with weak county and state participation is a Commonwealth tradition. "The people on the island generally know nothing about politics beyond the town," Shirley Frisch, one of Dukes County's three commissioners, said in a recent conversation. "They don't bother to because they don't think they can change anything." Mrs. Frisch, wife of the late Vineyard doctor, an R.N. formerly at the Vineyard Hospital, was elected a member of Vineyard Haven's Finance Committee four times for a total of twelve years, after she had stopped nursing work. "I thought I was a political person. Now I know what I read in books had nothing to do with politics," said Mrs. Frisch. "The Finance Committee was my biggest education." Before the present crisis, she was regarded as a liberal-minded commissioner, was energetic, involved, responsive to her fellow islanders, thought the county should be restructured, taking the court system out and putting in responsibility for the island's sewage, water, and health.

Communication between state, county, and town often breaks down. When town selectmen get behind on reading their mail, townspeople are uninformed about State House doings, Mrs. Frisch said. "As a result, we very often do not conform to the law." When the state decreed the end to garbage-dump burning by 1970, almost nobody knew about it. Burning, and resultant pollution, continued and the ruling had to be extended for the Vineyard until 1971. "The local official got the notice from the State House and either didn't read it or didn't pass the information along," Mrs. Frisch commented. "The *Gazette* has no political reporter, the selectmen are busy, but most of all, the people really don't want to be told what to do. They just don't want to lose their identity."

Identity, straddled between archaic town structure and the oncoming horde of off-island developers, who grind individual, town, and all into their homogenizing machinery, is in dire trouble. Anyone or any entity issuing orders is a threat.

The county has had very little to say. Chiefly an administrative body responsible for the district court, jail, airport, rat control, and other such functions, it serves as a liaison between state and towns, and has, Mrs. Frisch says, no power of its own. It even must have its budget, smallest of any county in the Commonwealth, approved by the State Commission on Budgets which, the candid commissioner comments, knows nothing about Dukes County needs.

In 1962 Dean Swift, one of the island's crack surveyors, whose father was in the business before him, was elected county commissioner. Swift is a fast-moving (he reads the Boston papers, finding the *Gazette* "too slow and too full of conservation matters"), intense, handsome man whose office, adjoining his Main Street home in Vineyard Haven, is crammed with files, reports, maps, and other evidence of his successful and busy career, becoming even busier as land sales and subdivision—all requiring survey—increase. The $3,000 annual commissioner's salary could not pay for the time required by the job, Swift said, because he very soon had surveyed the county setup and discovered that it could become more important in the total island picture.

Hearing that the county might be eligible for federal funds for a planning study, Swift journeyed to Boston to investigate. In the subsequent months and years he spent between five hundred and a thousand hours to establish the Dukes County Planning and Economic Development Commission. It took an act of legislature, a $50,000 grant (one quarter from the county, the rest from the U. S. Department of Housing and Urban Development), the assemblage of an appropriate body of citizens, before the Commission met for the first time in the fall of 1969, five or more years after Swift had started to bring it into being. Swift became the Commission's first chairman and its first act was to hire Metcalf & Eddy, a professional Boston planning and engineering firm, to make a comprehensive study and plan for Dukes County. The assignment was completed in less than two years, consisted of six preliminary reports and a final summary report.

"If by June, 1973, the recommendations made in this report for this date are not implemented, in our opinion, Martha's Vineyard will have contracted environmental cancer and by September, 1975, will not only have been fully 'raped' by the despoilers but also have contracted environmental terminal cancer."

TYPICAL APPEAL TO HYSTERIA. NOTE SEXUAL CONNOTATIONS. These comments, penciled in the margin of the above paragraph, were the reaction of one official reader (only the Commission, state and federal officials, and certain persons selected by the Commission were privy to the report) to the final words of the long-awaited plan. The paragraph was never published by the Commission, which was, in fact, so displeased by the plan itself that it refused to release it. From June to December a battle raged over what the *Grapevine* called the Vineyard's Pentagon Papers until finally a watered-down, cleaned-up version of this summary report was printed and distributed, with a disclaimer from the chairman pasted on its front page.

Meanwhile the Commission decided to end its relationship with Metcalf & Eddy and hire a full-time resident planner. By the end of 1971 Alexander Fittinghoff had been in the job for several months, coming to the Vineyard *de novo* from California with his wife and two babies. "I would like a set of policies to guide the future growth of the island," he told the Commission, remarking that its basic role was to set goals for the Vineyard and that this had not been done by the disputed Summary Report. It was agreed. "Alex shall develop goals and policies for the Commission," Chairman Swift decreed, and so, once again, an effort was launched to decide what the Vineyard's future should be.

The first effort to plan was judged a failure by the Commission which undertook it. Now it started a second effort. But there was no time left to make a second mistake. Crisscross gridiron development schemes poured into the Registry of Deeds in the county courthouse and by the spring of 1972 housing starts had escalated to a scarcely believable one per day, by summer a reported two per day. The single year of 1972 would see an estimated 500 houses built on the Vineyard while in the entire decade of the 1960s there were a total of 644.

The Commission had put itself into an uncomfortable spot. By holding back the Summary Report from public view, it had caused people to wonder what was in it that was unfit for their eyes. Since the Vineyard is as gossip-minded as any other rural place and possibly more so, being an island, it buzzed with rumors. What kind of plans would the new young planner from California make that were different from those in the rejected, unseen document? What was the Commission against and what was it for? But the core issue was not so much content—a plan can always be amended, altered, or vetoed—as it was conduct. "Don't the Commissioners have confidence enough in the people who elected them to trust these same people to judge the report?" a citizen wrote the *Grapevine*. "If so, why didn't they make it available to the press?"

Tempted by this Pandora's box, I obtained a clandestine copy of the Summary Report and read it with consummate care. It is a straightforward evaluation of a rapidly deteriorating island, and although I would not agree with some of the recommendations (particularly those which have to do with "necessary growth") and could criticize some of the planning technique, on the whole it appears to hold a mirror up to the Vineyard and makes some farsighted practical suggestions for immediate protective action. "The soundness of the recommendations of a plan have nothing to do with its acceptance," Edward Logue, one of the experts chosen by the Commission to review the document, told me. "I believe that the planners were way out ahead of their clients. The plan is more thorough and professional than such plans usually are," Logue said. "The Vineyard really got to those people."

The mirror was clear but the Commission didn't like what it saw. Overreaction to the word "rape" is a clue to the suppression of parts of the report. Kept from the public was a key suggestion for a public organization with the power and finances to both protect the environment and create economic opportunity, and the follow-up suggestion that, if this was not implemented by the state in 1973, it should immediately be requested of the nation's Department of Interior. The new agency thus created would supplant its creator, the Commission.

"It is unreasonable to expect the Commission to accept such a recommendation—particularly since it feels that the implied orientation is 'preservationist,'" a Commonwealth bureaucrat wrote an HUD regional official. (The Commission had often emphasized the economic development half of its title.) By this time, memos, meetings, phone calls, and explanations were in rapid transit between the State House, HUD, Metcalf & Eddy, and the Commission, trying to resolve the difficulties.

On the Vineyard end of many of these was Anne Hale, a vigorous, clearheaded woman with a master's degree in landscape architecture from Harvard, who had come to the Vineyard some years earlier when her husband Thomas took over the Vineyard Haven boatyard. Mrs. Hale, already deeply involved in many conservationist and preservationist activities on the Vineyard, had become the Commission's executive director at its inception. "I told Dean Swift I was interested in his idea when I first heard about it," Mrs. Hale says, "and told him I thought I could be useful. When the time came, he remembered." Because of her long, close work with the Commission, a talk with Anne Hale was revealing.

"The Vineyard study is a three-cornered arrangement," Mrs. Hale comments, "between the Commission, Metcalf & Eddy, and the Massachusetts Department of Community Affairs, which is a clearinghouse for state and federally funded projects." To get HUD money under its so-called 701 program, the department required a commission consisting of three county commissioners, one selectman from each town, and six representative voters. The members are the same public-spirited, conservative, overworked people who are cajoled, appointed, or elected to most Vineyard undertakings, including such as Ben Morton, executive of the Chamber of Commerce (since retired), Allen Look, first president of the Vineyard Open Land Foundation, fish merchant Everett Poole, real estate broker Nell Howell. A Citizens' Advisory Committee (also all voters) to help in the implementation stage, was still a gleam in some planner's eye.

From the start, Commission meetings were held once a month to take care of technicalities and hear information being gathered for the preliminary study by planner H. Calvin Cook, employed by Metcalf & Eddy for this assignment. "He was educating the group," Mrs. Hale says. "I was surprised that there were no big questions or fights. I didn't think it would go over with a business-oriented committee but it did. Of course the meetings were held at night, everybody was tired, bored with meetings, mostly half awake." In any event, it is generally agreed that Calvin Cook "had a way of talking to the islander," as Mrs. Hale put it, was accepted and well liked on the island,

and the preliminary report in six volumes, some of which was published in the *Gazette* ("Nobody read it," Swift complained. "Nobody knew anything about it"), raised no Vineyard hackles.

There was no reason why, in the first five volumes, it should have. Essentially a compendium of existing descriptive information about the Vineyard in its many aspects—land use, physical features, population, transportation, housing, natural resources —it is for the most part as controversial as an almanac or atlas and reads like a particularly detailed doctoral thesis.

In its sixth and final volume, however, the reader is roused by certain assumptions. Here Cook calmly accepts the proposition that, "based on future projections," the population of Dukes County will be 50,000 by 1990, and proposes what to do about it. There is something for everybody: open space for the conservationists, a new town with a "containment greenbelt" for the people business, and for those who like their planning murky, "ultimate residential densities which both respect the natural physiography and ecology, and allow for a liveable and flexible man-made landscape."

There was no argument, no fundamental questions were raised, according to Mrs. Hale's account. Swift's concept of the future matched Cook's. "I am not thinking about less growth," Swift tells a visitor, "but about how to get a sound economy for the island. I can't hire the staff I need for my business because there is no housing that they could afford. We can't stop people from coming here; we have to look at the problems and the projections and find out how to handle them." This view may have been representative of all the commissioners. In any event, their silence, and warm support of Cook's work in later days, suggests that at least this sector of the island leadership was probably in favor of and certainly unwilling to argue against anything as awesome as a population projection. Mrs. Hale was disappointed at what she felt to be a lack of understanding from the general public, thought there was "an endemic barrier to communication" since this writer was the first person who had ever even come to ask about the report. Nevertheless, she, Swift, and the Commission were content with Cook's work.

Then, for reasons known only to itself, Metcalf & Eddy fired Cook and assigned its assistant vice-president James Woglom to write a summary report. Although Woglom, and everybody else at the firm, consistently refused to be interviewed on the subject, it is clear that Woglom's approach to planning and to Martha's Vineyard was markedly different from that of the pleasant, easygoing, language-torturing Calvin Cook. Less smooth, less wordy, somewhat inflammatory, and a great deal more incisive, Woglom dared to call a threatened island a threatened island. "Jim was trying to do what he felt was right and I respect him for it," says Terry Ann Vigil, graduate of the Maxwell School of Social Science at Syracuse, and in charge of the Vineyard project in Massachusetts' Department of Community Affairs. Her estimate, however, was that his projections were "inflated and his document was not a plan but one idea— a superagency."

The term alone would have aroused power-sensitized Vineyarders who could not contemplate as mild a regional organization as an all-island fire department. Although Woglom did not say the loaded word, and devoted only six of his 131-page draft to the idea, the Metcalf & Eddy plan did call for an organization which would replace the present Commission, with power to act to implement the plan.

It was too much for town-tied islanders even to talk about. In June 1971 the Commission unanimously rejected the Summary Report, calling it "impractical, with no possibility of implementation. . . ." Swift says Woglom alienated the people. Anne Hale calls the report "much too divisive and much too much of a bombshell; it was much too far ahead for people—in

any numbers—to understand and be able to accept." This consensus was to bring unforeseen results.

The summer—during which development exploded on the
island—was set aside for a cooling-off period for island planning.
To print or not to print the report was the question to be ne-
gotiated. Woglom was upset by the rejection of his work, Mrs.
Vigil said, as was his firm, which had not yet been paid in full
for the project because of the Commission's action. The Commission was in a hurry to unload Metcalf & Eddy, worried that
it would lose HUD implementation money (some $30,000 for
the coming year), which would go elsewhere in the state if the
Vineyard had no satisfactory over-all design. Although it did
not have the power to fire the firm unilaterally, there being three
parties to the agreement, it said it was not interested in a re-
written summary, would take additional copies of the six study
reports instead, and started interviewing candidates for the job
of resident planner who could, Mrs. Vigil asserted, come up
with a satisfactory working paper based on Cook's reports
within six months.

Attempts at compromise stirred resentments further. The
Vineyard waved its fondness for Calvin Cook, who had now
set up business as an open space planner in Manchester, high
and wide in the summer breezes. He made several public appearances, speaking at the prestigious Garden Club where he
was introduced by Dean Swift, and at Felix Neck under the
aegis of its president Anne Hale. Mrs. Vigil went on record as
agreeing with the Commission about Woglom's work, believing
its criticisms were, if anything, understated. Official government
memos call the report divisive, accuse it of increasing dis-
harmony and needless polarization, say it is oversimplified and
unbalanced, permeated with poor English, bad grammar, and
"awful hyperbole." Metcalf & Eddy were urged to eat the bitter
crow of printing extra copies of the reports of its ex-employee

Cook to complete its Vineyard-HUD contract and close the case.

But the report did not stay in the top secret file. In late August, in a front-page *Vineyard Gazette* article, John Oakes, editor of the New York *Times*'s editorial page, noted conservationist, a founder and moving spirit of the Vineyard Conservation Society and a Vineyard landowner, called attention to its contents. "It is surely the business of the people of this island to know how gravely a respected firm of engineers views the prospects for Martha's Vineyard. . . . It is not so much any single part of Martha's Vineyard that needs protection," Oakes said, "as the complex organism as a whole." With liberal quotes from the Summary Report, he told readers how protection could be realized under the Metcalf & Eddy plan. Oakes said the report had been rejected and suppressed; an Editor's Note, following his article, said yes, it was rejected but "suppressed only in the technical sense. . . ."

Shortly thereafter, the *Grapevine*, trying to obtain the technically suppressed report, was told by Chairman Swift that the Commission did not have a finished Summary Report, was now in the process of employing a full-time planner, and thought "it most logical for he and the Commission . . . to work out long-range policies and plans" which would be released for publication hopefully by early fall. Since the new planner would not start work until October 1, the chairman's projections were optimistic if not misleading.

The field between my house and the brilliant blue Vineyard Sound was turning russet, its grasses, combed by the prevailing wind, accented by patches of scarlet cranberries, vivid goldenrod, lavender asters. Bright fall skies and mellow fall sunlight made the familiar view suddenly almost too poignant, with the idea of this entire, crucial summer of possible planning wasted by the determination of the Commission to secrete the thought of a superagency, awful hyperbole and all, from its fellow islanders.

Dukes County had come full circle from the time, some three centuries past, that the Provincial Assembly of New York divided the province into several counties, Banks tells us, including Kings (now Brooklyn), Queens (now Long Island), and Dukes, which was decreed to "conteine the Islands of Nantuckett, Martin's Vineyard, Elizabeth Island and Noe Man's Land." A few years later the charter of William and Mary moved the islands to the jurisdiction of Massachusetts, where there were only four counties at the time of the creation of Dukes. Nantucket became its own entity by an ensuing "Act for the Better Settlement of the Islands of Martha's Vineyard, and Islands Adjacent" passed by the General Court of Massachusetts in 1695.

The move to the Commonwealth was much resented by the reigning Mayhew, Major Matthew, grandson of Thomas, who thought the "pious greybeards" of Massachusetts "all deserved to be kickt into the dock." Challenged by Simon Athearn, a leading Vineyard squire "of considerable estate," Mayhew had trouble retaining his accustomed power but managed to hold it sufficiently well so that, in addition to his other offices, he was made chief justice of the new court of common pleas, set up by the Commonwealth for the islands.

The beginnings of town structure and town strength came with the settlement of the land. Divisions of new purchases, further acquisitions from the Indians, increasing numbers of settlers, gave Vineyarders more self-assurance, more independence from Mayhew dominance. Three men were chosen to administer town affairs in Edgartown as early as 1676, and soon the triad of selected officers were elected in each new settlement and called selectmen, then as now.

Land was central to the town, giving each its individual

identity. Edgartown's great harbor, the flat fertile fields of West Tisbury (named after the Mayhews' ancestral home in England which thrived on sheep farming, as did the Vineyard's Tisbury), the lively up-island brooks, supplying power for beginning industries, determined the life pattern of townsmen. Gradually the county assumed a judicial and general manager role, much as it has today; the towns were where the major business of life took place and, because of that, town government was dominant.

But now, once again, land merges into an undifferentiated whole. It makes little difference to an off-island developer who buys a couple of hundred acres at a good price whether those acres are in one town or another, as long as he can divide them into pieces and make a comfortable profit. The towns, when they saw what was upon them, moved toward zoning in the early 1970s, not realizing that this was no solution to what had become an all-island enigma. Actually, the circle might be thought to go from the days of an undivided continent, innocent and wild, which became the property of a new, hopeful nation, to the enigma of the contemporary nation which, although it has lost its innocence, struggles to retain some of that wilderness for future Americans.

The towns have not solved the over-all problem. The county tried its hand at a solution and failed. Protection of identity is central to the failures; just as Matthew Mayhew fought off the Massachusetts greybeards, so today's Vineyarders fight off the threat of control beyond town and county.

On a warm summer Sunday some years ago, a group of concerned Vineyard conservationists invited a contemporary Mayhew, the late Benjamin, the island's representative in the State House, and his wife Eileen, to journey across the Sound on an inspection trip of the newly opened Cape Cod National Seashore. With V.I.P. treatment arranged for the Mayhews and party, the tour of the Seashore with its superintendent was informative and impressive. Everyone was struck by the care which had been taken—even to a machine, busily planting thousands of stalks of beach grass on eroding dunes—and the protection of a unique area accomplished by the federal government in the public interest. "Well, Ben," one of the group asked on the way home, "how did you like it?" Mayhew was enthusiastic, discussed the planning of beaches and wilderness, the people and traffic control. "I liked it fine," he said, then added slowly and with emphasis, "but we don't want the Feds on Martha's Vineyard."

The incident was years before the present crisis showed itself, but the attitude remains firmly fixed in some Vineyard minds. Given the background and conditioning of the Planning Commission, what happened had had to happen. It was a beginning of a new way of thinking about the island, but just a beginning. The story of the Commission's effort revealed how immensely difficult it was to attempt to weld the island into a unit, and to do it in time to cope with the destructive forces already at its shores. Transferring power from a smaller to a larger unit was called divisive; planning for the island's future was seen as an undertaking "too far ahead for people . . . to understand."

On that crisp and shining fall day it became clear that the problem was bigger than the island and that its resolution would have to be at a level which the island alone could not achieve. The New York *Times* allowed me to relate the summer's story to its broad readership; I ended the piece with an appeal to Massachusetts Senators Kennedy and Brooke, and Representative Hastings Keith, to use one of the available federal solutions to preserve this endangered national resource.

The reaction was explosive. Such an unalloyed statement made at the exact time when the first subdivision plans had just been published, shocking unsuspecting visitors and Vineyarders out of their complacency, and when the Commission was being pressed for release of the Summary Report, set off a charge as neatly laid out as an expert time bomb. Everything that had gone before contributed to the detonation of a chain of events which are still unfolding on the island, in Congress, and the State House, as later chapters describe; it was like the hole in a sock which appears all of a sudden one day although it has taken many months to wear the fibers so thin that they ultimately give way.

The immediate response to the appearance of this hole in the sock was violent and revealing. Although the article was reprinted in full in a surprising number of papers on the eastern seaboard (including Nantucket's *Inquirer and Mirror*), the *Vineyard Gazette* gave it only a half-column summary which omitted the request for federal action. Robert Russell, president of the Vineyard Conservation Society, wrote the editor that federal intervention is "among the worst things that could happen to us. We lose control of the actions we think are necessary." Cook wrote that the report of his fellow professional Woglom was "basically deficient in tone and content . . . divisive and unbalanced." Dean Swift, who read the *Times* piece in the Boston *Globe*, called it an emotional display, revealing its author's "lack of understanding and knowledge of the real problems of the island." Shirley Frisch wrote, "I would like to be added to the number of people who want to bring [the article] to the attention of the local press," then urged immediate release of the "famous Final Report in the original form."

The *Grapevine* finally got its hands on and printed "The Pentagon Papers of Martha's Vineyard" in November, found its prose purple, tone supercilious, prophecies grim . . . and undeniable. Swift, who was soon to resign as chairman of the Commission due, he said, to the pressures of business (Edwin Tyra, a contractor, replaced him), announced that Metcalf & Eddy's revised report would be accepted "for publication but not for implementation so that we can get on with our own business."

Insularity, once revealed with all its terrors showing, could not be so easily erased. Too many people were aware, by now, of the kind of thinking that had gone into town and county planning to date, and what was likely to come in the future. The step toward self-study and self-planning had been taken; it was an enterprising and encouraging action, and although the Commission had not been able to go the whole way into a new planful era, it had achieved a collection of data and a plan, both of which were to be used within the year in unexpected quarters. And it had recognized the need to do more, clearly enough so that it put a full-time resident planner on the island for the first time in its history.

But to leave the Vineyard to the protection of the Commission alone was no longer possible. Too many people realized that the group, given its make-up, was only being true to its character when it accepted without question the projection of future population growth as a certainty, along with a new town to take care of more people, that it could not manage an open debate on the island's future. It was in character for the Commission to decide that Growth is Good, to suppress the idea of a regional governing body, to expect a satisfactory plan to spring full-blown from the mind of a newly arrived young planner in six months when a hard-working firm could not achieve it in two years. Too many people saw and understood that the Commission could only reflect its own hopes and fears.

And too many began to realize that the fragile island might only be preserved in what is left of its natural splendor if the country of which it is a part would move to protect it. Although there was often half-joking talk of secession, suggesting the wish that the threat of the Feds did not exist for the Vineyard, there were some islanders who began to reach for an answer, and off-islanders who wrote in considerable numbers, "What can I do to help?"

One interested off-islander, in spite of a painful Vineyard memory, took an unexpected, dramatic step. "Mr. President," said Senator Edward Kennedy on the Senate floor, "I am introducing today legislation to provide for a study . . ." The bill (S.2605) asked for $1.5 million to find the best method of protecting Martha's Vineyard, Nantucket, and neighboring islands and to suggest a plan for the future. The senator, quoting the *Times* article and his mail, emphasized that "we do not have years to reverse the trend, we have months. So let us not waste this precious time."

Action is born of action. The study bill has been supplanted by another and what had begun long before, when Dean Swift made his first trip to Boston on Commission business, now burgeons, as is related in later pages, in ways which none of the actors in the drama could have possibly imagined, but which they collectively made possible. As it turns out, the secret county plan by its very existence may save the island from itself after all.

CHAPTER SIX

When Lucy Dies . . .

Old family homesteads and farms on the Vineyard are suddenly and rapidly moving on the real estate market. As land values soar, so do taxes, and not many Vineyarders can afford to hold their acres intact. Land which has changed over the millennia from ocean floor to fertile plain, from meadow to forest and back to field again as its island stewards timbered or farmed or grazed their herds, now, for the first time, is to be radically different than it has ever been before.

What it will be might someday become the public's decision. When there is enough understanding and caring, men make laws to carry out their concepts and protect themselves by living under the law. But in the first years of the seventies, the future of Vineyard land depended in most part on the morality of the seller and the buyer. Except for the zoning brushfire, described in the next chapter, which spread across the island, sparked by the onslaught of development, and the newly sharpened attention to wetlands legislation, and to laws against polluting air and water, which caught the passing fancy of overworked town officials on occasion, there was not much between a man, his land, and his bank account except his conscience.

To forever alter a piece of the earth is a not inconsiderable responsibility. As the society begins to know that at least part of its salvation, its ability to survive if not to flourish, is in wise use of land, the responsibility increases. Land is no longer simply a commodity to be sold to the highest bidder or bought as a short- or long-term investment without concern for its future. Its history matters, and its character. It matters where it is, the kind of a town it lies within and the island that that town is a part of. It has miraculously firm limitations. To exceed them means destruction of land, people, town, and, eventually, island.

Land can speak for itself to people who will listen. One who did was a determined Vineyard lady, Lucinda Mosher Vincent, who lived on some sixty remarkable Chilmark acres which stretch along the ocean beach below the strikingly beautiful Wequobsque cliffs, sculptured by hidden water within and the pounding Atlantic without. Above the cliffs, streams run year round through moors and meadows, marshes and bogs, into a fresh-water pond which is separated from the salty ocean only by a narrow spit of land. There is a modest forest of tall trees and the remains of an old farm, its pristine white farmhouse behind a picket fence, facing the South Road for all the world like a two-dimensional stage set.

This seaside farm is pure Vineyard. Evidence of the glacier is in the scarred face of the cliffs and in the moraine's boulders, dragged by oxen in subsequent centuries to form sturdy, still-standing stone walls. The bit of precolonial forest, such as the first explorers might have seen, sets off a combination of plants which grow in proximity only when fresh and salt water are so neighborly. The place, which the *Gazette* calls "one of the most beautiful and significant in all Martha's Vineyard," is nostalgic in its pleasing recall of early settlement, typically Vineyard in the variety of its land.

If its grandeur survives, it will be because of Lucy, who died in March 1970 at the age of eighty-seven, "the last of the old South Roaders" as she called herself, and because of an oddly assorted company of people who came to respect her land's limits: her executor, her five principal heirs, three Chilmark

selectmen, a landscape architect, the president of the World
Bank, several ambitious off-islanders, a clutch of conservationists, and over a hundred developers. Close to half a million
dollars will change hands, the town will have a new beach and
a handful of new taxpayers, the character of the land will be
intact, and several people will each claim that the whole thing
was his idea.

This small but significant corner of the Vineyard is one of
the first on the island to demonstrate that the limitations of the
land can be its salvation.

Throughout the sixties, Chilmark abounded with rumors
about what would happen to the old homestead when Lucy, a
childless widow, died. Lucy, however, was "very quiet about her
business affairs," her friend Barbara Seward, wife of Menemsha's
postmaster and longtime storekeeper, says. Lucy was independent in the extreme, had in the past rented out a room or two
during the summer but mostly insisted on living alone, even
when she became quite blind and badly crippled with arthritis
during the last four years of her life. Chilmark's librarian for
thirty years, she was active in and unusually well informed about
town affairs. Except for vacations, she spent her entire life in
this small, rural, up-island town.

The land talked and Lucy listened. Like many islanders, she
was not an enthusiastic swimmer, but she would walk on the
beach a good deal, checking on the erosion of the sea cliff
(currently losing from two to five feet a year), occasionally invited certain of her relatives and friends to beach picnics, although one cousin, who lived not half a mile away, says she has
not been on Lucy's beach for more than twenty-five years.

Lucy was a skillful gardener and dedicated bird-watcher. She
initiated bird walks on the Vineyard. "Birds have seen more of
the world," she said, and cut paths through her woods for a better view of them, knew their calls, expected time of arrival on
the island, and other habits, just as she knew each plant in the

well-tended garden in back of her house. Even during her last years her enthusiasm stayed lively. A local lady came in and "did" for her three times a week, and David, one of the Sewards' sons, stopped by twice a day to do Lucy's chores, filling the bird feeders, fixing the fires, having taken over this job when Paul Mayhew, who had done it before him, died.

One afternoon David arrived quite late. Lucy was not in her room. Against doctor's orders, the lady had climbed out of bed, groped her way out to the garden where she intended to spend an hour or two enjoying the familiar sounds and fragrance of the place. It turned cold and windy, but Lucy had wandered too far to be able to find her way back to the house. David discovered her, huddled quietly in her garden, waiting for whatever would happen.

"Lucy never thought about dying," Faye Neumann Gilmour, a cousin, says. "She was always making plans for next year . . . a trip, a checkup visit to the dentist, new perennials." In line with her primary devotion, evident to those who knew and admired her, several hundred townspeople presented her with a telescope for window bird-watching at her eightieth birthday party in the Chilmark library.

It was irksome to Lucy when Roger Baldwin, Leona Baumgartner, and other renowned conservationists would urge her to leave her land to one worthy organization or another so that it would stay forever wild. "Lucy didn't like people to walk over her," Leslie Flanders, first vice-president of the Martha's Vineyard National Bank and Lucy's executor (until his untimely death in 1971), commented. In the last year of her life, Flanders said, Lucy had called him at eight-thirty one night, quite upset, having just had "one of those conservation visits." She asked Flanders to come to see her right then, an unusual request. Determined not to make a new will in the hospital because "they'll say I didn't know what I was doing," she expressed her profound feelings about her land to Flanders that night, and soon after went to the hospital where she died.

The farmhouse on Chilmark's South Road, built in the early 1800s, used to be a store, according to local sources, and was then altered into a two-family house which belonged to Lucy's grandfather. Since almost everybody in Chilmark farmed at that time, the land was probably a farm. Lucy was born a mile or so up the road in a house which her father had brought over from the Cape to its present hilltop site. "Houses were moved a lot in those days," a venerable Chilmark citizen recalls. "Land was cheap, lumber dear." Not far beyond her birthplace, Lucy's maternal grandparents, Mayhews, lived in a house overlooking Menemsha Pond which now shelters Jerome Wiesner, president of M.I.T., and his family.

Lucy was brought up in the South Road farmhouse with her cousin Leona, whose parents lived in the other half of the house. She was well on to thirty when she married Myron Vincent, a "successful and progressive trap fisherman in the palmy days of that industry," a friend recalls. Lucy, an only child, inherited the farm when her mother died and she lived there with Myron, although hardly a winter went by that they failed to take a trip—to Puerto Rico, Florida, San Diego—always bird-watching in some interesting place en route. When Myron, who was well off, retired at sixty, they spent winters in St. Petersburg, Florida, until his death in 1929.

Up and down the South Road and around Menemsha Pond, Lucy's family—"own cousins" (an expression used locally to describe first cousins), near and distant relatives in many generations—extended its landholdings, keeping them even when one or another branch of the family moved down-island or off-island. Leona, too, had married a Vincent although her husband Robert was no relation to Lucy's Myron. It is not known whether either was descended from the William Vincent who was registered as one of the first twenty-five proprietors of

Edgartown in 1654, became estranged from his son Thomas, and left him only one shilling, because "he hath not demeaned himself well toward me nor his mother, to our sad great grief."

If not related by blood, the early and latter-day Vincents shared this assertion of will power. When Leona's son was drowned in a pond, his wife and children—Robert, a teen-ager at the time, and William, some years younger—came to live with Lucy until they eventually moved to Schenectady, New York. Lucy had some strong feelings about how the boys' grandparents had disposed of their property as she did about her own, refusing to sell her "bride's lot" in Quitsa to Donald Hurley, a noted Boston lawyer whose land it adjoins, because, she explained to Flanders, "he's been too pesty."

When Lucy died, a rush of hopefuls who had been unable to do any land business with her descended on her executor, the tall, gray-haired, pleasant, and scrupulously fair Leslie Flanders. In his Vineyard Haven bank office he presided over a busy cashiers' department, answering the constantly ringing telephone with an unfailing, courteous "Yes, Ma'am" or "Yes, Sir." Flanders, who himself had Mayhews, Athearns, and other prominent Vineyard families in his ancestry, was firmly attached to the island, owned land in Vineyard Haven and up-island, including (with his sister) one of the crucial six lots on Menemsha Neck. Bombarded with propositions about Lucy's land before its proprietor had been properly buried in the cemetery on Abel's Hill, not far from where she had spent her life, Flanders was drawn into what became, he said, one of the most complicated negotiations of his more than forty-year career at the bank.

He was determined to see Lucy's wishes carried out. But her wishes were no more ordinary than the property she was leaving behind. She had hesitated for some time before making up her mind about the land. On the one hand her family ties were strong, on the other, her lifetime involvement with her home town and her intimate knowledge of its needs was important. Overall was a wish that the birds which had seen so much of the world would continue to see this part of it as it had always been.

During that memorable evening's talk, she told Flanders that she would leave her estate to her relatives. After some minor bequests and institutional gifts, half was to go to Robert Vincent —named for his grandfather, Leona's husband—who had grown up on the land, loved the place, and who, Lucy thought, had been unfairly treated in the wills of his relatives. "She felt she was righting a wrong," Barbara Seward says. The other half was to be evenly divided between other cousins—three widows and Robert's younger brother William. Lucy wanted the town of Chilmark to have the right of first refusal for the land if her heirs wanted to sell it. "But being very thrifty herself," Flanders said, "she was not sure she would want the town to buy the land as she thought it would not be able to afford it. She hoped Chilmark could come by it some other way."

Flanders was in something of a predicament. As Lucy's executor, he was bound to see that her heirs got what was coming to them. If they wanted to sell the land, he was equally bound to see that, if at all possible, it went to Chilmark without the town's having to pay for it. It was immediately apparent to him that offers from avaricious developers would not serve his purpose, any more than the proposals of certain individuals who wanted the land for themselves alone. He therefore embarked on the unusual undertaking of making a list of all prospective buyers in order of their appearance but refusing to listen to money offers. "I said that if they mentioned a figure to me I would not put their names on the list at all," Flanders told me. In this way, he explained, the land value would not become inflated and there would, perhaps, be a chance to do Lucy's bidding.

There was more than the average turmoil of rumors boiling in the small town pot when Lucy died. Fact, fiction, and imagination were peddled as inside information, many claimed to "really know," momentarily raising their stature until outdone by another self-proclaimed prophet. Big names and unknowns were in common currency as purchasers. Meanwhile, the town selectmen felt that somehow they had to get Lucy's beach for Chilmark, Lewis King, first selectman, says. It was particularly important to King. An émigré from New York where he had spent twenty-two years in the real estate business, he ran a successful guesthouse in his North Road estate, had extensive landholdings, but was still an off-islander. A coup, such as he was in the process of working on for the Vincent land, might, at long last, break down that barrier between himself and the native community.

It was no mere gossip that the land was appraised at $450,000, that Chilmark has a legal debt limit set by the state at $175,000, and with its harbor improvement project then under way, plus other undertakings, had bonds out for more than its limit already. Furthermore, even if the town had the ability to borrow the money and buy the beach, it would then be open to everyone as is its Menemsha beach. To keep it for Chilmark residents—the selectmen's aim—the town would have to lease the beach, much as it leases its Squibnocket beach, from an individual or organization able to impose limits.

Lucy died on March 4. On the twenty-third of that month, at a meeting of the Conservation Society, Joseph Kraetzer, a local insurance agent, suggested that the Chilmark Community Fund, a private, tax-free organization which could buy and hold land, purchase some of Lucy's property as a conservation memorial to her. On April 20, Robert Woodruff, the Society's executive, offered to meet with the Chilmark selectmen to discuss possible approaches, and in August the selectmen, in an open meeting with summer residents, asked for suggestions as to how to proceed.

There were plenty of ideas. Horace B. B. Robinson, chairman

of the Chilmark Town Affairs Council, later to become a controversial figure in the island-wide planning effort, had lined up a group of ten to twelve people to divide up some of Lucy's land for summer homes and sell the rest to the town for $150,-000. This solution was a combination of what Robinson had achieved in Blacksmith Valley, a summer community farther along the South Road, and in his community fund-raising.

Standing on top of the highest hill in the property surrounding his own house, he demonstrated what could be done when a group of friends from New Jersey got together. The once-open, hilly farm which had been in his family for generations is now a replica of a well-to-do suburb, dotted with neat gray-shingled houses on the hilltops and hillsides. The Robinson family and friends sail together in Menemsha Pond across the road where they have a common dock, use the exclusive Squib-nocket Association's private beach, socialize together, and are proud of Tom Robinson, who spent the summers of his Princeton years as director of the Chilmark Community Center which his father had guided into being.

"It is natural for me to deal with this Vincent beach business," Robinson comments. A member of a New York white-spat law firm, moderator of the Presbytery of New York City, he is a descendant of the Blackwell family, one of the first up-island summer families, which includes Dr. Elizabeth Blackwell, the country's first woman doctor. "It took a whole day to get here from Vineyard Haven then," Robinson says. "They had to change horses in North Tisbury." Robinson's position, experience, and friends, for whom there was no more room in the Blacksmith Valley environs, urged him to put together the Vincent proposal. Furthermore, he felt entitled to the privilege, commenting that he had done a good deal for the town, raising money to expand the library in 1963, and for building the Center in 1956 when he was one of the five summer people who guaranteed a loan for the town's share. "Summer and winter people can work together to develop the community and help it to grow," Robinson said. "The Town Affairs Council is proof of it." Some of his peers are less enthusiastic about his leadership.

There were other prospects. This was the summer that the Vineyard Open Land Foundation had come into being. It was a modified copy of the Lincoln, Massachusetts, non-profit, tax-exempt Rural Land Foundation, chartered to buy, plan, and sell property, keeping as much as possible in open space and preserving the natural features of the land. Lincoln has become an enviable Commonwealth model of what an aroused, informed citizenry can accomplish. It is a three-pronged effort: the Foundation, an active town conservation commission to acquire open space with the government paying at least half the cost, and a conservation trust to receive gifts of land. The Vineyard's Open Land Foundation announced that it would "focus its efforts on relatively large-scale tracts of significant undeveloped or underdeveloped open rural land . . . whose uncontrolled development could damage the Island's character and upset the ecological balance."

It sounded as though the Vincent property would be a perfect starting project for the new organization, and Selectman King appointed Herbert Hancock, a building contractor and fellow selectman, and Kraetzer to investigate. They reported that the Foundation was not equipped for the undertaking. A year later Edward Logue, its chairman, explained. "If we can show someone else how to do it," he said, "there is no reason to do it ourselves." Further, the Internal Revenue Service tax-free rating had not come through until late December and, last, if the Open Land Foundation had become the holding company, it would have had to give the land to local real estate agents for sale. "We must rely on them—plus some civilizing influence to correct certain practices," Logue said.

Thus, what the *Gazette* at the time of the Foundation's inception had called "the only program at all likely to shape the future as lovers of the Island would like to have it shaped" was not in shape for the future of Lucy's land. By 1972 the Open Land Foundation had become a land-development, planning, fee-charging service to put buyers, sellers, and plans together with Anne Hale as its executive secretary.

But its conception had sowed some inspirational seeds. Nicholas Freydberg, a New York social psychologist and onetime collaborator in Basic Books, Inc., had sold his house in Yorktown Heights, New York, to retire on the Vineyard with his wife. He had long admired Lucy's land and had, in fact, written to ask her if she would sell him some of it, gotten no reply. Reading the Open Land prospectus in the *Gazette*, Freydberg got the idea of forming a limited development. He would keep the old farmhouse and some land for himself, make three or four other house sites. "With my plan, each person involved would have to spend upwards of $225,000 for land, roads, electricity, and a house," Freydberg said. "Owning all the land was not important to me. I wanted to keep it as it should be and was willing to turn most of it over to conservation—not for public use—in perpetuity.

"If you are in a certain tax bracket and give land away, it is a better financial deal than selling it," Freydberg said. "The gift is deductible from your income." Knowing that he couldn't handle it alone, despite tax advantages, Freydberg discussed the project with his neighbor and financial counselor, Ralph Meyer, who was eager to join in the enterprise as he, too, would have liked a house site on Lucy's land. On Henry Hough's advice, Freydberg went to see Jerome Wiesner and Leona Baumgartner as backers for the proposal he would make to Leslie Flanders. He recalls that Dr. Baumgartner recommended a young landscape architect from Harvard's Graduate School of Design, Peter Hornbeck, although Hornbeck believes it was fellow land planner Kevin Lynch, a summer Vineyarder with a house in Gay Head, who suggested him for the job. In any event, it was Freydberg who first sent him to see the Vincent property and for whom he wrote a preliminary land plan.

Hornbeck's training had equipped him with advanced land-use planning tools. "The Vineyard has a capability which stops at point X. The planning problem is to identify this point," Hornbeck stated. It was standard operating procedure to him but a revolutionary manifesto on the island, which was at that moment pushing land use to its outside limits wherever development could get a foothold. To find point X for Lucy's land, Hornbeck peered at its fresh-water drainage process, soil development process, geology, vegetation, unstable cliffs, marine-salt water conditions. Freydberg and Meyer sent his first rough idea of point X and how to achieve it along to Flanders with a letter of intent.

The future of Lucy's land was still far from resolved. Robinson had one scheme, Freydberg and Meyer another, and Flanders, still not listening to money offers, still keeping his list, was still being flooded with offers and queries from avid developers, while the Chilmark selectmen scratched their heads for a way to secure at least some of the glorious beach for the town. Bobby Vincent had decided to keep the house and three acres. "He can manage if he's as careful about money as Lucy was," Faye Gilmour says. "She used to burn paper and kerosene when firewood got high."

Mrs. Gilmour and the other heirs wanted to sell their half of Lucy's estate. Although the land was well known and loved by them, Massachusetts property taxes had doubled in the last five years and were second in the nation to New Jersey (when measured as per cent of annual income). Because of this high rate, and the fact that, although twenty-four states give preferential tax rates for agricultural or horticultural land, the amendment to match this in Massachusetts was still not operative, it is increasingly difficult, as a *Gazette* editorial remarks, "for owners of any extensive open land to continue to pay taxes on it. They must either sell for 'development' or set aside some of it . . . for conservation purposes." The latter choice, thrifty for those in high tax brackets, would not be an advantage for Lucy's heirs.

This was another enigma. Although Lucy's younger cousins could use the money yielded by a land sale, they did not want to see the old farm that most of them had known for so long, broken up. "I can't imagine it being 'developed,'" one of them said. And there was Chilmark's right of first refusal to be considered; it was thought that the town was contemplating the exercise of this right.

At just such a state of affairs, somehow or other, Robert S. McNamara, president of the International Bank for Reconstruction and Development (otherwise known as the World Bank), former Secretary of Defense appointed by President Kennedy, former president of the Ford Motor Company, with an MBA from Harvard Business School where he was once assistant professor, got into the tangle of the Lucy Vincent estate.

McNamara was not looking to reconstruct and develop the Vineyard. He was in the market for a personal summer retreat, had spent some time visiting fellow Administration members on the Vineyard during the Kennedy regime (on one August weekend, three Kennedy cabinet members—McNamara, Katzenbach, and Udall—were on the Vineyard concurrently, and all three up-island, at that), and had often expressed his admiration for the island.

Lewis King said that he had "been advised by a friend" that McNamara would be interested in acquiring some or all of the Vincent land. King made a call to McNamara, not officially, he says, but "as an interested bystander," saying that if McNamara would put up the necessary $450,000, limit house lots, and keep the major part of the property in trust in its natural state, King could arrange for a hearing with the town officials (he himself being a selectman, that part of the arrangement was not too difficult) and with Lucy's executor, "but couldn't guarantee results." Edward Logue said that it was he who first talked with McNamara about Lucy's property, urged him to buy it, advised him to hire Boston rather than New York or Washington lawyers to talk to the Vineyard lawyers: "Mac listened, talked, and hired Boston lawyers," Logue recalls. Over on Nantucket, Roy Larsen said it was really *his* idea, as he had tried to get McNamara to settle on that island in much the same way, and more than a few of McNamara's former colleagues and many friends, summering on the Vineyard, let their importance in the Mac-snaring leak out on the cocktail circuit.

"Ed Logue first mentioned the property to me," McNamara said in an interview. "I went to the Vineyard, walked over the land, and fell in love with it. You could see the delicacy and fragility of the dunes and streams," he continued, "and as I discussed the place with Peter Hornbeck and Nick Freydberg, I was even more impressed with the need for careful preservation."

Hornbeck remembers his prospective new client's enthusiasm when he first saw the moor, the brook, the view of the ocean from the top of the cliffs. He pointed out to McNamara a huge blueberry bush that "the Vikings might have looked at, it's so old," the stone walls which revealed that the land had been a cattle or sheep farm. If it had been used for agriculture, Hornbeck said, you would find many small stones in the walls, thrown out of the field as it was being cleared for plowing and planting. "Large stones and a single-width wall mean animals, grazing." He showed McNamara how to estimate the rate of growth of a stand of white pines by counting one year for each straight section. The World Bank's president counted with curiosity, "like a little boy," Hornbeck said. "I wouldn't

want to impose anything on this place," McNamara told the
planner. "Let's work with what it has."

Point X was starting to become a reality. Working with what
it has included not only the particular character of the land
but its significance to Chilmark and the greater island. "With
our present morality, I doubt that there can be large stretches
of privately owned beaches any more. Ultimate use of beach
frontage," McNamara said in what is turning out to be an
extraordinarily prophetic remark for the Vineyard, and perhaps
for the country at large, "will be public."

The plan which McNamara, Freydberg, and Meyer now
joined in negotiating has several versions, depending on the
informant. Basically, the purchasers would keep four house
sites of five acres each and about eighteen acres dedicated by
covenant to open land for the communal use of the four future
homeowners. Bobby Vincent had the farmhouse and somewhere between three and seven acres. The town would have
the right to lease 2,500 feet of beach, including the beautiful
sand spit between pond and ocean, an access road and parking
lot, a total of some eighteen acres, which included the entire
knoll above the beach. Variations of this are the gospel according to Herbert Hancock, who said it was "a fancy lease" McNamara and partners had made with a restrictive convenant which
would not allow "another class of people" to use the beach. The
gospel according to Hornbeck said the entire beach was to be
public; Lewis King said the owners would retain 1,900 feet of
beach for themselves.

"Roy Larsen was my inspiration for the idea of giving the
beach to the town," McNamara said. "Over in Nantucket, ten
per cent of the land has been turned over to non-profit trusts.
Larsen and Arthur Dean have donated a good deal of it." Later,
Freydberg, unable to buy Lucy's house, bought a West Tisbury
farm, and another place on Stonewall Pond and dropped out
of the plans in the spring of 1971. McNamara said that he and

Meyer would conclude the deal by themselves, sell the two remaining house sites when it was completed.

By now it was clear that to keep the beach for Chilmark residents the town should lease, not own it. Its Squibnocket beach is leased from the Cape Cod Cranberry Company, a holding company for landowners Hornblower and Howland, Robinson said. He recalled that in 1904 when his father crossed that land, which then belonged to a Mr. Hammond, the owner objected. Robinson, Sr., sued, established that the way he used to get to the beach was a public road by testimony of eighty-four-year-old Moses West, an undertaker, who swore to the court that "I've taken people out that way all my life."

In this instance, the Chilmark Community Fund, which had applied to Flanders almost immediately after Lucy's death, would own the land, receiving it as a gift from purchasers McNamara et al. and renting it to the town at a dollar a year for ninety-nine years, with a ninety-nine-year option. There were a few serious disruptions; one of the heirs who was not fond of the Community Center (as many up-islanders and old-time summer residents are not, it being uncomfortably close to the suburbia look, hitherto foreign in Chilmark) said the name Chilmark Community Fund would set anybody's teeth on edge, insisted that it be changed, which it was, to the Chilmark Town Association, Inc.

Neighbor Howard Young, whose property overlooks the part of Lucy's land which was to become the town beach, was bitter at the way things were going, Flanders said, and threatened the executor with a lawsuit. To get his views before the people, he flew up to the island to attend a winter Chilmark town meeting but was not recognized by Lewis King in the chair, not being a voter. (Had Young been up on his law, he could have insisted that the meeting vote to exclude him, or to give its consent for him to speak; the basis for the notion that one not registered to vote in a town may not address town meeting without consent is, according to a handbook of parliamentary law, "historical and not relevant to a New England town meeting." It was established in the early seventeenth century by the English House of Commons struggling for parliamentary democracy against the power of the throne.) "I need hardly remind you," Young wrote to the *Gazette,* "that the western end of Upper Chilmark Pond has long been a sanctuary for wildlife." For this reason, he said, the parking lot should be a distance from the pond and there should be only "quiet locomotion allowed" on its waters, adding that whatever restrooms are constructed in his view should be built in as inconspicuous a manner as possible.

As point X continued to be refined, and individuals continued to make their demands on the slowly emerging solution, the purchasers were apparently steadfast in their devotion to the preservation project. More than two and a half years after Lucy's death, the deal had been within days of closing twice, McNamara said; Leslie Flanders died a few days before the first date, Kennedy filed his bill, which would affect all Vineyard land use, less than a week before the second date. Although Meyer preferred not to discuss his motives, reasons, or beliefs, or anything else about the undertaking, believing the deal still in danger "from tricky developers," McNamara talked freely about his love for the seashore and mountains which had started during his boyhood in San Francisco. "Major portions need to be preserved in their natural state," he said, "and this is very expensive to do now. The government must make more national seashores and parks." He regarded the present opportunity as fortuitous for him and for all concerned.

The sellers, who might have gotten about fifty per cent more for the land had they dealt with one of the developers on Flanders' list, judging by current land prices, did not feel that they were giving up too much by making this arrangement. Flanders said that each in his own way made it clear that Lucy's feelings about her land were paramount. "There was no idea of having made a sacrifice," Faye Gilmour says. "It's not our money, really, it's Lucy's."

Point X worked for Chilmark, too. Land which had yielded $100 annually in taxes would be shared by four additional residents who were expected happily to build handsomely taxable homes, more than making up for taking the rest of the acreage off the tax rolls and into conservation. The acquisition of an additional exclusively Chilmark ocean beach was a long-anticipated dream come true. Selectman Lewis King was involved in high finance and exalted circles; the gossip circuit was kept busy as one rumor after another filtered down along the wharf and through the daily gatherings on the post office porch. Without a murmur, the town passed an $18,000 appropriation to build a road for the "Lucinda Vincent Memorial Beach," $6,000 to maintain signs, police the beach, and provide a gate, hoping to reimburse itself by charging admission fees. True to its character, when someone suggested paving the access road with scallop shells to cut the cost, the motion was applauded.

"If you take it step by step, proper land development works," Hornbeck tells a visitor in his Cambridge office, where he keeps a watering can in the corner—"a sign of my calling," he says. Planning, economics, and regulations about town use of the beach were not arbitrary but based on what the land could take, its physical and visual tolerance, as Hornbeck puts it. Walking to the beach, for example, is restricted to footpaths because the dunes are too unstable to survive constant people pressure; sites are restricted to four because of the water-table problems of the soil.

Once the approach to the problem was defined, everyone said yes—the town, Flanders, Lucy's heirs, the buyers, even Horace B. B. Robinson, who had to accede to the new purchasers, disappoint his prospective buyers, and take an unaccustomed back seat in the negotiations. Add McNamara's and

WHEN LUCY DIES . . .

the mysterious Meyer's tax brackets, which must make possible
a generous public gift, Lucy's wish about her land, the pressure
of developers who made this solution even more palatable by
comparison, the dedicated Flanders, the admirably unselfish
heirs, and you have a remarkable potential for some remarkable
land.

By midsummer 1972, it became a reality. McNamara and
Meyer were joined by Richard Hodgson of the International
Telephone and Telegraph Company and David Ginzburg, a
Washington attorney, acquiring some 40 acres and 1900 feet of
beach for their own use, giving the rest to the town via the
Association. The town's half mile of beach had been known as
Jungle Beach in recent years, attracting hordes of nude bath-
ers; now it would be restricted to use of residents ($5.00 per
annum fee for voters, $30.00 for off-island taxpayers) and car-
ries certain obligations. The town has to build and maintain an
access road and parking lot, keep animals off the beach,
motorboats off the pond, impose a closing hour of 11 P.M.,
and other restrictions calculated to protect the purchasers who
provided for the possibility of each building himself a house,
guest house, swimming pool, tennis court and other amenities
if desired. All of these arrangements caused a certain amount of
name-calling ("feudal fiefdom," "Kennedy-style compound")
and the usual flurry of "unfair" outcry from some islanders,
fueled by a largely inaccurate account in the *Grapevine*, which
accused the buyers of "getting the best of the deal by far."

Emotions about Lucy's beach were so grotesquely out of focus that they created an untoward incident on the Vineyard-
bound ferry when a 26-year-old man—"an island youth"—
attacked McNamara and tried to push him overboard. The encounter, widely reported in the press, was said to be due to
the fact that the assailant was "upset" over McNamara's purchase of Jungle Beach.

"The prospect is now bright," the *Gazette* editorializes. "It isn't often nowadays that wisdom, practicality, and also a balance of dollars and cents can be combined. Some quality of genius is required to hitch them together."

The genius is in the land. Eloquent enough to communicate to generations of Vincents, to romantic off-islanders and unsentimental Chilmark voters alike, to insist on showing its history from the days of the rolling glacier to the patient sheep farmer, to demonstrate in its folded clay underpinnings, which slant drainage downward, just how much human habitation it can sustain without polluting the valued Chilmark Pond, this old farm, which has become the first outstanding example of contemporary land planning on Martha's Vineyard, has a quality of genius.

It did not, however, spring full-blown from a shellfish shell. Other efforts in other times contained some of the elements in the plan. The Blacksmith Valley Association which Robinson put together up the road on his family farm, reminiscent as it is of a transplanted surburban residential community, combines the need for neighbors, shared land costs, and some limits— numbers of houses, no houses built on the road; formed in the 1950s, it was for twenty families. "We had no idea of giving any land to the town," Robinson says. "It was never discussed."

Across the island, on the north shore, a large farm which contained the island's second-highest hill—Prospect Hill—was sold in the 1960s to a New Jersey couple who moved into one of its houses and prepared to develop the breath-takingly lovely rolling hills into 3- to 5-acre house lots which were recently selling at the breath-taking price of $35,000 to $50,000. Some limits were recognized by the developers here too. They took trouble about aesthetics of siting houses and passing on design but what they neglected to do was to listen to the land. As it turns out, the soil for the most part of the large tract has, a soil scientist reported, "severe limitations for on-site septic tank sewage disposal, homesites or roads."

In the course of this upset, it was discovered that town-wide soil surveys, which the Dukes County Planning Commission is belatedly undertaking, will not be completed until 1975. The developers must now revise and clear new plans for sewage disposal with the Chilmark Board of Health and apply to the town's Conservation Commission for any alterations in wetland areas. Because this particular developer has forbidden people to cross his land to reach the Menemsha Hills Reservation, lying serenely beyond it along the moors and cliffs of the island's north shore, his standing in the neighborhood does not augur well for quick and favorable solutions.

"With a bit of land, anyone may play the part of a god," a professor of geology, Nathaniel Shaler once said. Fascinated by the glacial character of the Vineyard, he taught summer classes here in the late nineteenth century and in 1882, Henry Hough tells us, bought his first Vineyard property in the north-shore hills of North Tisbury and Chilmark, overlooking the Vineyard Sound. Year after year he bought more Vineyard farms, "to satisfy a deep land hunger, until he owned a broad and picturesque domain," Hough says, six large farms in a total of several thousand acres. He often brought his Harvard geology students to study the morainal deposits of the land, having moved into the original farmhouse, built in the late 1700s.

This land is a sort of spiritual grandparent to the Lucy land solution. Its generous flat fields are backed by deep woods but were bare a century ago, according to Frederick Moore, who lives in the original Shaler house and has obviously communicated with the good professor's ghost or, at least, with the records of the times. The land once supported cattle, hogs, and sheep. When the British fleet captured Vineyard Haven in 1778, Moore says, quoting from a diary of a Major André, who took part in what was known as Grey's Raid, the British requisitioned 5,000 cattle and 10,000 sheep from North Tisbury and West Tisbury farmers, taking them on forty vessels to the New York area to feed the British Army. It can be surmised that a good proportion of these came from farms which were later Shaler's, and that there were very few trees on these farms, the cattle having kept down the growth.

Because he had to go through seven gates to get to his house, Shaler named his place Seven Gates Farm. In 1921 Willoughby Webb, Shaler's son-in-law, a lawyer, persuaded the six families living in onetime Shaler houses to join in what Moore describes as "an experiment in communal living—sort of an idealistic Utopian idea." Webb formed a corporation, had surveyor Swift (Dean Swift's ancestor) lay out thirty-six building sites of at least five acres each so that no one site would be in view of another. The rest of the land, including two ponds and the curving rocky beach, became communal, belonging to the corporation.

The experiment is in healthy shape today. Twenty-four of the sites are occupied, the rest held by various families for their children and grandchildren. The Seven Gates Farm Corporation has a board of directors, bylaws, rules and regulations which, according to Henry S. Patterson II, former mayor of Princeton, New Jersey, its present president, are "a means to preserve the property and to provide the money necessary to pay for farm expenses." The objectives of the Corporation: "To afford the families sojourning within its domain the protection and advantages of the community property and community shore frontage, on as simple a basis possible. . . ." This includes truck service to Vineyard Haven three times a week, trash pickup, ability to rent your house (with permission of the Admissions Committee), to cut down trees (by permission of the Environmental Committee), no dogs on occupied beaches, fishing and deer hunting for residents only, and such mundane matters as maintenance of roads, water supply.

"In general," Patterson comments, "the Farm has tried to have a low profile." Walking through its acres, one can sense the unadvertised marvel of the land which the geology professor fell in love with, dramatic heights over the sound looking far across to the low-lying Elizabeth Islands, wooded hills, wide green stretches of open land and winding dirt roads through now dense forests. No offending houses mar the views; each is hidden by a turn in the land, a stand of trees, a sheltering knoll.

Seven Gates senses its lack of a modern land plan. Although it may, and hopefully will, survive to refresh the spirit by its mere existence, to cheer passers-by with an endless stretch of daisies or golden black-eyed susans in its uncut roadside field, it was not and could not have been created in the 1970s. Shaler and Webb knew the beautiful land well and were remarkably sensitive to it; the arrangement that was worked out for its corporate ownership was, for the times, a forward-looking way to continue protection ad infinitum. In the half century that has intervened since its establishment, ideas about land use have undergone a radical change. Seven Gates could not have reflected it, Blacksmith Valley and Prospect Hill did not; for different reasons all are limited by their own boundaries and do not consider the larger requirements of town and island.

The complicated Vincent solution is a step ahead of the ancestral pace. It moves to include the town in its planning; McNamara, like Larsen on Nantucket, held that contemporary morality does not allow for large stretches of privately owned beaches any longer, believes that the government must act to regulate and control these lands. The plan that was worked out gives Chilmark residents the right to drive in, park, and use the beach; it might have been even more advanced had it made this exquisite stretch of shore available only to those who are willing to stretch their muscles and walk there, keeping heavy polluting vehicles and unappreciative crowds off the delicate lands.

The plan could be criticized in that it provides only for wealthy owners. No one who is not exceedingly rich could participate in the partnership devised for building on Lucy's land, the same partnership which made the gift to the town possible. But this was a condition of the state of planning on Martha's Vineyard. There was no way of knowing whether Lucy's land should rightly house a tent colony, a few fishermen's shacks, or McNamara and partners, until the entire island is planned according to its total limits, as well as the individual limits of its parts. There can be no cogent idea of housing density or housing mix, no way to tell how many people there should be on the island as a whole or where they should locate until the Vineyard is considered as an entity and defines its limits. The regional plan which puts the island into partnership with the nation, under consideration as presented by Senator Kennedy might accomplish these goals.

Given the state of the island when Lucy died, the absence of a regional plan, and the Vineyard's very tentative beginnings of contemplating a new land ethic, it is remarkable that this scheme—combining Lucy's dedicated understanding of her acres with newly forming ideas of land protection—emerged. It puts Lucy Vincent in a special Vineyard Hall of Fame along with others such as the Daggetts, Shaler, Mittark the Indian sachem, and many contemporary Vineyarders who care enough about the land's natural limits to act for their preservation.

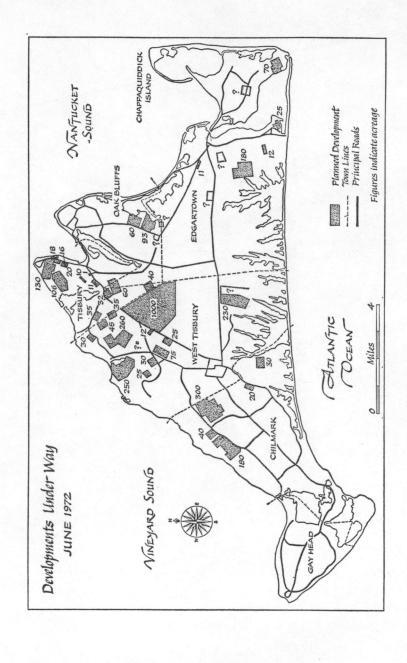

Developments Under Way
JUNE 1972

VINEYARD SOUND

NANTUCKET SOUND

CHAPPAQUIDDICK ISLAND

OAK BLUFFS

EDGARTOWN

TISBURY

WEST TISBURY

CHILMARK

GAY HEAD

ATLANTIC OCEAN

Planned Development
Town Lines
Principal Roads

Figures indicate acreage

Miles
0   4

CHAPTER SEVEN
Quarter-Acre Lots

One hundred and one years ago, a certain Charles Stewart sold his farm near the Vineyard's South Beach for exactly three times the price he had offered it at twelve months before. Henry Davis had ten acres which he "considered almost worthless a year ago," but sold, in 1872, for $1,000. In the same banner year for real estate, Tarleton Cadwallader Luce sold nine lots for $2,000; the Vineyard Grove Company collected $3,000 in lot sales in a single week. The land boom reached a high peak. A nineteenth-century chronicler says the new summer resort, Katama, had a year-round population of 2,000, a summer flood of 40,000. The Oak Bluffs Land and Wharf Company tripled its assets in two years, built the $102,000 Sea View Hotel, a chapel, wharf, gatehouse, bathhouse and arbor, pavilions, restaurants, shops. It invested a total of some $300,000 in what is now the town of Oak Bluffs. In those days, even in these, that, as the saying goes, is money.

A railroad was built to run from Oak Bluffs to Edgartown and Katama, and General Ulysses S. Grant, President of the United States, paid a visit to the wildly proliferating resort. By 1873 more than 2,100 down-island acres were chopped up into lots so small that they were measured by feet; Bellevue Heights, Engleside, Oklahoma, West Point Grove—subdivisions with oddly un-Vineyard names abounded. A year later, Tarleton Cadwallader Luce went into bankruptcy, the rolling stock of the railroads was in the hands of the sheriff, and the bright little stakes which marked out subdivision lots and roads were faded and overgrown by weeds and grasses. The nineteenth-century Vineyard land boom was history.

Today there are the same bright little stakes in the Vineyard's green fields and sandy dunelands, the same cellular layouts for subdivisions. "Design for the Future Reflects Spirit of the Past" is the *Gazette*'s consoling headline over a development scheme for 208 West Tisbury homes which shocked the unsuspecting 1971 populace when it opened its weekly paper. There are the same eager land sharks, the same quick inflations of land price, if on an elevated level. Two hundred and fifty Chilmark acres sold in 1968 for $250,000, changed hands six months later for $450,000, and two years thereafter were on the market in lots with a total value of $650,000. There are new, non-belonging names on knolls and meadows.

That is where the comparison stops. The present real estate boom is not "a little era . . . [with] the grand inflection of a fresh surge in human affairs," as Henry Hough affectionately regards the nineteenth-century development splurge in his detailed history, *Martha's Vineyard Summer Resort*. Nor is it possible that today's boom will disintegrate with the obliging speed of its predecessor—if it disintegrates at all.

When the massive land-use enigma, which troubles the entire nation, arrived on the Vineyard in the 1960s, the island as has been noted, was completely unprotected, its identity problem unresolved. In the first years of the seventies it had to make some fast decisions. Divided by town loyalties, by divergent goals and a variety of visions of the future, it grabbed the handiest solutions to its ever mounting problems, solutions which would lead it straight to the homogenizer, turning it into an extension of the mainland.

These actions alerted citizens and a senator. Whether the aroused Vineyarders—on and off-island—and the United States

Congress, in 1972, considering legislation to make a regional plan for the Vineyard and neighboring islands, will succeed in overcoming small-plot zoning, hot dog stands, and the shopping center syndrome for the Vineyard remains to be seen. But the actions which instigated this slim, almost miraculous last chance are the burden to be considered first, for it was these which revealed the need for something larger.

The nineteenth-century land boom was of quite a different character. The Vineyard had hardly begun its career as a summer resort then. Before the rise of great cities there were no summer resorts to speak of; anyone wanting to swim or picnic could walk or ride to the water's edge, or to open country, from the center of New York or Boston or any other town. Sulphur baths made Saratoga a place to go before 1800, but the Vineyard had to wait, Hough tells us, until cities grew up to be places to get away from in the summer.

The island was as pleasant an escape as Newport and other beginning resorts, if somewhat harder to get to. Contemporary literature advertises Vineyard advantages as "mild and balmy air of even temperature, superior bathing especially for children and invalids, excellent drives with sea or country aspects and the society of intelligent sea captains." Early promotion genteelly indulged in mention of Nathaniel Hawthorne's visit in 1830, and of Daniel Webster, who came in 1849 to escape hay fever, go bluefishing, and ride over the Great Plains to shoot plover (or perhaps the heath hen which would later perish there forever). Webster wrote three letters describing these pleasures which, Hough says, were quoted by Vineyard hotels and real estate agents for decades.

But the root of the island real estate uproar in the 1870s was the fun of the wild release to be found while worshiping the Lord in the great outdoors, amid hordes of fellow followers of The Word.

The zeal with which The Word was spread by John Wesley, eighteenth-century British evangelist and founder of Methodism, closed Anglican churches against him and his helpers; they took to preaching in the open air. By 1773 there were 10 English or Irish Methodist preachers in the U.S.A., a decade later there were 104 traveling preachers, 100 or so local preachers (who were laymen during the week), more than 200 licensed exhorters, and 18,000 members. At the turn of the century, an outdoor meeting in a Kentucky forest grove had the local population singing hymns, praying, and preaching with such enthusiasm that the event lasted several days and news of it spread fast and far, eventually reaching the Methodist pastor at Holmes Hole, John Adams, whom Hough describes as "a mighty shaker of the devil's kingdom." Reformation John, as he was known, held a week of meetings near the West Chop Lighthouse in 1827, first of what was to become an island institution, which built a town around it, attracted thousands of sinners every summer, and was responsible for most of what happened to Vineyard real estate in the nineteenth century.

Not to be outdone by their Holmes Hole neighbors, the Edgartown Methodists, led by a lay exhorter, Jeremiah Pease, undertook a camp meeting too. The spot they chose was to become one of the Vineyard's six towns, a grove of oaks, which, Hough tells us, were the largest in New England, near a sheep pasture on East Chop. At that first meeting in August 1835, according to the Reverend Frederic Denison's records, there was a small rough shed for a preacher's stand, 9 tents with straw and blankets, 1,000 in attendance and 65 conversions. By 1840 the half acre of pasture was leased and named Wesleyan Grove; in another two decades there were 320 tents, some houses built of wood, 15 acres, and 6,000 to 7,000 people.

Wesleyan Grove expanded fast. The circle of tents around the speaker's stand was surrounded by more circles, and a wide avenue went around the whole arc. In 1867 there were 570 tents, 12,000 people; a year later the Martha's Vineyard Camp Meeting Association was incorporated. The change from canvas shelters to the decorated, turreted, bescrolled, and balconied "wooden tents"—many of which still stand today—proceeded at a quick clip. Huge crowds came from the Cape and farther away; a Reverend Mr. Parks from New York called it "the largest camp meeting in the world."

Into this antique model of the modern encounter group—complete with Love Feast, sea bathing, and ceremonial professions of perfect love (150 in an hour)—crept the money-making motive in the person of a retired sea captain who sold the pasture adjoining the bursting camp grounds to the Oak Bluffs Land and Wharf Company, made up of himself, some other retired captains, and a sharp off-islander from Foxboro, Massachusetts, who supplied the necessary promotion for lots in the pasture—and for the expansion which eventually became a new town called Cottage City, until its name was changed in 1907 to the present Oak Bluffs.

The real estate boom which the success of the revival meetings in the oak grove had set off was no more lasting than the old-time religion which had brought it into being. The captains and other developers overextended themselves, counting on the continuing attraction of The Word out of doors. There was an assist from the Baptists, who started their own camp meetings, built a wooden tabernacle, and drew some new customers, and from the short-lived Martha's Vineyard Summer Institute, established "to combine study and recreation at an inexpensive seaside resort." But the help was insubstantial. Enthusiasm for revival meetings waned, fire destroyed many of the wooden hotels, promoters suffered injurious losses, and the 50 by 100-foot lots in The Region of Perfect Content, a onetime Chappaquiddick farm, went unsold and unnoticed in the general collapse.

An ironic footnote from real estate Boom #1 concerns certain other unsold Chappaquiddick lots which had been laid out in sizes varying from an eighth to a quarter of an acre. Although one-acre zoning has recently been adopted for Chappaquiddick, it does not apply to development plans filed before the bylaw was passed. In March 1972, as real estate Boom ⚹2 escalated, one of its biggest developers, Benjamin Boldt from Lexington, Massachusetts, bought forty-three of these tiny nineteenth-century-designed lots and put them on the market, thus circumventing even the modest regulations which attempted to govern building in the area.

The source of Boom ⚹1 was a fad, a God-given way of expressing pent-up emotions in a manner acceptable to that particular American era. What fooled the speculators, and then brought them to a sudden full stop, was that although it sounded like, looked like, and felt like religion, that most dependably everlasting habit, this was not religion, only one of its odd sprouts which blossomed bravely, brightly, furiously, and fast—and was gone.

Boom ⚹2 has no such gently entrancing characteristics. It is a pattern which is relentlessly cut on to rural America, particularly noticeable on the nation's two coasts. Along almost any highway you pass fields full of stairways, climbing to nowhere, waiting for their prefabricated encasements; you see miles of subvisions, punctuated by shopping centers, endless developments. When this national plague jumped the Sound and arrived on the Vineyard, romantics and engineers alike started talking about the rape of this island—the rape of the grape became a current quip—as though its land's tender delicacy could have somehow kept it virgin pure, untouched by what has hit the rest of the country—more leisure, more money, and many, many, many more people.

Getting to know what boom ⚹2 was made up of was shock therapy for even the most apathetic island-lovers. One man who was developing several hundred acres near the airport refused to discuss plans. "If I see anything else of what I consider a spurious nature . . . in your paper, you pay. Understand?" he told the *Grapevine*. A representative of the Maryland Investment Partnership answered a reporter's query with "Call my lawyer." It took the *Gazette*'s editor exactly six weeks to penetrate the new phenomenon. His pre-Christmas 1971 editorial said, "Land on Martha's Vineyard deserves to be thought of in terms other than money." By the end of January there was painful realism: "Now come the off-island developers to wave aside our own decisions and solutions, and to substitute for our goals their own objectives of profit-making. The lines are clearly drawn."

The lines were less distinct than they may have appeared. All off-islanders were not the bad guys; all Vineyarders were not the good guys. The vertical division wasn't working any more. Instead it was, as demonstrated by the group which worked out the proposed Lucy Vincent solution and others, a matter of land morality, and there was no consensus on the Vineyard about that. Builders, suppliers, hotel and restaurant proprietors, surveyors, earth movers, and the lengthening list of those who arrive with a spectrum of services where the people are, saw a healthy profit in developing the Vineyard. They were for it. Still, one builder whose craftsmanship is legendary, and whose up-island farmhouse embraces the visitor with a quiet sense of survival over centuries of winter storms and summer sun, despaired over the boom that could make him rich. "This is not what we came to the Vineyard for, twenty-five years ago," he said, and thinks of leaving the bright meadows to find a serene Vineyard somewhere else.

A particular kind of land morality emerged over the years in one of the Vineyard's first developers, a dentist whose interest in the land was aroused by the recurring mumble issuing from his dental chair: "What's going to happen to the island?" Beginning in the 1950s, Dr. Alvin Strock, with his brother

Moses, started to accumulate Vineyard land. He bought the Love Farm in Hart Haven (the largest dairy farm on the island, he says), Katama Farm, which has "the largest field in New England," from Al Brickman (whose clothing emporium is known to summer shoppers as Bergdorf Brickman's), a stretch of spectacular Gay Head land abutting that of the Hornblower family, the Island Country Club, which has the Vineyard's only eighteen-hole golf course, and dozens of other parcels, with and without superlatives attached, to total 2,200 acres by 1972, when, he said, his Island Properties, Inc., was one of the Vineyard's largest single landholders.

Strock, an affable, earnest man who speaks more like a professor than a real estate entrepreneur, had discussed his development approach with Hideo Sasaki who was at Harvard's School of Architecture. "It had a serious impact on my life," he said. His first enterprise—Waterview Farm—is a cluster of gray-shingled contemporary houses with traditional pitched roofs, overlooking Sengakontacket Pond. Half the acreage is kept in open space, the two-and-a-half-mile waterfront is and will remain free of housing. Island Properties was well advertised as "Preservation of an environment, an approach to conservation and proper land use," an unusual bad-guy slogan.

Nevertheless, when Waterview Farm became a reality, the Vineyard pressed the panic button. Strock, it was said, was a crass money-maker who would bring ruin upon the island. "I was the only one trying to do anything on that level and it came out as though I was a villain," Strock recalled. "I withdrew mentally into the lab." He retired from practice in 1966, continues to supervise Island Properties; although his brother has died, his son and nephews are part of the operation.

"Investment in non-development" is his future plan. If there is no protective action by the government in the next year or so, Strock intends to assemble a private partnership to put enlightened investors into the landholding business. "The only way left to preserve the island will be to buy land and hold on to it," he says. "It's no good to ask for gifts; people won't give, but maybe they will invest."

Despite his pariah image, Strock was less of a threat than two other warning signals which, because of their implications for the island, might have put the population on notice of what was to come. One was a young man's decision in the spring of 1971 to initiate the Vineyard's first night club.

"I plan to run a good restaurant-night-club operation," Edward W. Vincent, Jr., told the Edgartown selectmen, "in a structure in keeping with the character of the town in its design. . . ." His request was supported by his father, who thought it would be good for young people to have somewhere for dancing and name bands, and by friends, one of whom said it was "about time that this town had a place where the average person can go." William Parks, then chairman of the Board of Selectmen, felt he was being impartial in judging the matter, even though he was a relative of the Vincents. The state, he said, had increased the number of year-round liquor licenses for Edgartown; if this request were denied, reasons would have to be spelled out.

The people-business promoters lined up against the quiet-life-with-yacht-club proponents, many of whom were taxpaying non-voters. These Edgartown enthusiasts hired a Boston law firm, obtained 476 signatures on a petition, and in five months emerged victorious when young Vincent was persuaded not to pursue his plans. But he had thought it might work, as had his father and other relatives and supporters. Surely the *idea* of a night club and name bands had a message for the island, and just as surely, unless the direction changes radically, the idea will return as a reality before too long.

During this same summer Charles Feeney, Jr. of Sharon, Massachusetts, issued a semiconcealed but nonetheless telling challenge to the island. Having purchased nineteen acres, most of which were in the town of Tisbury, which had no zoning at the time, he applied for and got a Board of Health permit to build a family-type campground. It was well known that Feeney intended to add to the campground (there were already two on the island) an entirely new phenomenon for Martha's Vineyard—its first trailer park.

"A trailer park will irretrievably damage Martha's Vineyard," the *Gazette* said in June; in July it pointed out that Falmouth had barred trailers for many years. Robert Clark was chairman of the Tisbury Board of Health when Feeney got his permit for the campground, separate from the trailer park, against loud public opposition. In February 1972 it was reported that Feeney would move to open the 40-trailer park for the '72 season, though by May he still had not applied for a permit. At the same time it turned out that Clark and Feeney had a business relationship, Feeney distributing literature for rental houses owned by Clark, Leland and Clark, and Mrs. Feeney giving out Clark's number for reservations on houses. Selectman John Schilling suggested that Clark disqualify himself in any future Feeney hearings, and somehow the controversy was swallowed up in other conflicts. Knowledgeable Vineyarders maintain that trailers will be crowding the ferries along with the name bands as soon as Feeney can maneuver himself through the necessary legal entanglements.

The night club and trailer park were symptoms of the quarter-acre lot disease which was festering all the while in the island's innards. People who want to live in a development bring the need for a night club along with them; it doesn't much matter where the trailer is parked, or the lot is situated, as long as the accouterments of "civilization" are there too. Thus it might be said that it was not so much the Vineyard's special character that the newcomers were looking for, as it was Anyplace, U.S.A.

In August 1971 some of the off-island developers' plans,

long since securely filed in the county courthouse, saw the light of day. Plans for the quarter-acre lot subdivisions started being published in the *Gazette* and *Grapevine;* week after week, stunned summer people and island people alike gazed numbly at the apparently unending series of plans for hundreds of acres—in Edgartown, Tisbury, West Tisbury, Chilmark. Since not all towns require that building plans be filed, it was impossible, then, even to estimate the extent of land Boom #2.

There was some variation. One developer decided on an equine motif: "Horses will be compulsory in front lots facing State Road," owner Boldt decreed for Martha's Vineyard Island Farms, "to preserve the rural look." Tea Lane Associates in Chilmark favor cluster housing, hope to put ten houses on four acres "with open land all around," but when owners Julia Sturges and Eleanor Pearlson consulted Peter Hornbeck about their plans, he advised that they stop everything and look at what there is on the land. "I suggested that they do their homework first," Hornbeck says.

By and large, the effect of the honeycombed newspaper pages and stepped-up rumor factory—talk of a high-rise condominium on Vineyard Haven's Main Street, apartment houses on Katama, summer rentals on Menemsha Neck—was to hurry the towns into zoning.

As early as 1958, over ninety per cent of the Massachusetts population lived where there was zoning, a mechanism unknown in America before the 1920s. Two thirds of all Commonwealth towns were zoned; of the 102 which were not, 5 were on Martha's Vineyard (the sixth island town, Oak Bluffs, locus of Boom #1, had adopted a rudimentary zoning bylaw in 1948). Not that the idea hadn't been discussed here and there on the island. "The old idea of individual liberty carried with it the idea of individual responsibility too," the *Gazette* commented in 1953. "But now we need zoning." A year later Edgartown started talking about it "to encourage the most appropriate use of land . . ." and when Nantucket set up its Historic District in 1955, and nearby Rockland, threatened by trailer parks, passed zoning, as did Falmouth, overwhelmed by too many gas stations, conversation was more lively and determined. The Garden Club ran a "Zoning Facts" column in the paper, polled voters in 1959, and found zoning "heavily favored."

"Restriction of the individual for the good of all is nothing new," Joseph Allen, island philosopher and historian, said, recalling the institution of the hog-reeve, a person whose duty it was to impound stray swine lest they destroy individual crops, a move ahead from the days when pigs ranged the village streets, ate garbage thrown from the houses, and rampaged where they would. Allen, favoring zoning, believed people would realize its fitness as they understood the need for a hog-reeve.

It took Edgartown fifteen years of talking to finally pass a zoning bylaw in 1969. Part of the town, Chappaquiddick, had been zoned some years ago, as had West Chop, part of Tisbury. But big, sprawling Edgartown took its time, ultimately legislating residential and business areas, lot sizes, height of buildings, and other standard zoning regulations. While its selectmen struggled with an expanding building program and population influx—suddenly there was a swarm of pale, long-haired hippies in their tie-dyed shirts and jeans, lounging on the courthouse steps, an odd meld with the Lilly-dressed ladies of North Water Street and the well-tanned yachtsmen—they took the time to request the owner of the Coffee Shop to move its pool table upstairs "as it was not the intention of the board to grant a license for a pool table to be located on the ground floor."

The same admixture of the big and little problems showed up in West Tisbury, where zoning talk started more than twenty years ago. The late Joseph Howes, in his nineties, wrote a protest; in sixty-odd years, he said, West Tisbury had lost a long list of buildings including 2 churches, 4 school-houses, a lumber yard, brick kiln, 4 grocery stores, a furniture factory, slaughterhouse, tavern, gristmill, 3 ice cream parlors, and some 30 barns. It had gained one new house a year, Howes said, some non-resident owners of shore-front property and 5 rights of way to the Great Pond . . . no reason for zoning. But a town committee continued to look into the matter until, in 1966, it voted down a zoning proposal by one vote, defeated it again in 1967, and finally passed it in a hurry in 1971 by a 4:1 ratio, the moderator of that victorious town meeting being the island's only resident psychiatrist, Dr. Milton Mazer.

"We feel that all towns are on the threshold of a disaster," Lewis King told the Chilmark town meeting, which discussed at one meeting whether to allow Bingo in town (the vote was close, but negative) and at another a zoning proposal for one third of the town which it passed in December, 1971, by a vote of 101 to 21. "A clear and decisive mandate . . . to go on to more extensive zoning," King said. An attorney representing some objecting clients was denied permission to speak for them at the meeting, King again ruling that non-voters are not permitted to talk in town meetings. A second portion of the town was zoned five months later by unanimous vote. Here, two-acre lots were included "to encourage medium-income home builders." The other compelling reason for this lot size, according to King, was that the first zoning, with only three-acre lots, had almost not been passed by the Massachusetts attorney general's office as "there was no state precedent for lots this large." King told the town meeting that zoning without two-acre or smaller lots would probably not get state approval.

"Three cheers for Chilmark on the passage of its partial zoning bylaw," the Conservation Society's executive Woodruff said to his organization. "Tisbury is working hard on a zoning proposal and has begun a large-scale selling job which promises to dispel some of the fears . . . which killed it a year ago. Gay Head is next." Even at this late date, one of the few evidences that I could find of thinking about the island as a region instead of as a collection of six towns came from County Commissioner Shirley Frisch. "It's important for everyone here to call all their friends in Tisbury and get them to vote for zoning," she said at a meeting. "What happens in one town affects the whole island."

In mid-'72 there were dozens of developments under way, as the map of as many as could be located shows. These slipped into place before zoning, or sprouted in Tisbury, not zoned until May 1972, and in Gay Head. There were enough developments, if all are built and occupied, to completely change Martha's Vineyard. Already the towns with zoning found it an inadequate protection; Edgartown, where there were seventeen developments under way in mid-1972 (one with 30 by 60-foot lots), was the first to pass a subdivision control law to make developers pay for their own services—water, sewer, roads—and conform to certain town-imposed rules. "We can't demand gold streets," a planning board member said, "but we can impose certain controls and limitations."

Twenty years had passed since zoning was first seriously considered on the Vineyard. In 1972 the island was on its way to completing a town-by-town "victory" of adopting zoning laws. During two short decades it had changed from looking at zoning with suspicion (I remember an influential Vineyard Haven shopkeeper insisting that it was a form of communism) to welcoming it with unanimous votes, cheers, and self-congratulations. There were irate discussions, of course, but it was the rare voice now raised in question of the basic idea. Ed Cuetera, a busy West Tisbury architect, noted the self-fulfilling nature of zoning: Tisbury land along the State Road, for example, proposed as a commercial zone, became commercial almost overnight, crowded with new stores, gas stations, markets, instead of a placid view of trees and fields, before the bylaw was even passed. Cuetera suggested the appointment of a planning board. In Chilmark, Julia Sturges spoke to the idea of an over-all town plan instead of bit-by-bit zoning; the *Gazette* warned: "The prosperity of the Vineyard depends on rejecting, not copying, mainland standards."

The Vineyard wasn't listening. Because there was no preparation for what was coming, no agreement on whether it was good or bad, no consensus on the island's future, no one thought that zoning, which worked well on the mainland, was not appropriate for the island. No one thought to challenge the attorney general's reported desire for a maximum size of two-acre lots; no one, to my knowledge, publicly protested the zoning method of protecting the Vineyard.

Zoning, as undertaken by the Vineyard towns, was prejudging the island's future. Zone it like a suburb and chances are it will become a suburb; zone it like a subdivision and it will attract subdivisions. An overcrowded, overdeveloped Vineyard future had been in the making ever since the disputed Metcalf & Eddy report, with its projections of 23,000 new year-round residents by 1990, its plan for a new town to hold them. "If you prepare for that kind of influx," the *Grapevine* said, "build your sewage systems and water supplies around it, then it will appear." In a pro-zoning column, James Reston, the *Gazette*'s publisher, commented: "We are going to have more people and more business regardless of what anybody says. No editorials in the *Gazette*, no matter how eloquent, are going to stop the trend."

Reston said what most islanders were thinking. The zoning mentality—which takes for granted that the most that could be done for the delicate Vineyard lands was to keep houses an acre or two apart from each other—had dug in deep. Almost everything that happened was considered in terms of The Trend.

Sewers and water, for example, now became something to worry about. What was satisfactory for the island's pre-boom population would mean trouble when there was a house on every quarter-acre lot—or every three acres. Some of the costs of The Trend are public sewer systems (there were none on the island) and a public water supply. The County Planning Commission, promoter of growth, was told by a state official that "co-ordination of sewage systems and water supply is mandatory," but towns continue to do their own thing about such basics with more or less success. Edgartown got more than a half million federal dollars for a sewage plant to be completed in 1973. Another half million in federal funds for a water-quality study by the National Environmental Protection Agency to be undertaken in 1972, completed in 1975; such a study will be a requirement for every town for future government funding of sewage plants.

All these millions in sewers are spent to prepare—for suburbia.

The Trend infested the already people-minded Steamship Authority, which invited bids for two new boats, stepped up their TV and radio advertising campaign for the Vineyard and Nantucket route. It penetrated the tourist bus operators, who sent more and more 9,000–10,000-pound juggernaut buses across the Sound and around island roads, causing slippage in East Chop's fragile banks and undermining the road to Menemsha village.

Even the Vineyard Conservation Society, successor to the Friends of Martha's Vineyard, which did battle for Menemsha Neck and its birds, back in the halcyon days before subdivision gales had swept the island, began thinking in The Trend. "A consistently negative approach will only further the already wide gap which exists between development interests and preservation interests," Bob Woodruff said. He was in favor of Feeney's campground: "Except for its high density, he [Feeney] is planning a high quality development," the voice of island conservation said, warning that "we will lose the support we now have from the business community if we exhibit blanket opposition to all development. And we NEED the support of the business community." He did not say for what.

The Conservation Society had slowly altered its governing body and membership; involved as its executive director Woodruff was in dozens of conservation matters behind the scenes, advising, putting people in touch with each other, co-ordinating the clutch of like-minded island organizations, the Society's leadership—many of the same people who went to all those meetings, wearily, night after night—was less than dynamic. In 1971 it stated that its major concern was to get people to put conservation restrictions or easements on their land. In 1972 its hope was in its new young activist board members.

There were a few holdouts. Most tenacious and effective was the Concerned Citizens of Martha's Vineyard, a group brought into being in the spring of 1970 by the airport issue, a drama which ripped into the Vineyard with the force of one of its mightier hurricanes. One founder of the organization is Gerald Kelly, editor of the *Grapevine*, a rotund, ubiquitous journalist, born in Wisconsin, who came to the Vineyard in the late sixties from a stint in Mexico where he edited a magazine. Kelly now lives in West Tisbury, glides around the island collecting stories, writes for and edits the weekly paper that started to give the *Vineyard Gazette* some competition but in 1972, inexplicably switched to an openly biased propaganda sheet which carried little weight. James Alley, the other founder of Concerned Citizens, is West Tisbury's postmaster and storekeeper like his late father before him, sports a Texas-type hat, has a profound determination to protect the island where he grew up, and a motivating affection for his two children who, he believes, should have the same privilege as he did—to roam the island's beaches, fishing wherever the fishing is good, knowing most of the island's terrain.

"Jesus Christ, Henry," Kelly remembers saying to fellow editor Hough, "they're bringing jets to the Vineyard!" In June two hundred people and some dogs witnessed the arrival of a rather soiled yellow and white Northeast Airlines jet. There was applause when it landed, someone called out, "Beautiful!" and Alley, Kelly, and friends went home to do some serious thinking. "It was a good gut issue," Alley says. "Everyone cared, summer people too, and because it was summer we could raise some money." The issue centered around cutting down the trees in some twenty acres of state forest adjacent to the airport, to accommodate jets. The runway had already been extended by 500 feet the year before, and the road grade lowered to accommodate jets (causing a rash of opposing bumper stickers, "Save the Sub-Standard Bump"). Now the trees were to be axed by order of the F.A.A.

In the airport battle, the Concerned Citizens (who had considered naming themselves the Society for Having a Haven Here—S Triple H) demonstrated what a straight-thinking, hard-working citizen group can do, vis-à-vis a Trend.

John Alley, James's brother, was the first president of the organization, which accumulated membership fast, raised some money, hired lawyers, had well-informed representatives testifying at every hearing, kept people up to date about what was happening, took a poll of voters (fifty-six per cent opposed to enlarging the airport), refused proffered compromises. "The airport expansion is a virtual character assassination of the Vineyard," Alley said at the time. James Cagney, who has a farm in Chilmark (daily pointed out to busloads of tourists through a break in the trees near his house), commented, "For more than thirty years, I have watched the Vineyard go downhill. . . . Now they're talking about jets. Please give it some thought." A Sierra Club official did. "The frequency of fog in the area," he said, "makes a jetport on Martha's Vineyard an absolutely insane concept."

The case dragged along, step by step, with every possible bureaucratic barrier put in the way of the Concerned Citizens, including threats from Nantucket's representative to the Massachusetts legislature, Arthur Desrocher, who suggested—in a disturbing reminder of McCarthyism—that the organization be the subject of an immediate investigation by the Secretary of State. After the Citizens had encountered more powerful legislative opponents and thoroughly displeased the airline lobby, another disturbing, tougher (for the island), if less direct threat appeared. It was reported in the press that the state's Department of Public Works and the Aeronautics Commission had embarked on a two-year study to see whether the Vineyard airport might feasibly act as an alternate landing field to Logan and other large airports in the Boston area. Lost in the political power play was the reluctance of Northeast to continue jet service to the Vineyard.

"To every vacation area, transportation is the life line of its business," the island's Chamber of Commerce secretary testified to the F.A.A. "In an era when you can have lunch in Boston and tea in Bermuda, it is not unreasonable to expect a safe, modern, efficient airport on Martha's Vineyard." Robert Carroll, then chairman of the Edgartown selectmen, who was to figure importantly in a later Vineyard bout with Senator Kennedy, joined Trend promoters, reminding the hearing that direct air service to the Vineyard from New York and Boston was "important to over-all economic development."

The forest vs. jets battle reached the senatorial level with the issue of installing an instrument landing system. Massachusetts Senator Edward Brooke, meeting with local and state officials on the island, completed an opening statement before he realized that reporters were present, then insisted that members of the fourth estate withdraw. He had already ruled out further discussion on jets with a firm, Trend-type statement: "Whether we like it or not," he said, "we already have jets on the Vineyard." Brooke was there to act, not debate. "Saying nice things about trees is like saying nice things about motherhood," a *Gazette* editorial remarks. "Senator Brooke referred gently to the trees of the Vineyard's state forest before, a minute or two later, condemning them to be cut down."

The airport was enlarged. As a part of the forest was being mercilessly cleared for jets, Northeast, the sole Vineyard jet operator (carrying only 1.9% of all Vineyard traffic), filed a request with the F.A.A. to drop the Vineyard from its route. Delta Airlines, which absorbed Northeast in 1972, follows the same policy.

The Concerned Citizens do not consider their efforts wasted. "We had not lost," Kelly said, "we had merely defined the nature of the battle." By 1972 the organization had an excess of 1,000 dues-paying members, an annual budget of $5,000 to $8,000 (dues are low—$5.00 to $10 a year—to allow a broad membership base and because of the organization's lobbying, are not deductible), holds regular open monthly meetings, regards itself as a watchdog, aims to get more qualified people into public office. "We need a legislator who will do some work for the island," the founders said, "somebody who is responsive to his constituency." Despite his distinguished Vineyard heritage, Gregory Mayhew, the incumbent, does not fit their requirements.

Other aims are to control the flow of people to the island, oppose use of mass media advertising, stop the building of a radio station on the Vineyard, try to weld people together in face of important issues. The Citizens are repeating their airport confrontation with the Steamship Authority with unflagging zeal, challenging the profit-minded actions of this semipublic service, have already succeeded in getting its advertising budget reduced, and at least a consideration of the problems inflicted on the island by the Steamship Authority's attitude of building up the island's people business, and its own.

The Concerned Citizens apparently has the confidence of members. When it needed money for a special cause—to fight the dumping of garbage in Nantucket Sound—it asked the public for $500, got $800 in a single week. It has a new president, Carleton Parker, who came to the Vineyard to live, in the late 1960s, from Williamstown, Massachusetts, and believes that "the quantity and quality of the frustrations evidenced by our concerned citizens" produces the results which the organization is getting. Parker is concerned about Vineyard citizens: "The reaction of islanders to fears brought about by pollution, real estate developments, increased tourism, potential government takeover of the seashore," he notes, "runs the gamut from utter lethargy to talk of suicide."

The island environment arouses strong loyalties in the catholic assortment of people who choose to live in it. To lose it is indeed devastating. But those who would transform the Vineyard to Anyplace, U.S.A., will lose money if their present efforts should, by some miracle, fail, and it is not as easy to rout the Devil in dollar dress today as it was when The Word was shouted and sung in the Vineyard's oak groves, a century back. Despair in the face of impending disaster will only encourage avarice; neither lethargy nor suicide is an effective opponent to greed. Neither will help. And help is needed. The large-scale land-use dilemma facing much of America must be defined for the Vineyard in terms which deal specifically with this particularly special place. Solutions which may fit mainland suburbia are grotesquely unfitting for the island of Martha's Vineyard. It requires—and can have—its own answer.

CHAPTER EIGHT

Answers in Other Places

The Vineyard, by reason of circumstances which have been noted, is late in confronting the land-use dilemma, years behind less exposed places with less exquisite resources to worry about. Crucial time has been lost. The one advantage of this otherwise unadvantageous delay is that during the ten or more years, a number of different ways of protecting land have been created and put into effect across the country. Although the Vineyard is unique and its problem is critical, there are now some new and intriguing precedents for what to do about it, ideas, plans, structures, laws, which can be used in deciding what should happen next.

One principle governs the emerging land ethic. Land is no longer simply a commodity to make money for its owner. It is increasingly regarded as a resource to be used for the public good. And the public includes the entire environment, the ecosystem, "the interdependent web of life" as it has been called. Until now the environment seemed infinitely capacious, able to regenerate itself no matter what we did or how we lived. No one even thought about it much. Man was the boss and acted as he would—cut forests, filled swamps, dumped garbage, leveled ground—getting rich on the land, keeping large portions of it in individual ownership.

Now the environment informs us that our arrogant splurge is over. Man has to be a member, not the master, of the ecosystem.

We have to think of land as part of a scheme where plants, animals, air, sun, and water—and man—live together, or in all probability we will not live.

Part of the new necessity is to make rules about land. People can still own, buy, sell, and build on it, gain a portion of a fortune if they are clever about it, but they are subject to regulations, or, if they are not now, soon will be. "Americans are beginning to change the rules that govern the use of their most basic resource: the land. . . . The change promises to affect nearly everyone from big land developers to individual home owners," the *Wall Street Journal* comments. "Public rights to environmental quality, enforceable at law . . ." is the central issue of law professor Joseph Sax's recent book on the environment; in another book on the subject, Richard Saltonstall says the modern presumption is that "all land is subject to restrictions to prevent its abuse at the public's expense."

The idea of planning land use has finally caught on in the U.S.A. Amazingly, it is discovered that protecting the land with long-range vision does not harm the would-be profiteer but more often than not enhances land values. Although this is not the primary purpose of the new land ethic, it is more immediate and tangible than the solemn idea of saving our lives which still seems remote, a vaguely placed threat. Regulation of land use changes from minus to plus for landowners whose first reaction was that this is an infringement of their inalienable rights. Gradually, America is beginning to look at land differently than it ever has before.

The move is away from the primitive form of regulation— local zoning—which a current survey describes as "a feudal system controlled by thousands of individual local governments, each seeking to maximize its tax base and minimize its social problems." The move is toward regional control, which fits land use into a larger plan. It can be accomplished by any one of countless permutations of private and public bodies, by a place of any size. A few that have worked are described in the next pages. These examples are by no means an encyclopedic review or even a scientific sampling but they do tell a tale of ingenuity, innovation, experimentation, from an east coast island to a west coast bay, from a midwestern city to an entire New England state. By their extreme difference, one from the next, they suggest that wherever we are, we may have the capacity to restore the balance between man and land.

Imagine Martha's Vineyard almost unoccupied and in the hands of a very few owners—wild, empty, quiet. Such was Cumberland Island off the coast of Georgia, the same twenty-two miles long as the Vineyard, with fresh-water ponds, dunes, long open beaches. A brother of Andrew Carnegie bought the island in the nineteenth century, his heirs still held most of it in mid-twentieth century. The National Park Service had had its eye on Cumberland since 1955 when it had made a survey, *Our Vanishing Shoreline*, of the Atlantic and Gulf coasts. "Foreboding is the only word . . ." it said, finding only a few accessible and underdeveloped beaches left, and only six and a half per cent of the shore line in federal and state ownership for public recreation uses. Cumberland was first on its 1955 list for prompt acquisition.

Nothing happened until 1968 when Charles Fraser, developer of the widely acclaimed Sea Pines Plantation on nearby Hilton Head, acquired 3,000 Cumberland acres from three Carnegie heirs. He brought David Brower, former executive secretary of the Sierra Club, friend of the earth and eloquent champion of the ecosystem, to Cumberland to discuss its development, a visit reported by John McPhee in *Encounters with the Archdruid*. " 'You, Charles Fraser, have got to persuade the whole God-damned movement of realtors to have a different kind of responsibility to man than they have,' " Brower said. " 'If they don't, God will say that man should be thrown away as an experiment that didn't work.'"

Together, Brower and Fraser worked out some tempting schemes for Cumberland: ten per cent development, ninety per cent a National Seashore. (Fraser was afraid that if he managed a successful development, its value would soar and bring in developers of a different caliber who would detract from it, but he could not afford to protect the rest of the unprotected island himself.) They decided to cluster use in one area, keep the rest wild (as in Yosemite, a Brower favorite), rule out all automobiles ("'Whatever you do,'" Brower said, again thinking of Yosemite, "'don't give the island to Detroit. Zermatt is carless. Stehekin in the State of Washington is carless'"). Food and services would be brought in in mini flying boxcars, jeep trains would get people around the island, or they would walk.

Cumberland was bound to change, one way or another. Then worth at least $10 million, now three or four times as much, it was, McPhee says, "A beautiful and fragile anachronism. . . . Need, temptation and realistic taxes would eventually wrest the island from its present owners. They would not be able to afford it." Fraser couldn't keep his foothold there either. His purchase set off what McPhee calls "one of the great land-use battles of recent times," resulting in heavy pressure on Fraser to sell his acreage.

There was no chance for realtors to show God that the man experiment worked, after all, at least on Cumberland Island. The Andrew W. Mellon Foundation made $6 million available to the National Park Foundation to buy the privately held lands on the island, and the first acquisition, in September 1970, was Fraser's property.

By the summer of 1972 the transformation to the Cumberland Island National Seashore was still not complete. The Foundation had still not acquired all the land; greed showed itself, even in this paradise, or perhaps because of it. One owner asked $22,000 an acre for land he had bought two and a half years before at $1,000 an acre, an informed source says, other owners asked for life tenancy; some members of the Carnegie and Rockefeller families asked for the right to pass their lands on to heirs ad infinitum. Little Cumberland Island nearby will not be acquired if the organization which owns it puts sufficient restrictions on the land to insure scenic preservation; if it doesn't, the Foundation will acquire that too, in addition to 12,000 acres of submerged land and 4,000 acres of estuarine land. The new National Seashore will have to control volume and actions of visitors to protect it properly. The Department of Interior proposes to limit access to boats only—ferries or personal craft, no cars. To keep fragile inland areas intact, visitors will be escorted from docks to beaches by mini-bus or jitney; only trails will penetrate the island's interior.

In a recent conversation, George Hartzog, director of the National Park Service, politically embattled protector of its lands, says he is pleased with the Cumberland transaction, particularly as it demonstrates "use of new tools for land acquisition." The U. S. Government would have been hard pressed to come up with the amount necessary for outright purchase of Cumberland; private funds and privately inflicted land restrictions make the government's appropriation within the realm of possibility, if not a downright bargain. If it all works out as planned, Cumberland will become part of a scheme much larger than itself. The Foundation will give it to the U.S.A. and it will be fitted into the roster of public lands, subject to the decisions of the democracy.

It could be among the last of such clear-cut and relatively simple solutions. There are few Cumberlands left, few Frasers who will surrender to the public good, few Mellon Foundations able (as land prices soar) and willing to buy. But even if the process is never repeated in the same way, it clarifies what happens elsewhere. The dilemma of an enlightened developer in an unplanned area, the burgeoning flexibility of the National Park Service, are part of the Cumberland story. So, too, is the terrible (and terribly expensive) time lag between recognizing the need for a land-use plan and doing anything about it. Fifteen, twenty years . . . we can't afford to wait for the endless surveys and studies any longer. In the 1970s, land moves fast. But Congress, even under these best of circumstances, with land and money almost all readily available, moves with deliberate speed.

Could the Vineyard ever be carless, supplied by flying boxcars? Could it, in the present circumstances, set a Brower or a Fraser to scheming? No enlightened developer would gamble on the Vineyard if his only protection was local suburban zoning. The quality of the Vineyard's land might still inspire some sort of federal protection but to enact it, before it is too late, will require extraordinary pressure on Congress.

In 1970 President Nixon delivered an Environmental Message to Congress which, he said, was "an historic milestone." So, too, was the statement of a predecessor. "Nothing, in my opinion," George Washington had said, "would contribute more to the welfare of these states than the proper management of our lands. And nothing . . . seems less understood." Apparently things haven't changed too much. Nixon told Congress that today was "the first time in the history of nations that a people has paused, consciously and systematically, to take comprehensive stock of the quality of its surroundings. It comes," said the President, "not a moment too soon."

Nixon set up the Council on Environmental Quality (for policy analysis and advice) with Russell Train, former head of the Conservation Foundation, as chairman, and the Environmental Protection Agency (to combat pollution in air, water, and land). Congress passed the National Environmental Policy

23. The island's first federal highway—"People begin to forget what
a quiet island road looks like"

24. "Town strength came with the
settlement of the land"

25. Lucy's house—"pristine white farmhouse behind a picket fence"

26."Lucy died at the age of eighty-seven"

27. Stone walls tell the history of the land

28. "Bescrolled and balconied wooden tents still stand in Oak Bluffs"

29. Boom #2 begins

30. Boom #2 continues—condominium houses on once-wild Katama moors

31. The island relies on the people business

32. The Vineyard becomes Anyplace, U.S.A.

33. Waste disposal is a problem

34. Before the crowds arrive

35. "Vermont keeps some of its green mountains green"

36. Bolinas—town, lagoon, and ridge

37. K. Dun Gifford meets with Vineyard citizens in Edgartown

38. "Trading up"—Beinecke's Nantucket restoration

39. Edward Kennedy—"He genuinely
cared about the islands. And acted."

40. All beaches—forever wild

41. West Tisbury—"an eye-catching flock"

42. "The end is the beginning"

Act (NEPA), which requires all federal agencies to prepare environmental impact statements for all proposed legislation or major expenditure of public funds. After some two years on the books, NEPA was reviewed by the Conservation Foundation, which finds it "revolutionary—and tormenting—for a bureaucracy," lacking in authority to enforce standards, threatened now by commercial and bureaucratic interests which rebel at being held up by the courts. The real issue of urban growth and land use, the reviewers say, still stays with the local power structure, which does not have to make NEPA reports.

In 1971 Nixon asked Congress for a national land-use policy act "to reform the institutional framework in which land use decisions are made." This, in effect, passes the buck for planning and regulating land to the states, for which the President requested $20 million a year for five years. Priority was for states in the coastal zone, particularly to protect areas of critical environmental concern, "areas where uncontrolled development could result in irreversible damage to important historic, cultural, or aesthetic values, or natural systems or processes, which are of more than local significance . . . coastal zones and estuaries, shorelands, rare or valuable ecosystems, scenic or historic areas." (Martha's Vineyard defined?)

In the election year of 1972, Nixon's bill (S.992) for a national land-use policy was still being considered in Congress—and Murphy started building on the rare valuable shorelands of Menemsha Neck.

Meanwhile, some places weren't waiting for the nation or for the states. In the Twin Cities of Minneapolis and St. Paul there is a Metropolitan Council—a regional co-ordinating agency of local governments—the first such body in the nation. It has authority over functions that affect the entire area—sewage, highways, environment, growth patterns—and was the result of acute problems of the 1960s. The central city was deteriorating, pollution on the rise, police protection and public transportation inadequate, land use chaotic. Local governments fragmented function; there were 2 million people, 320 government units, each with a tax jurisdiction, seven counties.

The co-ordinating Council, created in 1967 by the state legislature, was chosen as one of the nation's nine important innovations in land regulations by the President's Council on Environmental Quality, which also describes its chief problems: the resistance of certain major agencies, such as the Airports Commission, increasing friction with local governments (who fear the Council's involvement in purely local business) and with certain legislators who worry that they have, indeed, created a Frankenstein. However, in 1971 it achieved a law which provided that each local government in the region had to contribute forty per cent of tax growth moneys to the Council for redistribution according to population and need. The operation of this law, observers say, will be "viewed with interest throughout the country."

> *Would Edgartown be willing to share* forty per cent of its tax growth with Gay Head, a poverty-ridden town which could use some help? Are Twin City residents endowed with so much more sense about co-ordination in their area than citizens on Martha's Vineyard, which is, in camera, a Twin Cities equivalent? Call it what you will, a regional agency with authority over the six Vineyard towns is worth considering.

In Boulder, Colorado, there is determination not to let the city grow wild. Its City Council is studying optimum size and hopes to stabilize Boulder's population at about 100,000. To protect its foothills, it established a "blue line" beyond which the city would not furnish water to new subdivisions, Stewart Udall, former Secretary of the Interior, tells us, then evolved a master plan for purchase of 13,000 acres of open land to add to the 5,000 the city already owned—"a necklace of open space."

With work on its buffer lands, bikeways and anti-pollution programs under way, the Boulder plan, Udall says, is "almost revolutionary."

What body can rule on the optimum size of Vineyard towns? Or protect its special scenic wonders?

The great San Francisco Bay, sweeping in from the Pacific, is unexpectedly vulnerable because it is shallow (two thirds of it is less than 18 feet deep at low tide) and therefore easily filled, to make land where there was water. In a little over a century, it has been reduced from 680 square miles to 400 square miles today; around the bay there were 300 square miles of marshland; only about 75 are left. The bay continues to be tempting to private developers and local governments. Ownership is divided; roughly a quarter is in private hands, a quarter belongs to the cities and counties, about five per cent to the federal government, and the rest to California.

At the rate that it was being filled, it would be half its present size in fifty years, in some places little more than a river. "With a rapidly growing population (from 2.7 million to 5 million between 1950 and 1970 and a projected population of 7.5 million by 1990), some 36 communities felt that they had to have the tax revenues generated by new development, particularly on the valuable waterfront property, and construction," a contemporary description says. "A truly remarkable outpouring of conservationist sentiment as well as working alliances between many groups, leadership by two legislators . . . led to a reprieve."

Californians, much affected by the sight of their magnificent bay, determined to keep this natural resource more or less intact. They created the San Francisco Bay Conservation and Development Commission, which was appointed by the California legislature, authorized it to prepare a plan for the future of the bay, adopted a temporary moratorium, then the plan, and made the Commission a permanent body which passes on all proposals in or along the bay.

The Commission opposes almost all development other than for water-oriented uses and has had a considerable impact. It has forestalled development proposals for miles of shoreland and thousands of acres of bay land. It has inspired similar bodies—such as the Commission for Florida's Tampa Bay—and is being studied by public agencies as far away as Canada, Australia, New Zealand, and even translated so that the Japanese can take a look at it in regard to their harbor planning.

The twenty-seven-man commission (two federal representatives, five state, seven public, and the rest from various levels of locals) makes the grade as one of the nine important land-use innovations in the U.S.A. Federal observers believe that the crucial question of its future is whether it can now lead to broader regions of planning, so that the bay will be part of land-use regulation in the mountains and fertile valleys around it to preserve the distinctive character of California's Venice.

The Vineyard's harbors, which give its shore line the character and excitement of variety in these havens, are unprotected. You can pollute them almost as you will, build on them if you can afford to. They need a commission which will keep a water-oriented protective eye on them. Without viable harbors, an island must perish; a man can come close to perishing should he perchance fall overboard and swallow a gulp of a Vineyard harbor's water.

As California, with its Bay Commission, has provided land-use control for what is known in ecology jargon as critical environmental areas, so Wisconsin requires its counties to protect the shores of lakes and rivers with a model ordinance, although so far it lacks the authority to enforce it. Massachusetts has laws on its books to protect its wetlands although there is, as has been seen in the instance of Menemsha Neck, a lag between law on paper and law on land; after nine years of the law, only a third of the state's wetlands are under some protection.

Three states have embarked on statewide land-use regulation—Hawaii, Maine, and Vermont—and all three are groping. Although the legislative frame, experts say, is sound, goals are still confused.

Hawaii has a land-use law but no land-use consensus. Tourism has replaced agriculture as its major source of income, the President's Council tells us, resulting in the familiar (to Vineyarders) conflict between those who would develop the land, destroying the scenery, taking away the possibility of agricultural employment, making the state an undesirable place to live, and those who would conserve Hawaii's lush lands, preferring sugar and pineapple crops to people crops. "It is probably to the Commission's credit," Council evaluators say, "that it is not too popular with either the builders or the conservationists." In Maine, a Department of Environmental Protection co-ordinates all land-use regulations, but there is, as yet, no over-all state planning, so decisions are based on inadequate criteria.

In the spring of 1972 Hawaii passed a trail-blazing law which empowers the state to control transportation, limiting the number of cars, airplanes, and ships that bring passengers to the islands. It expected a court challenge from the automobile lobby and airlines, believed that state protection of residents should be held paramount. The outcome will be an important step for all overwhelmed and overrun places.

If the federal push for states to take over control of land use within their own boundaries is to really work in any one of the innovators, Vermont is a likely candidate. Small, relatively homogeneous, with large areas of non productive land, it appeals to people who want to privatize it, improve it, keep intact the natural resources which bring them there in the first place.

Frank Michelman, professor at Harvard Law School, with special knowledge and interest in land use, says that Vermont appears to have more concern than most other New England states. "There was enough sentiment there at an early stage, before investment got to a level too high to stop, to make at least a paper law possible," the professor says. While New Hampshire, next door, becomes "increasingly a mess," Vermont has a chance to be an environmental haven, Michelman comments, except, perhaps, for its southern section.

Vermont decided to involve itself in land-use planning and land-use control in 1969, when it became evident that small-town officials couldn't handle the deluge of vacation home developments. Governor Deane Davis established a commission to identify problems and make plans; the General Assembly, almost unbelievably promptly, made the resultant three major environmental bills into law in 1970. One is for special control of shorelands, a second for pollution abatement, the third, known as Act 250, is the land-use and development law.

Act 250 requires three implementing steps. An inventory of existing land use and natural resources (reminiscent of Metcalf & Eddy's preliminary reports on the Vineyard) plus policy guidelines has been completed and adopted by the legislature, Bernard Johnson, Vermont's assistant director of planning, says. Expected by 1973 are social and economic guidelines and, finally, a land-use plan based on the foregoing.

Vermont is, corporately speaking, against ecological sin. The first report makes some pleasing ecosystem statements. Citizens, the planners say, want development to conform with basic characteristics of the environment; soil erosion and stream pollution are "assumed undesirable," wildlife "a benefit," existing land form "a contributor to landscape," preservation of artifacts and scenic qualities are goals.

Seven regional task forces involve citizens in listing problems —strip developments, protection of lakeshores, taxes—and the

Commission continues to collect information on the state's natural resources, its waters, flora, and fauna. It finds that the "raw material for the non-skiing tourist business" (4 million people come in a year, spend some $84 million, stay an average 2.4 days) is "the beauty of the landscape, the quality of the environment, the quaintness of the more leisurely pace in a rural community, and the friendliness of the Vermonters. The public," the planners say, "has a vital interest in assuring that Vermont remains beautiful. . . ."

To keep itself beautiful, the state not only is pioneering in statewide land-use control but must also figure out its relation to federal planning above and local planning below, a subject in complete confusion. "The bulk of land development decisions," Johnson says, "must still be made at the local level" and local officials, he says, are often unable to stand up to irresponsible land developers.

What is clear in the tangle of Vermont's reports to date is that the state, like Cumberland Island, will change. The effort is to make that change as consistent and as harmonious with what exists as possible. Evaluating the effects of Act 250 so far, the planners say that the quality of land development has improved but the quantity has not slowed.

At least part of the reason is in the act itself. Planning, according to the new Vermont law, must include social, economic, and environmental matters; it must achieve "orderly growth and environmental preservation." The two may be inimical. Growth means change and change means destruction of the environment unless the ecosystem is the undoubted, clearly stated, first priority.

The Vineyard can't count on Massachusetts for a statewide land-use plan or a regional plan in the foreseeable future; the state is too varied, too industrialized. In June 1972 the Commonwealth shelved a bill which paralleled

Vermont's Act 250, changing it to a feasibility study. Arthur Brownell, commissioner of the Department of Natural Resources, says the Vineyard has a low priority in his Department, is not a unique natural resource, and does not have enough active interest in preservation to get much help from him. Secretary Charles Foster, who heads the new Office of Environmental Affairs, one of ten cabinet-level agencies formed in a reorganization of some three to four hundred state departments, will be ready with his recommendations in May 1973, a system of regional offices where local participation will merge with state supervision. Lack of leadership on the islands, Foster said, makes it doubtful that they could be a region unto themselves. "We'll have to design something special to fit Martha's Vineyard," the secretary comments. Governor Sargent said that he is "anxious to provide leadership" in finding a solution for the Vineyard, added that State House involvement needs local participation.

A revealing and realistic note on Vermont's effort in the report of the President's Council says Americans don't look kindly on planning for its own sake, pay attention to it only when it immediately affects decision-making. Thus the best way to achieve a state land-use plan—or any other—is to start, as Vermont has done, with a few goals and gradually expand. "To insist that the planning precede the regulation," says the Council, "is probably to sacrifice feasibility on the altar of logic."

An eloquent example of the small, feasible start is what has happened to a shallow lagoon, a mile wide and three times as long, separated from the Pacific Ocean by a sand bar, some twelve miles northwest of the Golden Gate. When the tide is out, great blue herons, pelicans, and snowy egrets feed on the mud flats and an occasional harbor seal suns itself on Kent

Island near the mouth of the inlet. This is Bolinas Lagoon, subject of a remarkable amount of ecological attention.

Descending from the forests of Bolinas Ridge, which divides the coastal area from the rest of Marin County, California, to come upon this peaceful scene is a surprise. Considering what has gone into figuring out the land use of this place, one expects more arresting grandeur. But the very lack of drama is part of its special character, unexpected because lagoons in California are on their way to extinction, not often to be seen. Most have become harbors; dredged and developed, they are soon transformed into crowded recreational areas for recreation-minded Californians, their floats, boats, and cokes.

Bolinas is one of the very few natural lagoons left undeveloped on the California coast, one of the remaining opportunities to understand the marine environment of such an estuary. It survives more because its rescue was feasible than because it was logical, do-able rather than planned, a bold, entrancing undertaking which has much to say to more celebrated, large-scale accomplishments.

How this glistening lagoon, where a couple of mallards and four white egrets rested on a rusting dredge near the salt marsh, was there to be seen seemed so unlikely that it was more impressive, even, than the huge redwoods in the Audubon Canyon Ranch nearby, where the great wading birds nest each year, the two state parks—Stinson Beach and Mount Tamalpais—and Point Reyes National Seashore, all in the area. Innumerable developers have coveted the lagoon. "Properly dredged," Harold Gilliam, San Francisco *Chronicle* columnist, comments, "it would make a fine marina, the nearest small boat harbor beyond the Golden Gate."

Chief protector of Bolinas Lagoon is Pierre Joske, a personable young landscape architect who had come from the Los Angeles Department of Parks to be director of parks and recreation of Marin County, a department which was just seven

years old in 1972, had increased its share of Marin's total budget
five hundred per cent in six years, Joske said, by adding an open
space program. "Nobody could have done it alone," he remarked. "It's orchestrating . . . you have to orchestrate."

It started with an Audubon theme. Breeding colonies of
herons and egrets had been disappearing from the San Francisco Bay shore line, Gilliam notes, displaced by subdivisions
and marinas. At Canyon Ranch, then a dairy farm, the birds
were still undisturbed, but when the dairy business waned, the
ranch was to be subdivided. Instead, the Marin Audubon Society, which had never before raised more than $200, set out
with the help of other Audubon groups in the area to collect
the necessary $337,000 to buy the 500-acre ranch, overshot its
goal some years ahead of schedule. Development proposals
made by the Bolinas Harbor District, which had been given
jurisdiction of the lagoon and its surroundings by the state,
were dampened by the evident intention of citizens to preserve
the entire area.

"I spent more time with the people of Bolinas and Stinson
Beach than with the county supervisors," Joske said. "While the
advocates of development were lobbying in Sacramento, we
were taking advantage of the conservation-minded orientation
here. The bridge wasn't built until 1936; all those years in
Marin—second richest county in the U.S.A. after New York's
Westchester—there was the chance to live with nature and
without crowds."

The five county supervisors were split, three to two, all the
way, Joske said, with the majority on the side of conserving the
area. A photo finish ended the possibility of Harbor District development when Audubon members, the Marin Conservation
League, and the Nature Conservancy joined to buy Kent Island,
key to the lagoon, from its co-operative owner in secret, presented it to the county's Board of Supervisors. The Board
wanted to consider for a week, then for a few days—or even

until after lunch, Joske recalls—but the donors, wanting to prevent any condemnation proceedings or other possible difficulty, insisted that the gift be accepted immediately. It was.

The state then transferred Bolinas Lagoon out of the development-minded Harbor District, which was dissolved, into the custody of Marin County, which had three years to submit a plan for its use and protection to the state (accomplished in 1972), five years thereafter to put the plan into effect. In further orchestration, the county asked for and got the planning help of the Conservation Foundation, Washington-based professionally staffed organization "dedicated to encouraging human conduct to sustain and enrich life on earth."

This Foundation serves as a catalyst, does environmental studies, surveys, demonstration projects. Arthur Davis, its exceedingly well-organized, energetic vice-president for operations, is refreshingly clear-minded about conservation activities. "Environmentalists," he tells a visitor, "are succeeding old-line conservationists; now we have to accommodate to a limited set of natural resources and that takes a different approach and a different kind of mind.

"We are here to see that destruction doesn't happen," Davis remarked firmly. Key to his strategy is to ask three questions: What is the cost of growth? How shall we grow? Should we grow? Although his top priority in the early 1970s was urban areas, plus such extended projects as the Alaska pipeline ("It's about the whole energy policy; do we really need more power?"), Davis is open to any and all requests for question-asking. "What will your actions result in? What are the alternatives? Why pay Vermont farmers not to grow hay? The farmers don't like it and the land is rendered useless." In a published booklet, the Conservation Foundation's Bolinas study recommends environmental protection as a goal for the lagoon, spells out ways to achieve it, long-range and immediate, with no-nonsense orders: "The Marin County Board of Supervisors

should . . . The Citizens of Bolinas and Stinson Beach should
. . . etc."

I asked Davis if the Conservation Foundation would come
and take a questioning look at Martha's Vineyard, analyze
its problems, and suggest a program, as it had done for
Bolinas. "Some official or group would have to ask us,"
he said. "To my knowledge, nobody ever has."

The plan based on this advice and that of California's Department of Fish and Game proposes that the lagoon and lands
surrounding it, private, semipublic, state- and county-owned,
should become an ecological reserve under county jurisdiction.
Land use will be limited so as not to damage any of the lagoon
resources; control of the watershed which is responsible for the
health of the lagoon is strict, limiting logging, certain damaging
agricultural uses, and development.

An unlikely marriage between computer-minded modern
man and ancient nature is an innovation in the proposal for the
lagoon's future. What is planned for the life-giving tide-water
marshes and flats is an "environmental early warning system"
which, its engineers say, will monitor what's going on in the
ecosystem (such things as stream sediment discharge, for example), process and interpret the data from seven subsystems
so that "solutions to terrestrial and aquatic environmental problems can be formulated before damage to natural systems reach
the acute stage where only a cure and clean-up approach
remains." All institutions contacted to assist with this innovation
have been enthusiastic, Joske said, but when asked whether they
would work within it, decline because of lack of staff or money
or both. He is hoping that a university or other institution will
help in implementation.

While willing Marin conservationists work on the lagoon
plan, new threats to the treasured place appear. There was the
Black Tide in January 1971, when two oil tankers collided

and volunteers worked day and night to keep the bird-killing oil out of the lagoon; there is the continuing battle to stop highways from being built through this part of the county, building up footpaths, bicycle trails, and ferries as alternate means of transportation, and the saddening decline in nesting success of herons and egrets.

An ornithologist's observations, reminiscent of the heath hen's decline, are reported by Gilliam: "In 1969 there were 55 nesting attempts by 55 pairs of herons; 48 nests succeeded and 111 young were fledged. Two seasons later, in 1971, there were 56 nesting tries by 44 pairs of herons; only 30 nests succeeded and only 59 young were raised. Meanwhile the eggs of both herons and egrets have become thinner . . . and laden with pesticides. Only half of the breeding pairs of egrets are producing young." The interlocking nature of the global ecosystem, or at least the California part of it, becomes overwhelmingly apparent when it is noted that the great birds spend their non-Bolinas half of the year wading in the shallows of San Francisco Bay and the Sacramento-San Joaquin Delta. "The waters there," Gilliam says, "are heavily laced with industrial, agricultural and domestic pollution."

Surroundings start to press in on the small lagoon in other ways. Trouble in this paradise of ecological awareness might serve as an early warning system to less well-endowed settings. Bolinas, after all, is in a state where outdoor living is a fact of cultural life, with the largest state park system in the country (800,000 acres of scenic reserves, parks, campgrounds, beaches, other recreation areas), where nature has long been noticed and enjoyed. It is in a county where a quarter of the land has been set aside for parks and open space, a staggeringly high proportion (the Vineyard's Dukes County has slightly over nine per cent, a large part of which is the impenetrable state forest). In Marin County the magnificent Point Reyes National Seashore was fought for for years by little old ladies in sneakers alongside the new-type environmentalists, and will include some one hundred square miles (the size of Martha's Vineyard) when acquisition is completed. It is in the area where the citizenry made the massive effort resulting in the protection of San Francisco Bay. But with all these remarkable resources conserved, there is trouble.

There is too much traffic and too many tourists. Roads to the area are narrow and winding, getting there on a weekend is an agonizing bumper-to-bumper crawl. Having arrived, visitors drive their cars in and around the magnificent virgin forests, open meadows, and along dunes and beaches, affecting the wildlife, wildflowers, the sense of wilderness.

Bolinas Lagoon, snatched from acquisitive developers just in time, rescued by an army of enthusiastic understanding, protective people, studied, planned, monitored by experts, is nevertheless subject to the pressures of its surroundings. Marin is the fastest-growing county in California; this, plus an exploding metropolitan population across the bay in San Francisco, so close to the exquisite new National Seashore and other public lands, creates an ecosystem enigma which works its way along coastal Marin, even into the quiet lagoon. Should everyone who wants to drive out on a Sunday come, unregulated? Should there be a mass transit system, eliminating the automobile? Limited mass transit within and without the parks? What, essentially, is the place of man in the wilderness?

People in the little settlement of Bolinas (pop. approx. 1,700) asked themselves the question. Many discouraged, puzzled young people had found refuge in one or another of the 700 houses near the lagoon and on nearby hills. The saving of the lagoon started some of them on a quest for protecting their small area, which is not a town but part of the county, but with its own public utilities district. "You can make those amorphous districts into almost anything you like," said Orville Schell, distinguished China scholar and author, who lives in Bolinas in a house he built himself. Schell had been ready to leave, sure that Bolinas was about to turn into another overdeveloped plastic place, when he and some others decided to see if they could stop the trend.

"We started with man's most basic issue—his waste," Schell said. "There were plans for a $9 million sewer plant all ready to go; no one understood it, or knew that it would be a disaster, bringing development in with it." A thorough study of waste disposal gave Schell a new, provocative set of facts. "I am all out about sewers." From this beginning, the group educated their community, bringing together all generations and levels of citizens, captured the local political power, electing four of their number to the five-man Public Utilities Board.

Bolinas has "unbeatable power" in the county because all its citizens turn out and vote on every issue which affects their community. They have embarked on agricultural experiments to see if the land can be reclaimed, people employed where they live, and the area made sufficient unto itself "so we don't need tourists or a General Motors plant." A planner and two architects work on an over-all Bolinas plan, Schell and cohorts on the Public Utilities Board "have won every holding action, ask the county for everything and get most of it." The county is impressed by the community's activism and evident unanimity about its future, Schell says. "We go to hearings and tell the supervisors, 'There are fifty guys sitting in the back of the hall, ready to devour you if you don't give us what we need.' Now we are ready to work on getting the best county supervisors possible elected. We can progress from kid-stuff protest—cutting down all the signs on the road which point to Bolinas so people can't find it. We have a community that's real and a political system that works for it. Bolinas now thinks of itself as an entity."

The small feasible start—saving the lagoon—has led to enormous questions. Because of them, Bolinas has demonstrated that decentralized community action within a larger entity can work. Marin County has made a plan for itself which deals with matters "beyond the capability of any single jurisdiction to handle alone," a link between them and regional, state, and national agencies. "A Marin County that speaks to such agencies with a single voice on countywide matters is going to receive better treatment at their hands than a balkanized collection of small soloists," the plan says.

The region, too, has had to broaden its vision. Late in 1971 final approval of the Southern Crossing, a new bridge to cross the bay, was held up by a NEPA statement coming from the Coast Guard, which had to approve the bridge, suggesting that the entire area's growth policy be reviewed before another bridge, and new highways to feed it, were built. This set off a public controversy of gigantic proportions. Governor Ronald Reagan vetoed the bill which would have stopped the bridge; the matter was then taken to the electorate of the six counties bordering on the bay. In June 1972 the Southern Crossing was finally and firmly defeated by an overwhelming vote, an action which should encourage Vineyarders who believe a bridge from the mainland can be literally and otherwise built over their heads. It may also encourage the growth of NEPA into a law which can plan for land use, growth, changes in social and physical environments.

By the time the National Park Service gets ready to put its announced major recreation areas near America's big cities, it will, perhaps, be able to look to San Francisco and Marin County for an answer to the still unresolved dilemma it creates. Joske believes that by then there will be flotillas of ferries bustling back and forth across the bay, bringing people to and from the Seashore and the parks, that there will be dozens of bicycle paths added to the one he presently uses to get to San Francisco, keep trim, and see the scenery en route, that people will learn how to walk again, if walking is the only way they can use the parks, that man, in sum, has the ingenuity to join, not destroy, the ecosystem.

Perhaps inspired orchestration of federal, state, regional, county, and local interest will bring together the best thinking man can achieve, which will ultimately filter down to the herons nesting in the tall redwoods, the swarming life of the lagoon waters, the seals asleep in the sun on Kent Island . . . and to himself.

There is no one answer to this, a monumental assignment of our times, the necessity to figure out man's place in the natural world. Bits and pieces of answers are assembling across the country. There are fire-and-brimstone leaders like David Brower who threaten to have God call man an experiment which failed, pragmatists like Arthur Davis, prototype of the new environmentalists, who probes with questions, uses expert consultants, there are developers with a conscience, planners with inspiration, government influentials like George Hartzog and Russell Train, men in Vermont, the Twin Cities, in Boulder, San Francisco, Marin County, Bolinas, men of whom these are but a small sampling, who are inventing, experimenting, reaching for answers.

The common theme is interdependence. We are discovering that all places are related to each other, all life. No piece of land, or town, or park—no man—can be single and apart from the surroundings any longer. Each must define its own goals and work for its own salvation, but in the process discover where its limits are, where it must act alone on issues which concern it alone, where it must become part of a larger unit.

Not only is no man "an island entire of itself," as John Donne wrote in the seventeenth century, no island is an island. The Vineyard can take advantage of what has been discovered elsewhere, apply painfully acquired knowledge to itself. It can know that the hard slogging of community action, based on conviction as it was in Bolinas, can work on the island, too, stopping unnecessary sewers, revitalizing shellfishing and agriculture. It can move toward becoming a six-town entity and enjoy the fruits of a co-ordinated policy, such as is demonstrated in the Twin Cities and in Marin County where a collection of small soloists is now a chorus. It can keep its waters clean, protect its land and its culture. It can become part of a region and part of a nation, in this way securing the particular place in the wider ecosystem to which it is entitled.

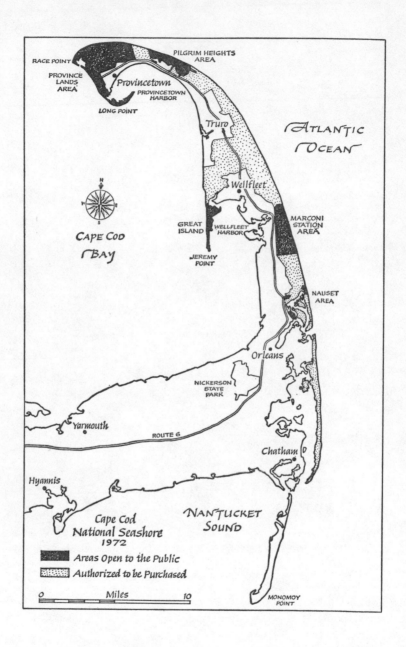

RACE POINT

PROVINCE LANDS AREA

Provincetown

PROVINCETOWN HARBOR

LONG POINT

PILGRIM HEIGHTS AREA

Truro

ATLANTIC OCEAN

Wellfleet

GREAT ISLAND

WELLFLEET HARBOR

JEREMY POINT

MARCONI STATION AREA

NAUSET AREA

CAPE COD BAY

Orleans

NICKERSON STATE PARK

Yarmouth

ROUTE 6

Chatham

Hyannis

NANTUCKET SOUND

Cape Cod
National Seashore
1972

Areas Open to the Public

Authorized to be Purchased

0   Miles   10

MONOMOY POINT

CHAPTER NINE

Nantucket-Vineyard Time is Five Minutes to Midnight

The Vineyard entered a new phase in the autumn of 1971. The first shock of Boom #2 had subsided, there was now mounting alarm at its realities. Fresh-cut roads darted into woods and fields; from the air the island looked as though it had had a bad accident, sustaining dozens of long, vicious wounds. The towns struggled with the multiplying problems of zoning, water, sewage, and other planning necessities, brought about by an unprecedented number of people. There were those who rejoiced, anticipating swollen profits, those who rebelled, others who were silent . . . overwhelmed.

Most people concerned with the island shared the presentiment that it was, as someone said, five minutes to midnight for Martha's Vineyard (and for Nantucket, as ensuing pages relate). The next months would decide whether the island would be transformed into Anyplace, U.S.A., or would retain its own extraordinary character. A shadow loomed over the future. Those who settled in for the winter, and those who went away, back to home and work, had the uneasy sensation that it would be a different Vineyard next year.

"The United States is backward in thinking of new arrangements about land," Senator Edward Kennedy told a visitor in a recent conversation about the state of the Vineyard. "The British," the senator said, "are more flexible, imaginative, and innovative." Kennedy was determined to discover some preservation concept that would work for what he called "the total environment" of Cape Cod's offshore islands. It was at this moment that he asked Congress to authorize a study of the Vineyard, Nantucket, and neighboring smaller islands, which would come up with an answer for their protection within six months. "The islands," Kennedy said, "are beginning to show the fact of disastrous lack of planning, commercial development, and sometimes cynical lack of foresight."

He listed three possibilities. The islands could be made an extension of the Cape Cod National Seashore, or become the first of the Department of Interior's plan—published but not yet implemented—for a series of National Island Trusts, or some combination of these alternatives. "We'll get three plans," he said, "see which is best and which is do-able—and do it."

It was almost exactly ten years since President John Kennedy had signed into law the legislation establishing the Cape Cod National Seashore. The wording of the senator's one-paragraph study bill ("To determine whether the islands should be made part of the Cape Cod National Seashore") and the praise he lavished on the Seashore in his introductory remarks ("Almost without exception, everyone is pleased. . . . We have struck a delicate balance which worked uncommonly well") convinced Vineyarders that the senator had already made up his mind in favor of this alternative. Many would quickly answer in the affirmative to senator-watcher William Honan's second-guessing-Kennedy piece "Will He Say: 'Help Me Finish What My Brothers Began'?" Unlike Honan's campaign focus, Vineyarders' thoughts were on the Seashore.

"National Park Here?" was the *Vineyard Conservation News* headline for a comment that "massive numbers of people would come" and that the Vineyard would better determine its own destiny. President Robert Russell, who had been writing to the *Gazette* that federal intervention was the worst thing that could happen to the island, could read in his house organ that "Island people should carry the ball." Mary Wakeman, active Edgartown conservationist, wrote the senator: "I can only assume that you are understandably in ignorance of some of the efforts which are being made to protect the desirable qualities you mention on the islands. . . ." And there was poetry:

"A Federal Possession?
Oh, Better Secession!"

"Recognizing at last that Martha's Vineyard is not only a natural but a national resource," a New York *Times* editorial said, "Senator Edward M. Kennedy has just proposed a study . . . which should give both the Interior Department and State and local agencies the needed impetus. . . ." To some it seemed a long-overdue act on the part of the Commonwealth's senior senator; others probed for hidden if not Machiavellian motives.

The senator's stated reasons for his study bill were clear enough. Citing his mail, which "indicates that there has been some sudden and not wholly tasteful commercial development in recent months," this writer's New York *Times* article "To Save the Vineyard," which "suggests that the balance is suddenly erupting," and the fact that 30 million people live within a one-day drive of Cape Cod and the islands, he made his concern for the islands' future clear to the Senate. "Unfortunately it is that which is closest to us that we sometimes fail to see in our endeavor to preserve and protect," Kennedy said, stating that he thought the islands to be "within our power to make enduring."

Undoubtedly his strong ties to Hyannis and its environs and the anniversary of the Seashore were also in his mind. "John Kennedy had always wanted to extend the Seashore to include the islands," an aide said, "but had put the project aside until the Seashore itself could be assembled." And there were those who were determined to connect his action to the Chappaquiddick incident; as far as I know, their ruminations, like most conjecture, remain in the area of fiction. At this juncture, Kennedy was showing a new and incisive self. "What has come over him?" Honan queries in a recent biography and answers, after a series of in-depth interviews with Kennedy, that the Senate Whip fight had "freed him to speak out" on things which he cared about.

To all appearances, he genuinely cared about the islands. And acted. If caring carried political plus signs for him, aligning him with the increasingly popular and powerful environmentalists, this, according to an educated guess, could hardly be considered a primary motive. Kennedy was making his political impact on a dozen fronts; at this time he was chairman of five Senate subcommittees, two of which—Health and Refugees—were of major importance, a member of seventeen others. "I expect to continue to be interested in conservation and preservation matters particularly as they affect Massachusetts," he said. "While I don't expect to be assigned to a committee dealing with this area specifically, I look forward to working with my constituents . . . implementing existing programs. . . ."

Kennedy was being pushed and pressed to be on his party's presidential ticket in 1972. He could make the dash from his teeming, frenetic office to the Senate floor to vote in a couple of minutes, return, pick up a sentence exactly where he had dropped it at the sound of the warning vote bell. It was unlikely that he would have taken up the island issue if it had not mattered to him.

"The issue raised by Senator Kennedy is the vital one we have all been facing," the *Gazette* remarked; "what is the best method of protecting the essential character of Martha's Vineyard? The whole project . . . ought to command cordial support."

There was, instead, guarded suspicion, a New England version of wait-and-see, accentuated when there appeared on the island a tall, handsome young lawyer, K. Dun Gifford, who had been Kennedy's legislative aide until 1970, when he resigned to join the Boston real estate firm of Cabot, Cabot and Forbes. Gifford, who summers on Nantucket, explained his Vineyard visit to the local press. Kennedy, he said, had asked him to do some preliminary work on the study which had begun three years before but got nowhere while Interior's Island Trust preliminaries were under way.

"Sitting on Muskeget Island [off Nantucket], we were talking about it," Gifford told reporters, "and Ted said, 'Whatever happened to that study? Do you think we could get it going again?'" It is not unusual for senators to take on former staff or other qualified people for a limited assignment, and Kennedy chose Gifford to quarterback the island effort, along with Mary Murtagh, an able, witty young woman who is, she says, the senator's Massachusetts Desk. Gifford moves fast, his restless energy producing rapid-fire sentences. He enlisted the aid of three Harvard law students under the direction of Charles Haar, professor at Harvard Law School, who had worked in the government for President John Kennedy and President Lyndon Johnson. "He is probably the nation's leading expert in land-use controls," Gifford said. "We bounce ideas off him."

The team worked with dispatch. Six weeks after Kennedy had filed the bill for a study, he brought the matter up again in the Senate. His mail on this issue, he reported, had been considerable, nearly all of it favorable. He took this as an indication of the severity of the need for immediate action, and of the widespread recognition of the need to move swiftly. At this time he filed with the Senate a memorandum from the

Harvard Law School Legislative Research Bureau, signed by the three students.

The foundation stones of a bold structure which Kennedy would propose in the months ahead were in this memorandum. It gave him the information he needed to move for the islands, move faster and farther than anyone had anticipated. But before he could decide on the next conclusive step with Haar, Gifford, and various other advisers, the background had to assemble. An assessment had to be made of the Vineyard, Nantucket, the possibilities of the Cape Cod National Seashore, and of an Island Trust, as a solution.

Nantucket and the Vineyard, geological and geographical first cousins, have developed differently. Like most relatives, each believes its own way superior. Nantucket, being farther out at sea and half the size of the Vineyard, is a separate county, equivalent to its one Nantucket town (Siasconset, or 'Sconset as it is known, is a village, part of the town). It is more of a unit than the Vineyard, more homogeneous, having attracted the same stylish conservative society summer people for generations, and is somewhat behind the Vineyard in being attacked by developers. When Gifford started working on the island project, the Vineyard was immersed in Boom #2 but there was little awareness, he said, on Nantucket of what was coming, and indeed had come. He told his father, a governor of the Nantucket Yacht Club, to drive out with some friends and look at the new developments. "Dad and the rest were shocked," he said. "They didn't know what to do about it."

There are three excellent reasons why they didn't. Nantucket thought itself an impenetrable fortress, protected by a triad of well-known undertakings of recent years. The island's history, and men of wealth and influence, had made them possible.

The entire island—moors, beaches, Nantucket town, brambled thickets under the pines—is an Historic District. No other cran-

berry bog, moor, or dune in the Commonwealth is thus dignified. It took a series of special acts of the Massachusetts legislature, beginning in 1955 and culminating in 1970, to achieve
this distinction which the said moors, bogs, village, and town
share with some houses and streets of Boston's Back Bay and
Beacon Hill, of Lexington and Concord, Harwich and Sandwich, communities in which there is, according to the rule of
the Massachusetts Historical Commission, "an area, building,
site or object, historically, architecturally or archeologically significant to any period in the development of a town or city or
any portion thereof."

"It's a form of zoning but we don't call it that in Massachusetts," Richard Hale, the state Commission's acting chairman,
said in an interview. "We're a great state on local options."
Hale believes Nantucket was misusing the Historic District
designation "or at least using it very broadly. It is zoning, but
intellectual zoning, a kind of control. But it allows subdivision
of land for 'compatible purposes'; now the Nantucket heath is
full of ranch houses."

Preservation of historic properties is a federal program under
the U. S. Department of Interior, where there is a National
Register, funds for half the cost of the states' surveys, and plans
for Historic Districts. In this program, a particular favorite of
President Nixon's, the local citizenry has to make inventories,
learn histories of places to be preserved, catalogue and eventually administer the H.D. This same method now applies as
people look to the future instead of the past, cataloguing natural resources as they are doing in Vermont, for example, to
get the statewide land-use plan under way.

Applying H.D. to Nantucket started properly enough, with
the admiration of the populace for the old colonial houses
which had survived the island's great fire of 1846, and for the
houses and churches which prosperous whalers put up to replace the third or more of the town which had burned down,

building in the architectural style of the times—Greek Revival. "The restraint, the power of mass composition and the simplicity of classic detail appealed to those men," an architectural account says. Local sentiment about these old houses and the cobbled streets of the town initiated one of the Commonwealth's first two H.D.s (the other was Boston's famed Beacon Hill). To establish the District, the town's history buffs must follow a procedure which occupies some twenty-five single-spaced pages of instructions. If the request is enacted by the legislature, it must then be voted in at town meeting. H.D. can control exteriors, driveways, changes in existing houses; in general, a local commission, appointed by the supervisors, sees that streets, signs, and other accouterments of history remain as nearly unchanged as possible.

"It took a catastrophe to get the Historic District for the whole island," a Nantucket planner said. Intellectual zoning had appeared to work well for the island for more than a decade before developers appeared; when the catastrophe—the first condominium—hit, it was natural for Nantucket's powerful summer people and local officials to reach for more of the same, scurrying to the State House for an extension of H.D., so that it could take all of Nantucket under its protective wing. Since the local commission could decide what was compatible for the open, rolling moors, the island was soon in the situation of so many other places across the country where local control of land use is parochial, lacking regional and long-range vision.

A master plan for Nantucket was not much help either. Charles Foster, the state's secretary of environment, had encouraged the creation of the plan when he was commissioner of natural resources. "I approached the selectmen, asked if they would be interested in examining the island, then they requested the study," Foster said. "We sent a team in and a plan resulted; it defines environmentally sensitive areas." Foster had been planning to get around to the same procedure with the

Vineyard, which would have been much more difficult, given the complexities of dealing with six towns instead of one, when other priorities intervened. The Nantucket plan, accepted and filed by selectmen, was not put into effect by the town, but there was a notable by-product.

"Larsen and Beinecke bought up most of the sensitive areas," Foster said. These two Nantucket summer residents—Roy Larsen, vice president of Time, Inc., president of the Nantucket Conservation Foundation, and Walter Beinecke Jr., heir to a Green Stamp fortune, whose activities on Nantucket are described in the next pages—have separately and together contributed a great deal of the land in the Conservation Foundation as has Arthur Dean, renowned New York lawyer. Founded in 1965, in 1972 it held between twelve and thirteen per cent of the island's acreage. "The planning report was forgotten by the locals," Larsen said. "The selectmen didn't even read it —or at least didn't do anything about it. Four or five of us did what needed to be done, putting the land under conservation."

Larsen, a vigorous septuagenarian who lives in 'Sconset on a one-acre lot, hoped that "those Scandinavian houses out there on the moor will blow away in the next hurricane." In the meantime, he continued his active work with the Conservation Foundation, with the abiding satisfaction of knowing that in one of his gifts to it (with his wife)—a 513-acre tract called Larsen Acres—there lies a fundamental development control, the island's primary source of ground water. Nantucket's expression of the wish to protect, its Conservation Foundation, had a fast-growing membership. Larsen had a Time-type slogan at hand—Everybody's In It But You—and a design for a car windshield membership decal. "It's the thing to do, now," he said. "Everybody's a member; we shamed them into it." It had employed a full-time director, collected some $25,000 a year in dues, and in the last three or four years had undertaken a broader-based land acquisition program.

The Foundation's strong if feudal presence and the island-wide H.D. were two of the three supports for the presumption that the island was safe from unwanted development.

A Nantucket citizen whom I interviewed on a recent visit to that island slipped a lapel button into my hand, in the manner of a tipster at the racetrack, saying that it was now a collector's item. It was my introduction to the third prop. Against the button's familiar Green Stamp background was the legend NO MAN IS AN ISLAND.

Walter Beinecke, Jr., to whom that button, and another— BAN THE B—referred, spent the decade of the 1960s "trading up" Nantucket, to use one of his frequent expressions. "To trade up," Beinecke explained, "is to sell something of greater worth for more." He had spent fifty years on Nantucket in the summers, growing up there in his parents' house; he analyzed the island's character with two key words—fragile and scale. Beinecke decided that the island could and should prove that a limited capacity was economically viable, and this he set out to do. "Fewer bodies spending more was what I was after. I had to invest enough capital to prove that this was better than staying on the mundane level. Tiffany versus the five-and-ten," he said. "There have to be limited opportunities—and Nantucket should be one of them."

Although Beinecke insisted that he would have preferred to share the risk, responsibility, and fun of trading up Nantucket town with others ("It would have been better to involve more people, investment-wise, politically and philosophically," he said), his highly individual style and candid elitist approach suggested that it was in character for him to do it alone. The resultant anti-B buttons and the public sentiment they expressed did not bother him, he said. He was too involved, economically and emotionally, in what he was doing. Besides, he was in a typical hurry. "Mr. Beinecke likes to do things fast," John Welch, who was the executive of Beinecke's Nantucket firm, said, and, as the record shows, he did.

After buying some key properties such as the White Elephant Hotel, which he tore down and reconstructed into a luxury hostelry in less than two years, the prized Jared Coffin House, transformed in a massive undertaking into a hotel in months, and other commercial real estate, Beinecke went to work on the waterfront. In his terms it took patience (a total of six years from start to finish to completely reconstruct it) and help. When he began, the town's front yard looked like its back yard, he said, with coal sheds, oil tanks, lumber and ice sheds and run-down wharfs, no facilities for yachts. By 1970, it vied for the distinction of the finest marina in New England, charged a minimum $10-per-night docking fee, and was at once an as-good-as-they-come reconstruction (which Beinecke compares to Williamsburg, Virginia, and Ford's Dearborn Village in Michigan) and a viable shopping center.

Beinecke accomplished this by escalating downtown real estate values. "Moving the A&P to the waterfront was the spark that put the whole thing together," he said. With the First National on the edge of town, there was fractured economic flow; downtown needed year-round traffic and Beinecke sold everyone concerned, from the chairman of the board of A&P to the local management, on a waterfront location, built them a color-co-ordinated building, in scale with the old houses he had moved onto the wharfs. "There are no historic supermarkets," he said.

What Beinecke did was small-scale regional planning with an economic loyalist twist, announced and carried out. By the time he had assembled the money for this undertaking, eighty per cent of which came from commercial lenders (chiefly a midwest insurance company), and about three quarters of the town's commercial real estate, he had added two parallel activities. "It's like playing three-dimensional chess," he said of the interlocking nature of his business, his Historical Trust (started by his father, revived by Jr. in the sixties to buy various non-profit buildings and keep H.D. on its historic toes), and the Conservation Foundation. For "leverage," he contributed staff to the Historical Association and to the town's Planning Commission. All this, Beinecke thought, would get the island moving in the direction which he regarded as essential for the limited quality product he believed Nantucket should be. (Independently, Hough, for the Vineyard, came to a like conclusion: "Quality experience," he wrote, "is indispensable in the heritage of mankind.")

Beinecke's fall-back position is to change from quality to volume, install pizza parlors, motels, and hot dog stands. Although this would be economically profitable, it would be a massive disappointment. Nantucket was more than a business venture to Walter Beinecke; one might conjecture that it represented at least a part of his reach for a quality immortality.

Nantucket could not depend on Beinecke to keep it pure. Despite a sturdy appearance, the quality of his endeavor was, by his own admission, just as destructible as H.D. zoning or the good will of conservationists. The triad that had seemed so convincingly protective now confounds the island with the unexpected sight of Scandinavian condominiums scattered on its virgin moors. In 1971 Nantucket, like the Vineyard, was open to development. The first break in the fortress had been made; land speculators, subdividers, and developers poured into the enticing opening, shocking islanders and summer people out of their insularity.

One of Kennedy's proposals was to include the Nantucket Sound islands in the Cape Cod National Seashore, or at least to preserve the most vulnerable, important natural resources of the islands in this way. They would then be blessed and damned with the protection of the National Park Service. A marked advantage of this method was that it could happen comparatively quickly by amending existing legislation, a much faster process than starting, *de novo*, to make a law.

While Vineyarders fought off the idea of the Seashore— "glutted with yowling tourists," "a sea of parking lots," "withering into an obscenity"—there was serious doubt whether the Seashore would consider the Vineyard. George Hartzog, National Park Service director, was not enthusiastic. "The Vineyard does not fit the traditional park concept," he said in a recent conversation. "Although there are values which should be preserved, we would need to adopt new preservation tools, new legislation. Compensable land-use regulation is one idea I have in mind for such situations, where the government could not possibly afford purchase." Another barrier was the particular interest of President Nixon and Secretary of Interior Morton in historic preservation and cultural parks.

Long before, when the National Park Service had examined *Our Vanishing Shoreline* in the fifties, Cape Cod had been one of its sixteen priorities and one of the five areas "not overly populated," preservable by the Seashore concept. There was less enthusiasm about the islands; an interdepartmental memo says that in Nantucket there was marked antipathy of the residents toward public ownership, that the Vineyard had three public beaches (one state, two town-held) and believed Dukes County should be responsible for control of the rest. The islands were moved down the list for consideration later.

But the Great Cape Cod Beach and its environs, a ribbon-like stretch one to four miles wide and some forty miles long running along the coast from Provincetown to Chatham, was, as its proponents stated, unquestionably Seashore caliber. An ocean-blue-covered, liberally illustrated pamphlet proposed the Seashore in 1959 and in the first session of Congress that year, Leverett Saltonstall and John F. Kennedy, Massachusetts' two senators, introduced a bill to establish the Seashore; Congressman Hastings Keith put an identical bill before the House.

The Seashore would set the National Park Service on a new course in several ways: location, acquisition, and use. Most national parks were in isolated areas in the West; the Seashore was within easy traveling distance of major eastern population centers. Parks were generally open land, either transferred from other government agencies or given as a private donation; the lower Cape, inhabited for centuries, would have to be bought from homeowners. "A pioneer park," the then Secretary of Interior Stewart Udall said, "a reversal of the shortsighted policy of refusing to pay from the public purse to acquire scenic masterpieces for all the people." To the traditional park activity of communing with nature, the Seashore added "physical recreation"—swimming, hunting in season, cycling on bicycle trails near the ocean, driving beach buggies across the dunes. In the 1950s, all this was a major switch for the Park Service, agreed to against considerable opposition by old-line nature communers, because it was said to be what the people wanted.

The plan was to acquire 44,600 acres of beach and upland with a $16 million government budget, some contributions of state and federally owned land, and considerable agile invention. Some land would not be in federal ownership at all, but controlled by local zoning which complied with the purposes of the Seashore, thus keeping the property on the tax rolls. Some would be condemned and purchased outright, some acquired by various other methods. To keep the expected uproar at a minimum, people in houses within the boundaries of the park could elect to stay for a fixed period, or for life, keeping at least three acres of land. Enough undeveloped land was left outside the park to give the six towns involved room to grow. This mélange was presented to the public.

There ensued what one observer calls "the bitterest controversy that ever split the Cape," violent local opposition.

Such was the hurricane force of the oratory, protests, and mis-interpretation of what was proposed that a new and objective economic study was ordered by the Department of Interior to quiet fears of adverse impact on the towns, of declining real estate values and loss of taxes; the Park Service issued an additional detailed statement about land acquisition methods. Even so, the plan might have died a-borning had it not been for an event which clinched the establishment of what the Cape Cod Chamber of Commerce viewed with horror and the Secretary of Interior called the protection of the last of the great seashores.

In November 1960 one of the proposers of the bill and its insistent champion was elected President of the United States. Nine months later President John Kennedy signed the bill into a law. "We commemorate here today a love affair with the land," Secretary Udall said at the dedication ceremony, ". . . a masterwork of nature." It had taken until 1966 to assemble enough acreage to formally establish the Seashore. By 1968, the $16 million had been spent and some 21,000 acres acquired; in 1970, after two unsuccessful attempts, a bill introduced by Edward Kennedy produced $17.5 million for purchase of the remaining 7,500 acres to round out the Seashore.

Old-line conservation of the magnificent beach and new-time physical recreation were joined in the Cape Cod National Seashore. By the time Senator Edward Kennedy reviewed the place with the islands in mind, some results of the mating could be seen.

Chief economic effect was on private land values, which rose an extraordinary 106 per cent in the first eight years. Otherwise, because the area was already relatively urbanized and tourist-oriented, the Seashore's economic impact has been marginal rather than fundamental, an economic study made for the Park Service states. "Its largest impact has been the intended one of environmental preservation."

The Seashore's Visitor Center, visually exciting, mentally stimulating, makes one impatient to get out to see the beach plums and wild roses, the shore birds, creeping dunes, and roaring ocean *in situ*. Paths and signs allow for a tolerable further education, intelligently planned and organized. There are beaches for those who must drive within yards of sand; parking areas and bathhouses near these "heavy-use" centers bespeak crowds coming to pursue physical recreation in the waves. There are roads for jeeps, leading to wilder beaches; there are footpaths for those who can and will walk to find emptiness as a reward. The nationalization of these extraordinary lands produced careful planning, determined divsion of use, and gave the place the devotion and knowledge of its trained ranger staff. It was eye-opening reassurance, at least to this visitor.

Its total effect is mixed. "Cape Cod is a classic example of the good and the bad, the promise and the problems . . . ," reporter Robert Cahn, who made a survey of the national parks for the *Christian Science Monitor*, wrote. He said that although it was too early to pass judgment on the Seashore *in toto*, such difficulties as beach buggies tearing the plant cover off sand dunes, black-top poured on some of Thoreau's most admired fragile areas for parking lots, bicycle trails and new roads to the beaches, are already intruding on the preservation goal.

So, too, is the new national camping craze. Camping, in this age of the non-walking human, means wheels. Wheels require roads which there never seem to be enough of in places people want to go to. And campers require places to camp, not a few feet of a fragrant pine grove on which to pitch a tent or spread a sleeping bag, but a campground to park whatever one- or two-room campers arrive, electricity to plug into, water supply, trash cans, toilets, and preferably an eating place and an outdoor movie. No new campgrounds have been added to the three in the Seashore and the four at its borders. The place is

a magnet to campers; a dramatic rise in their numbers is anticipated when new Cape highways are extended to reach it.

First priority in the Seashore's 1970 revision of its master
plan was a transportation study. No further plans could be
made for use of the park until it could be decided how people
should get to the Seashore (on a warm summer day the traffic
backs up for miles) and how they should move around within
it, where they should camp. "Without careful planning outside
the Park, more aggressive action about highways, and more
accommodation for campers," an evaluation said, the impact
of the Seashore could be "sharply and negatively altered."

Here, regional planning is a glaring requisite. The solution
requires a policy, budget, and action which go far beyond any
decision the Seashore and its six towns could make for themselves. "Don't give the island to Detroit," Brower had said
about Cumberland. In the 1970s, George Hartzog confronts
the camping dilemma: "We have given up trying to build
campsites fast enough to accomodate everybody who wants one
at the peak of the summer season," he told *U. S. News & World
Report* in 1972. "We are working hard to encourage private enterprise to open campgrounds adjacent to our most popular
parks." Hartzog is also considering mass transportation to and
in the parks, before taking the long-considered step of limiting
numbers of vehicles, certain to set off a public explosion.

Fallible as the National Park Service is—and it is a favorite
target for those who want their preservation pure as well as for
those who want physical recreation at the door step of their mobile homes—it is more qualified and capable of regional planning than one place alone. It can and must consider adjoining
towns, roads, facilities, the movement of people from near and
far.

Now it faces a paradox which many believe is built into the
new park concept. "The parks were created as 'natural areas to

be preserved for public use.' How do you preserve while using?" one commentator asks. Henry Hough puts it a different way in the *Vineyard Gazette:* "It's not how many [will use the place]," he wrote, "but first and always how? Survival hangs on that question."

Stewart Udall, whom many believe to have been one of the century's outstanding Secretaries of the Interior, considered the question while spending a vacation on Martha's Vineyard in the mid-sixties. He dedicated the Gay Head cliffs as a national monument, listened to the worries of conservationists, tested their willingness to act toward making the Vineyard part of the Seashore and found it wanting. "You have to have leadership," he said at the time. "The Park Service will not move into an area, no matter how appropriate, unless there is pressure for it to do so. Where's the pressure here?" Udall conjectured that the Vineyard was just about at the turning point then, back in the 1960s. The island was already more thickly settled than most areas in the Seashore had been when acquired, he said; it would soon be too developed to even be considered for acquisition as an annex or extension of the Seashore. "Imagine the uproar, even among all you dedicated conservationists," he said with prescience.

But as Udall walked the island's great South Beach, inhaled fragrant meadow grasses, examined the messages of life everlasting on chipped slate tombstones from colonial days, and read Thoreau out loud in the warm summer evenings, he was inspired, he recalled recently, to the idea that some special preservation plan for the island might be devised. With this in mind, he initiated what became the country's first inventory of its offshore lands—*Islands of America*—and a suggestion for their conservation. In the report, submitted to Secretary Walter Hickel in 1970 by Interior's Bureau of Outdoor Recreation, the that it might first become a reality in the very place where it was conceived.

"In man's imagination, islands have always been lands of promise," the report begins, then lists the country's 26,000 islands (twenty-two per cent of them and about three quarters of total U.S. island acreage is in Alaska), giving statistics. It says there are almost a million acres of prime, largely undeveloped potential recreation land on islands near America's metropolitan areas, "a major untapped national resource with valuable recreation potential." It recommends public control of some islands, restoration and maintenance of environmental quality of all American islands, and picks Maine's Casco Bay Islands (324 of them totaling 17,000 acres, 100 miles NNE of Boston) as a pilot project for a national system of Island Trusts. After the Platte River Island, Nebraska, and the San Juan Islands off the state of Washington, the next possibilities listed are, in order, the Sea Islands, Elizabeth Islands, and then Martha's Vineyard and Nantucket.

Exactly what the BOR had in mind for these lands of promise was not clear. At best the report is an over-all plan for all bodies of land surrounded by water. It acknowledges that islands are different from each other but have in common the fact that they are fragile, vulnerable, and that most are still relatively undeveloped. Manhattan, a notable exception, which would have fitted into the New York list between Maloney Island (% developed—none; county—Onondaga; acreage—22; body of water—Seneca River) and Maple Bend Island Group (% developed—none; county—Washington; acreage—151; body of water—Lake Champlain) was sternly omitted from mention.

Besides its atlas aspect, the report made two important contributions. One is an instrument—the National Island Trusts Act—which, with a suggested Executive Order from the President, could start the program on its legislative way. The second

is to show us that the land-use dilemma along with the pres-
ervation-recreation puzzlement survives on the nation's islands
as on its mainland.

The small promised lands have, perhaps, a better chance
of finding answers. Island Trust conservation requires enabling
legislation from the state concerned, clearing titles to assure
public access, providing statewide zoning. Local governments
would have to adopt approved long-range plans to conserve
island resources, acquire land for recreation, open space, and
conservation, assure public access to the shore line by acquisition, easement, or tax incentives. A commission would govern. The weapon to push traditionally provincial town interests
into such a regional plan is the federal instrument which says,
in effect, "Do it, or else. . . ."

The "else" is federal acquisition. There would have to be
new techniques developed for this, BOR official A. Heaton
Underhill said when interviewed on the intent and method of
establishing Island Trusts. Direct purchase of most island land
would be prohibitively expensive for the government even to
consider; here, Hartzog's compensable land-use idea would
be a valuable innovation. Underhill was also concerned with
priorities. "There would have to be a popular ground swell with
strong citizen support to get an island on the Trust list," he
said. "Of all present governors, Sargent could be the most help-
ful. He's a real conservationist. It would be good to start with
his interest."

Instead the start was made in Maine for the Casco Islands.
By the end of 1971, as the Vineyard and Nantucket were
waterlogged by developers, and Kennedy's study bill was in
front of the Senate, the brave Island Trust idea foundered
on the rocky legislative coasts. Senators Muskie and Smith had
taken a wait-and-see attitude, a Maine report says; in Congress
the bill was not even at committee stage. The state bill had
been amended "to a virtually impotent state." Principal op-

position was from the city of Portland, which was worried that it might lose its zoning control of the islands. "A new approach is needed," the report said.

On Martha's Vineyard, where it was five minutes to midnight, time for devising new approaches was running out. Efforts had been made to persuade Congressman Keith (rated as President Nixon's third best supporter in the House between 1968 and 1970) to file a bill to match Kennedy's Senate proposal. "I don't file bills for publicity," the congressman, who after fourteen years in Congress had just announced that he would not run again, told a visitor. Reminiscing about having filed the Cape Cod National Seashore Bill, Keith said he had caused unfavorable comment by insisting that the Seashore emphasize conservation over recreation. (There is disagreement on his commitment to matters environmental. Gerry Studds, Keith's defeated opponent in the 1970 congressional race and possible successor, said that on this issue, "of the twelve Massachusetts congressmen, Mr. Keith ranks twelfth.")

Keith announced that Senator Brooke was planning to file a Vineyard bill "much broader than Kennedy's," and that he himself was making such plans. "My bill will be more serious because it will be a recital of objectives and ways of accomplishing them," he said, but did not elaborate on what those would be. "I'm going to stay in character, which is to co-operate with local, county, and state people who share the interest. It's my way to start from the grass roots and work up, not from the top down."

On a freezing January day (4° below zero arriving at the airport) Keith confronted a shivering collection of grass-roots voters and a few disenfranchised taxpayers from the Vineyard, Nantucket, and off island in the Edgartown Town Hall. He had brought with him a proposal for another study bill (never filed) and an assortment of government employees to explain what their departments—Park Service, BOR, Army Engineers, and so both —could offer the islands. Their presentations were painfully long, lacked application to the urgent problems at hand. "Bureaucrats wrap themselves in a flag and you've had it," an embittered resident said; another remarked that Dean Swift's introduction sounded like a reading of the congressman's last campaign brochure.

It was not until after the visiting dignitaries had been entertained at lunch that islanders had a chance to let Keith know their thinking. By that time many had gone home to take off their Sunday suits, either from boredom or from irritation. "A Political Day," the *Grapevine* said. "A massive insult to the intellect."

But it had served a purpose beyond its intent. With innuendo and bombast, the power structure—which would make a bitter fight to keep the island for its own delectation in the months to come—began to reveal itself. The islands' state representatives walked in "Hasty" Keith's footsteps. "When the federal government makes a study it's a cover-up for the real thing," Arthur Desrocher of Nantucket (who had once suggested an official investigation of the Concerned Citizens) said; there was loud applause. Gregory Mayhew was not far behind: "If we're not careful, the cure may be worse than the disease." County officials Swift and Shirley Frisch (who was to become alarmingly partisan in the months ahead) thought that the County Planning Commission—which had kept the secret county plan hidden from its constituency—should be the central place for all information and action to assemble. Builders, real estate owners and agents, contractors, the Chamber of Commerce—the lineup behind Keith was not surprising, replaying the script of the lower Cape.

Kennedy's Massachusetts Desk, called on by the congressman to speak to the meeting, remarked that the senator's statement had said, "What is the best way?" that no one, including the senator, is committed to any one way. "We're waiting," Mary Murtagh said, "to hear from you."

Most political leaders must maintain the delicate balance between listening and leading to satisfy their constituencies. In the instance of the future use of the islands' land, this feat required unusual skill. Do you give the people the answer they want or the answer you think they should have? The problem, here in microcosm, was among the most stupendous difficulties of the nation in the 1970s.

Environment was a top public concern and the islands were particularly well-known natural resources. They would not slip into extinction unnoticed. Furthermore, as was already evident, they inspired men to propose and do something about their preservation. There had been private efforts, like those of the early conservationists who had donated land, raised amazingly large sums to buy land for preservation, or who thought it would be enough to preserve the roadsides, hiding development behind hedges. There had been commercial efforts such as the aborted shellfish hatchery, the restoration of Nantucket town. There was H.D. and local zoning.

But there was little evidence that the islands were looking at themselves as part of a larger unit, or, in the case of the Vineyard, as a unit at all. Grasp of the convoluted planning problems of these times was painfully parochial. As late as 1971 Vineyard planning was confined to a group with a vested interest in development which could not make use of a professional land-use plan; Nantucket's state-sponsored master plan was filed and forgotten.

It was fast becoming clear that the only way the islands can survive is to be part of something larger than themselves. Then they can be what they are, a limited resource, so used and so regarded. All the problems of the continent need not be confronted and solved in these delicate lands; they can be known as special, set aside for special use.

If they were to become part of the Cape Cod National Seashore, they would inherit the unsolved dilemmas of conservation vs. use, the flood of campers and of traffic; methods by which the flood could be stemmed and the staggeringly expensive island land acquired are not yet established. By the time they are, it would surely be too late. If the National Island Trust was used, chances are that a solution would be held up by required state participation, to say nothing of national legislation under the aegis of the BOR, which would slow the progress of the plan from paper to law by bringing in the exasperating recreation issue.

Land-use experts, lawyers, and legislators could see that the islands—neither undeveloped nor, quite yet, overdeveloped—could be a part of a wider plan. A national arrangement which would include the Seashore, its assets and problems, as a neighboring fact of life, and the Island Trust as the germ of an idea, could give the islands sufficient protection so that their value, intact, could become part of the region and of the U.S.A. Such a plan, conceived and carried out, would make history.

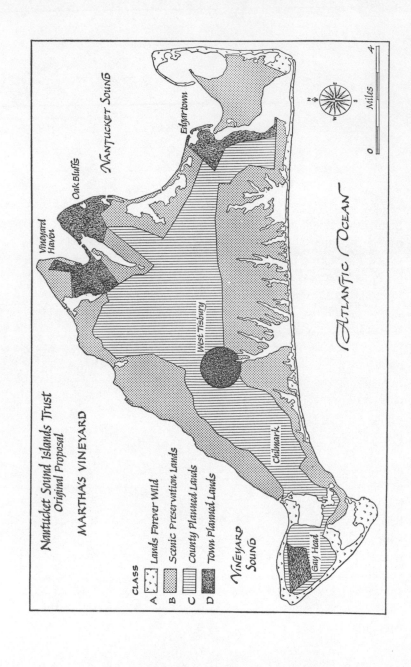

Nantucket Sound Islands Trust
Original Proposal
MARTHA'S VINEYARD

CLASS
A Lands Forever Wild
B Scenic Preservation Lands
C County Planned Lands
D Town Planned Lands

Vineyard Haven
Oak Bluffs
Edgartown
NANTUCKET SOUND
West Tisbury
Chilmark
Gay Head
VINEYARD SOUND
ATLANTIC OCEAN

Miles
0   4

CHAPTER TEN

The New Bird

Strutting through the aromatic Vineyard pine woods and dense oak groves are some long-tailed, unusually marked pheasants which had never been seen on the island before 1970. Their pedigree abounds with romantic ancestors: a pheasant with a four-foot tail from northern China, a variety found in the snowy mountains of Tibet, another which feeds on buds and tubers in the densely wooded hills of Honda, an island off the Japanese mainland. Crossed with ring-necked pheasants familiar to Americans, these birds and others have produced a new bird, prosaically named the wood pheasant by the Massachusetts Division of Fisheries and Game which bred it to flourish in the woods. Concocting a wood bird started when the pheasant population began to show an alarming decline, giving way to the exploding human population. Because of the shrinking acreage of open fields, accustomed pheasant cover, the birds were reproducing only about a third of the annual hunters' harvest where, twenty years before, natural replenishment had been seventy per cent. It was thought that wood pheasants which could live in forested parts of Massachusetts, or in submarginal lands not likely to be developed, could be a self-perpetuating population. Once bred, hundreds of wood pheasants were released in various sections of the state.

It could be a coincidence, a quirk of fate, or a gesture of the Almighty that the only place in all the Commonwealth in which the new species thrives is, amazingly enough, on the very island where not too long ago another bird species, the heath hen, perished. Scientists say that the Vineyard's marine climate and lack of predation explains the new birds' unexpected environmental selection. Although occasional birds are sighted on the mainland, it is possible, according to the state's chief game biologist, that the breed may not establish itself within the time allotted to the experiment.

Whether they make it or not, the odd proud pheasants, picking their aristocratic way through Vineyard woods in these critical years, are a striking symbol of what must be invented to replace what once was on Martha's Vineyard.

The island's natural balance has disappeared forever. After many centuries of absorbing the men who paddled, sailed, and eventually came to its shores in their flying machines, this land, lying quietly in the waters off Cape Cod, will from now on be the conscious product of the nation. One way or another, people will decide what the Vineyard will be and will make it that way. To do nothing is to donate it to the rest of overrun, overdeveloped America, just as doing nothing to manage the genes of pheasants, given the present predatory habits of hunters and land developers, would be consigning that species to oblivion.

A new bird in land use, ideas put together and tailored to fit the environment of the Vineyard, Nantucket, and other islands in the area and the complex of elements thereupon, was presented to the United States Senate early in April 1972 by the senior senator from Massachusetts. He combined certain features from the Island Trust concept, the Cape Cod National Seashore, from Senator Hart's legislation for Sleeping Bear Dunes on Lake Michigan, from the Department of Interior's new techniques for restricting land use, and other federal innovations. Adding these to recommendations of studies made of the Vineyard and Nantucket, to the judgment of advisers, and his own instinctive feel for the do-able, Edward Kennedy introduced a bill—S.3485—to establish what he called the Nantucket Sound Islands Trust.

The fate of this bill, like that of its feathered companion, awaits the impact of history. It may die in committee; it may be so strengthened, altered, or weakened as it winds through its legislative course that it will be unrecognizable. If it becomes a law and is put into effect, the way islanders live with it will be a telling force. It is and will be a product of the times, the result of interaction between man and land, man and man, the work of many minds in the social, economic, and political framework of the U.S.A. in the last decades of the twentieth century.

Whatever the islands and the nation make of this bill, in 1972 it was by its very existence the single most important event of Martha's Vineyard since Gosnold set foot on the island three hundred and seventy years before. It may become a law or it may serve its purpose by inspiring other action; it has already brought the islands' ordeal to the attention of the people. Timing is what gives it its extraordinary importance. LARGE SCALE REAL ESTATE TRANSACTIONS INCREASE RAPIDLY IN ISLAND COMMUNITIES was a three-column headline in the *Gazette* as Kennedy's idea came before the nation, and a bill for a "major bridgeway" to join the Vineyard and Nantucket to the mainland and make possible concentrated development of the area "in the style of Fort Lauderdale, Florida," was proposed, though defeated, in the state senate. As these words are written, S.3485—some version of it or successor to it—is a chance, one last chance, for the rescue of Martha's Vineyard.

The bill in essence would put the federal presence and local effort into partnership on the islands. The power does not exist in the town, county, or state law to accomplish a regional plan. A fundamental reason for the bill, Kennedy said in answer to a query, was "the lack of authority under existing laws to implement effective land use controls. S.3485 provides the necessary authority to develop effective controls . . . the best way of implementing a controlled development and preservation policy within the near future."

Unblinkingly it took on the preservation vs. use conflict, even in the same sentence ("to preserve and conserve the natural ecological environment and improve the recreational potential of the area"). It was an effort to blend the idealistic and the pragmatic, to make a structure "in which change can occur without tearing the essential fabric which makes [the island] so unique." The senator, noting in masterful understatement that "the forces and pressures of development are far stronger than the local governments and local private organizations can successfully withstand," presented a land-use plan for the region and an organization to carry it out. "We cannot delay in acting on the Nantucket Sound Islands," he said, "for if we do we have failed."

Kennedy's proposal moved the Vineyard into the main arena of the national political scene. In its original form it made these key provisions:

Land is divided into categories of use (as shown on the map). Forever wild lands where scenic or ecological values are so great that no development will ever be permitted on them; scenic preservation lands in which development shall not be increased over what it is; county-planned and town-planned lands where future growth can take place.

A governing commission, made up of members representing federal, state, county, and town governments and private conservation groups, to carry out provisions of the Trust.

All beaches are in the forever wild category and all forever wild lands have open access, although access to them is not necessarily open.

A *freeze on all new construction* of any kind from the date of the bill's introduction forward, with exceptions made where need is demonstrated.

The bill provides for acquisition of land by a mixed bag of methods, urging voluntary scenic easements which restrict land use with the big stick of condemnation and direct fee acquisition. It includes erosion and pollution control, retraining and new jobs for residents.

This bill dodged the central issue—preservation vs. use. It acknowledged the supersensitive subject of limits but did not resolve it, directing the U. S. Secretary of Interior to figure out a way of limiting access to the islands to "reasonable numbers" and to solve thorny transportation problems. It adopted the currently popular all-beaches-for-all-people concept but did not spell out what part of the beaches would have public access, or what to do about related tourist camping facilities which have been giving the national parks so much trouble. It took the present use of Vineyard land as a pattern for its division into categories, superimposing room for growth. Without a stated philosophical basis, the boundaries appear at best haphazard and at worst a response to pressure from special interests. How much or how little the islands should grow was not defined.

In one of the least daring (and to some taxpayers the most disappointing) of its proposals, the bill put the pivotal matter of growth up to the towns. Despite the record of Vineyard voters in the past few years, which demonstrated over and again that the dollar dominated decisions, Kennedy allowed for a generous portion of town-planned lands; therein, "all decisions regarding further development rest with the boards of selectmen," he said. "I feel that the legislation strikes the necessary balance in allowing for appropriate growth while at the same time preserving the unique characteristics of the islands' resources. I do not envision this limited and planned development rate as destructive of the islands." He may be proved right; but Vineyard history, and examples of land use elsewhere, demonstrate that such compromise—a little development to satisfy the business interests—is often a victory, long range, for Anyplace, U.S.A.

The bill was a beginning; Kennedy stated and re-emphasized that it was intended as a basis for discussion, refinement, and amendment. To carry out its provisions, he asked Congress for $20 million for land acquisition and $5 million for development.

"CHAPPAQUIDDICK: A BILL TO SAVE IT" was the Washington *Post* headline for a story which (inaccurately) describes the bill as designating Chappaquiddick a national park. The theme was picked up by the New York *Times* in the "Notes on People" column: "Kennedy Plea for Chappaquiddick," it said. The senator's press secretary commented that they had been aware that such remarks might be forthcoming. "What kind of a senator would he be if he hesitated to introduce a bill because Chappaquiddick was involved?"

The national press reaction was mild compared to the explosion on the Vineyard. The bill was announced to the island's elected officials at a meeting called by Thomas Hale in the office of his shipyard. Hale explained that he was part of a group which had been working on a similar proposal that had been sent to both senators and to Keith, that the group had reviewed several versions of Kennedy's bill, hoped people would see that it is "not a heavy-handed federal take-over of the islands," which the Seashore would have been, that the commission would have a majority of islanders. The bill, Hale said, "holds great promise for all of us."

A week later Mrs. Hale found it impossible to go to the supermarket without sustaining violent verbal assaults, sent substitute shoppers. Alexander Fittinghoff, the new county planner, had to make a lengthy explanation of his part in preparing the bill, and the bill itself was attacked as arbitrary, unfair, cold-blooded, a mockery of the legislative process. "I am dismayed, angry and completely outraged," Hope Mayhew Flanders, up-island real estate agent, wrote the *Gazette*. "This is the kind of thing we would expect in Russia. . . ." Fred Morgan, Jr., Edgartown selectman, said "an underhanded conspiracy had been perpetrated on the people," Cyril Norton called the bill "this rape of the Islands." Vineyarders expressed their outrage at everything from the way the bill was presented to them ("secretive," "calculated to offend") to its contents ("a gross violation of the rights of Island people as guaranteed by the U.S.A.").

Before a fortnight had passed, the Chamber of Commerce, Dukes County commissioners, All-Island Selectmen's Association, had held emergency meetings and were calling for immediate withdrawal of the bill. The Garden Club and the Conservation Society reserved judgment, the Concerned Citizens endorsed the spirit of the legislation.

"Kill the Bill" was the slogan of the angered citizens, and the Island Action Committee was organized to carry out the murder. Chairman was Robert Carroll, new chairman of the Chamber of Commerce, owner of an Edgartown restaurant, a real estate business, and a charter plane, and known to have been a friend and supporter of Edward Kennedy's. Carroll's fury did not suffer from indecision; in full-page ads in island newspapers ("If We're Not For Sale, Why Sell Out?"), in speeches and mail appeals, he swung at the enemy. The bill was "a complete lie," he said, "an unreasonable seizure," "insults the democratic process." Kennedy, according to Carroll, wants to close the island up the way it is now, to keep it for a few people. Asked what the conflict would do to his personal friendship with Kennedy, Carroll said he "had never considered him that much of a friend." "[Carroll] sees himself as the Vineyard's version of George Wallace," George Moffett, Jr., wrote the editor, "leading the populist revolt against effete snobs like me." Henry Carreiro, outspoken Oak Bluffs contractor, said at the time that there was nothing worse than a politician left out of the action or a woman scorned.

"The mob spirit . . . unleashed against the bill was outrageous," Henry Hough said, and it was indeed startling to many to confront the violence which erupted. Having read some of the fat volumes of transcript of the hearings on the establishment of the Cape Cod Seashore, I was startled only at how parallel the reactions were, so close, even in choice of language, that I was often overcome with a sense of *déjà vu*.

"We know enough to keep away from a rattler," Herbert Hancock, Chilmark selectman and contractor, said in the *Gazette*. "This bill is more dangerous . . . than all the rattlers in the U.S.A." A clue to the rage was in the images used—rattlesnakes, conspiracy, rape, the kind of thing found in Russia—which express fear of something one cannot control, the same kind of fear which, as has been seen, kept islanders from joining together in an island-wide fire department, health department, police department, or in an island-wide regional plan. It was the dread sensation of not being totally in charge.

A great deal was made of the fact that islanders had not been consulted in advance about the bill and its provisions. Forgotten were the bill's widely reported precursors—the bill to study the islands and the law students' report—and the intervening months during which neither of these measures attracted much attention or interest on the island. The matter of advance consultation on the bill was partially clarified, *post facto*, by Dun Gifford. "If some small number had had advance knowledge, they could be accused of using the information for personal gain," Gifford said. "It would have posed a real legal difficulty." Creating a land-use plan fast enough to save the islands was only possible in the way it was done, according to Gifford; there was no time for the long slow process of educating an entire citizenry to the pros and cons of new planning tools and techniques, or for what was bound to be (and later turned out to be) a lengthy and acrimonious debate.

"Something has to be done for the Vineyard, that is certain," Kenneth Jones of West Tisbury said in the *Gazette*. "Can we protect ourselves from ourselves? We have so many differences of purpose among us. . . . Can we ever get a Business Booster to sit down with an Ecology Nut to exchange views? We cannot hope to get together," Jones continued. "We can only expect one group to prevail over another." In this man's view, compromise was not workable.

The Vineyard was in no mood to recall that the definition of a camel is a horse designed by consensus. Loss of face and loss of power spiked fear—and hostility. When Kennedy wired the Board of Selectmen in each town, asking for suggestions and changes for the bill, Oak Bluffs, Tisbury, and Edgartown refused to discuss it; all we want, they said, is complete and unconditional withdrawal of the bill. In Chilmark, ex-New Yorker Lewis King joined fellow Selectmen Hancock and Mayhew in telling Kennedy to withdraw the bill: "We natives can and will protect these islands as well as anyone in Washington."

The threat of a new body politic which the bill proposed—the governing commission—stirred Shirley Frisch, a concerned, involved county commissioner, to become a prime kill-the-bill spokesman. Vying with Carroll in colorful language and attention-getting announcements, she stood up at one meeting to read a telegram from the town manager of Provincetown, congratulating her for her strong stand against the bill, warning her not to let it go through and citing Provincetown as a horrible example of what happens when the Feds move in. "Federal zoning standards on Martha's Vineyard will be a catastrophe," Gregory Mayhew, the island's elected representative to the legislature, said. His interpretation of the bill, widely shared, was that residents would lose politically and economically while the general public "would gain unlimited access to the Islands. . . . It's a fight for local control."

Fear of loss of control zeroed in on the freeze which threatened bank accounts as well as autonomy. Ten days after the bill was introduced, Senator Brooke's office released a Justice Department's opinion that the freeze was in violation of a clause in the Fifth Amendment. "The freeze is off," an Oak Bluffs selectman announced at the regular Thursday meeting. "We will continue to give building permits. . . ." "That's wonderful," a builder said, "I can sleep better tonight."

Elsewhere there was indecision; whom to believe? If the freeze was legal, any building started now ran the risk of having to be removed if the bill became a law. Although Mrs. Frisch said the whole freeze was "ridiculous" and architect Ed Cuetera thought it "an irresponsible gesture without any basis in law" no one was quite sure. Even so, housing starts went up to an estimated two or more a day before the bill was a month old.

The forever wild beaches were another major hostility target. The bill's provision moved the islands' sandy edges from private to public protection. Massachusetts and Maine are the only two states where the land between high- and low-water mark is not governed by the common law brought over from England which gives it to the King, thence to the governing bodies of the colonies, and subsequently the states. A colonial ordinance of the 1640s gives the seashore in these two states to the upland owner as far as low-water mark. This proprietary interest has been consistently upheld by the courts, expert Moses Frankel's book on the subject tells us, although the same ordinance gave struggling colonists the free fishing and fowling rights so badly needed then to eke out a living in the not very fertile wilderness. Access to the seashore for other purposes (except for sailing to another man's house) is not part of the law.

Kennedy proposed to put into law the change from colonial to contemporary view of beaches; the needs of man in the ecosystem of the 1970s were somewhat different from those of man in the uncultivated wilderness of three centuries earlier. "The difficulty is that the public may not find ready access," a spokesman for the Conservation Law Foundation of New England remarked, while on the Vineyard many assumed that the change would open the beaches to mobs of tourists and Hancock added to the alarmist talk with a statistical ploy which proved that there could be 528,000 people on the island's beaches at one time.

Few stopped to question how the mobs would get to high- or low-water mark. Nor did those who concentrated those first hostile attacks on the Secretary of Interior stop to consider that his prominence in the bill ("The Secretary is directed to, The Secretary is authorized to, The Secretary may, shall, will . . .") was a matter of legislative language, a way of expressing the idea of a partnership with the federal presence. Instead it was often assumed that, from this day forward, whoever occupied the chair of such as Harold Ickes and Stewart Udall would spend his days in office exercising his power over the island of Martha's Vineyard.

"The bill in its present form is not acceptable to me," Senator Brooke wrote in an open letter to the islands. Keith, in his open letter, agreed, said he planned to meet with the two senators, state and local officials to see if "a way to control the island's development" could be found. Most Vineyarders who would support the bill in the months ahead, were not heard from in those first weeks. I did not attempt to follow the reaction on Nantucket and the other islands in the proposed Trust.

The kill-the-bill invective swirled through the Vineyard with cyclonic force. I undertook to describe it in the Boston *Globe*; immersed in the material for this book, the need for a strong regional plan was overwhelmingly clear in my mind, as was the assemblage of facts herein set forth which suggest that the island could not achieve such a plan independently, any more than most places in the nation have been able to do. I expressed this conclusion and urged people who care about the island to work on the bill and see it through Congress. By the time the piece appeared in early June, the wind's force had somewhat abated and some islanders had begun to support the bill. Nevertheless, I was in for a public scolding from the executive secretary of the Martha's Vineyard Chamber of Commerce in the *Globe*, from Shirley Frisch in the *Gazette*, and from the *Grapevine*, which reprinted the piece with a scathing comment entitled "Simonizing the Island." The experience deepened insight of the difficulties facing islanders who might also want to challenge the status quo.

Meanwhile, from the senator's office in Washington, where the Massachusetts Desk calmly took endless phone calls and sorted out bags of mail, and from the ubiquitous Gifford, busy interpreting the bill on the islands and in off-island gatherings in Cambridge, Boston, and New York, came the word that Kennedy had no intention of withdrawing S.3485.

Kennedy's interest in the islands and his intention to do something about it went on the record when he proposed the study bill back in the fall of 1971. As the crisis mounted during the pivotal winter of 1971–72, the major all-important move was made: the problem was brought before the national forum, "a completely different circumstance," Harvard law professor Frank Michelman, a land-use expert, said. "Here local real estate interests and narrow parochial power plays don't reach." "The United States is undergoing a value revolution in land use approach," Russell Train, chairman of the President's Council on Environmental Quality, said; ". . . it is essential to extend the public's authority over private lands if we are to provide some order and preserve some beauty in the very complex urban society of the late twentieth century."

The power plays were on a national level, giving a national perspective of the islands' needs a better chance and suggesting that the new conservation is *au fond* a political matter. Contemporary land use is not decided by the parochial mind alone, nor by latter-day Thoreaus, the tender pleas of poetic mystics, nor even by generous philanthropy. Tough, rough, and often mysterious politics is what will translate at least some of the intentions of ladies in sneakers and barefoot idealists, of engineers with early environmental warning systems and planners with plans, into reality.

Assorted political pressures played into the production of S.3485. The co-operation of the National Park Service was important. George Hartzog, director of this division of the Department of Interior, told Kennedy that he had the resources to do the study of the islands without enabling legislation, suggested that the senator get Massachusetts Governor Sargent, Senator Brooke, and Congressman Keith to join him in requesting the Service to make a study and recommendations for the islands. The elected representatives of the Commonwealth, in an unusual show of togetherness, signed such a letter with the hope of a reply "at an early date."

They had a long wait. It was not until two months had gone by that the answer arrived, a jumble of verbiage "calculated to make your blood boil," Dun Gifford said. It was an incoherent brush-off addressed to the honorable Massachusetts quartet by one of Hartzog's associate directors. "I was out of town when that letter was written," Hartzog said. "I travel a lot in my job." It is not every day that the Park Service director gets a request from four high officials, a reliable source says, nor is it every day that a staff member reverses the director's commitment to one of them; insiders suggest that the negative was directed at Kennedy and came from the White House.

Kennedy was the only one of the four signators who had taken a specific federal-level step for the islands to date. Senator Brooke, a Republican and long-time Vineyard summer resident, after cosigning the letter, promptly wrote the *Gazette* that he believed "decisions directly affecting a community should be principally decided by those most immediately involved," that he saw his role as senator "to clarify options available at the federal level." Brooke is one of the few people, of some seventy in public and private life, who, despite many requests, would not discuss his views about the islands with me for the purposes of this book; his position on matters Vineyard, therefore, is taken from the sparse public statements he has made.

Congressman Keith, unquestionably concerned about the islands, was not then ready to join Edward Kennedy in more than a letter. He was offended, he said, that he had not been consulted before the study bill was filed. "I worked closely with John Kennedy preparing the Cape Cod National Seashore legislation," Keith recalled, "and I was the one who introduced it in the House." Increasingly conscious of his loyalty to Nixon and of his approaching retirement from Congress, he was ready to proceed to do something about the islands, but in his own way.

"I want to take aggressive leadership on behalf of the islands," Governor Sargent had said, having worked for their preservation from various state positions during the many years of his service to Massachusetts. Sargent was ready to endorse a Kennedy bill and to testify in favor of it; at home, however, he had to deal with a legislature which, a politically wise Bostonian commented, "is not likely to be persuaded by poetic ecological argument." In fact certain politically potent people would be made unhappy by any drastic move on the part of the state to take the islands out of the private profit arena. Sargent's strongly protective position had support in an unexpected Commonwealth corner—the Department of Commerce and Development, which had made a study of the state's tourism potential. Growth of tourism was not advocated for its own sake; ". . . it may be wiser to by-pass opportunities for expansion," the study says. "The deferred social and economic costs, like environmental pollution and abuse, cannot be ignored against short term and short-sighted returns." On the subject of the islands: "Utmost caution needs to be exercised in the selection and development of new facilities." Sargent's signature on the letter enabled him to endorse such views.

But to Kennedy, the obfuscated negative from the Park Service was, in a roundabout way, a pressure to move ahead. The bill which Haar, Gifford, Mary Murtagh, and others on and off the islands who remain unidentified, had been working on since the Harvard students filed their memorandum, was taking shape. Gifford was sending out third and fourth drafts for comments and suggestions: "Ted is in Bangaladesh now," he said, "but when he comes back I think he will introduce the bill." When the Park Service letter finally arrived, Kennedy's staff regarded it as more of an encouragement to the senator than anything else. "Don't forget," one of them said, "he's Irish."

More significant was the little-known fact that the Islands Trust was to be administered by the National Park Service, an item quietly tucked away in Section 11b where it is mentioned only by number of the enabling legislation. Presumably the authors decided that public mention of the Park Service authority in connection with the islands would add unnecessary fuel to the already leaping flames. "Besides," said Gifford, "where else would you put it? Under the Bureau of Outdoor Recreation?" Because of this connection, Kennedy needed Hartzog's okay; and Hartzog's okay had to come from a study;

and the study, which would take several months, according to
Edwin Winge, director of the Park Service Office of Information, "could not begin until Congress and the President
have approved the Interior Department appropriation for fis-
cal 1973 . . . and I cannot predict when it will."

Putting the islands under the Park Service wing at a rela-
tively bargain price would perhaps be more persuasive to the
Nixon administration than the united front letter had been.
Thus it was in Kennedy's interest to get on with the bill.

National sentiment, moving quickly toward doing something
about the environment, was another pressure. Its urgency was
felt in the nation's Capitol. "After nearly two hundred years
there appears to be a chance that the United States will begin
to plan the uses of its land," a New York *Times* editorial said,
supporting the "giant step" in this direction of Washington
Democratic Senator Henry Jackson's Administration-approved
bill (S.632) to finance the states in making comprehensive
land-use programs, such as had been pioneered by Vermont
and Hawaii. "A growing number of planners, land-use experts
and government officials agree: The era of total local domina-
tion in the field is over," the *Wall Street Journal* said, reiter-
ating that the move is toward broadening state control, while
federal concern with areas of national value kept dozens of
ecology-centered proposals circulating through congressional
committees.

Early in 1972, while Kennedy et al. were awaiting Hartzog's
reply to their letter, Senator Jackson entered the island lists
himself, with a proposal (S.3164) which he described, in answer to a query, as legislation which could "preserve the recreational and environmental qualities of . . . approximately three
million acres of undeveloped or minimally developed island
lands." Jackson thought the Islands of America proposal "completely inadequate," remarked that since neither it nor any alternative had been introduced by the present Administration,

he had made his proposal "for a nation-wide islands conservation and recreation program." His bill noted the rapidly increasing recreational demands of the nation's citizenry for water-based activities, recommended a two-year study.

Jackson was chairman of the Senate Committee on Interior and Insular Affairs; its Subcommittee on Parks and Recreation would hear S.3485. His interest in islands encouraged Kennedy and influenced the decision about beaches, Gifford said; "Jackson's bill is evidence that it's the way the country is moving." Furthermore it was a threat of another study—more delay.

There were at that moment on Martha's Vineyard either contemplated, under way, or just completed, a study of low-income housing, a study of the airport, a study of the Steamship Authority, studies of shellfish, waste disposal, natural and historical points of interest, offshore drilling risks, an erosion study, a $500,000 water resource study, a sewer study, and others too numerous to list, to say nothing of the voluminous research of the island in the 1950s and '60s and the major Metcalf & Eddy report which came to its mournful conclusion in 1971. Money and, more importantly, time were being studied away.

"I'm an old Vineyarder and a conservationist, too," Roger Baldwin, founder of the American Civil Liberties Union, wrote to Kennedy. "The combination prompts me to applaud your intention to get some federal action to protect the islands. . . . I gather there must be some hitch." Paul Warnke, Vineyard summer visitor, Washington lawyer and former assistant secretary of defense, working with a group interested in protecting the Vineyard, had reviewed Gifford's drafts and encouraged Keith to file a bill in the House: "I have concluded that comprehensive regulation by the Federal Government is the best way to assure the Islands' preservation," he wrote the senator. "Dear Ted," wrote Gilbert Harrison, editor of the *New Republic*, who with his family lives in the summer on the edge of Menemsha Pond, "Unless some prompt, firm action is taken, a unique natural preserve will be gone—and forever. If you have a wand, wave it."

Quite suddenly, on a balmy April day, Kennedy introduced the Nantucket Sound Islands Trust Bill. "A legislative bomb," the Boston *Globe* commented. "The islanders have had two or three centuries in which to get going and time is what they no longer have." The remaining question, said the *Globe*, is whether the islands can be preserved "under a distant bureau in Washington."

The senator's timing is a matter of feel and experience, according to Gifford: "He does it when the vibes are right." Having spent three years in Kennedy's office, Gifford was neither surprised nor annoyed, he said, at not having been informed that the suitable vibes had arrived on April 11 and that on that date the legislation which he had spent some months preparing was being presented unbeknownst to him to the U. S. Senate by his former employer and friend. The bomb caught him on his way to Florida.

"Nobody ever leaves the Kennedys," a knowledgeable government official said. "Once you work for them, you always work for them." The nub of truth in what must be an overstatement might in part explain Gifford's willingness to give up months of weekends, vacations, evenings, and working hours in behalf of S.3485; it was not for a salary as he was not being paid by Kennedy—"didn't even think of asking," he said. "Land use and control is part of my psyche," Gifford commented. "I know a lot about it; the first problem Ted gave me when I went to work for him in 1967 [after a post-law school stint as special assistant to Charles Haar] was to deal with a proposal for a bridge to Naushon [one of the Elizabeth Islands] which the Forbes family was protesting. I am fascinated with the idea of preservation and my wife and children [boys ten, eight, and six], feel the same way about it. That's important."

Gifford's interest was such that during the bill's first three months he held over thirty separate meetings with various groups on the islands, charmed some, offended others, was in constant communication with Kennedy, he said, and sure the bill would go through. "I feel confident about it because I plan to be involved," he said. "I want to continue to vote in Nantucket and live in Massachusetts." If he had other ideas about the future which contributed to his intensive work for S.3485, the vibes were not right for sharing them—at least with this writer at that time.

The first big break in the kill-the-bill sentiment came in West Tisbury where year-round residents are of a less conservative cut than those in the larger, more commercial down-island towns. The old farm community which stretches across the island from Lambert's Cove on the north shore to Tisbury Great Pond on the south shelters Alley's General Store and post office, fairgrounds for the annual Agricultural Fair jamboree, complete with a ferris wheel and dart throwing; there is a quiet shady street of houses, one with the original diamond-shaped leaded glass windows, and a pond where a pair of swans faithfully produce an eye-catching flock of small cygnets each summer.

While rude refusals went to Kennedy from the selectmen of other towns, unwilling to discuss the legislation, the West Tisbury town meeting voted to have its selectmen inform the senator that the town was interested in discussing the bill; Gay Head followed the same course. Two telegrams immediately went forward to the selectmen from Kennedy: "I am delighted to hear that you will urge the residents of West Tisbury [Gay Head] to forward their suggestions to me and that there will be future meetings of the residents to discuss the bill. I look forward to meeting with you soon." A second break was when Tisbury voters refused, by a large majority, to instruct their selectmen to follow their original no-talk-just-withdraw position. These two events, according to Gifford's pulse-taking, began a shift in known island sentiment.

"VINEYARDERS ATTENTION!! VINEYARDERS ATTENTION!!" An advertisement in the *Gazette* some six weeks after the bill had appeared announced the formation of "Vineyarders to Amend and Support 'The Bill' "; John Alley, first president of the Concerned Citizens, whose brother had been one of its founders, signed the ad as recording secretary. "The Kennedy Bill with suitable amendments will become OUR BILL, an ISLAND BILL," the ad read, announcing that the organization's purpose was to gather ideas on amendments, forward them to Kennedy in Washington. Two weeks later the name had been shortened to "Vineyarders to Amend the Bill," committees organized to study beach access, commission authority, employment, boundary lines, and fair market value. Over 400 supporters were listed; in another month there were several thousand.

By the time the *Vineyard Gazette* editorial, "The Kennedy Bill Must Be Enacted," appeared on the front page of the paper late in May, supporters had come forward in its letters column, in meetings, in the endless talk all over the island. "The price of crow on Martha's Vineyard is going to go up," James Alley wrote the *Gazette*; "we can be part of the final draft if we work at it now." Stan Murphy, distinguished island artist whose murals decorate Vineyard Haven's refurbished town hall, wrote that the bill needs farseeing study, wondered how this can be accomplished "in the face of so much self-serving antagonism." Alvin Strock, the island's first developer, came out strongly for the bill as did William Honey, president of the Martha's Vineyard National Bank, and Henry Hough. "If I have to give up being a contractor," said Henry Carreiro, "I can learn something else. . . . In two years the island would have been shot." Carleton Parker was "absolutely for this bill," and would remove himself from the Concerned Citizens, of which he was president, if they were not. He did not have to. Now, official support for the principles of S.3485 came from the Vineyard's Concerned Citizens, Conservation Society, Open Land Foundation, Garden Club, with more or less emphasis on the need to study, change, or amend. The *Grapevine*, editor Kelly said, was "waiting for the real Kennedy bill to please stand up."

Kennedy sent a series of open letters to the island, circulating suggestions which had been made, asking for more, insisting that S.3485 was a working model, open for alteration. Definition of use vs. preservation began to take shape; limiting numbers of people became the subject of serious discussion; the ability of selectmen and county commissioners to think through a plan for the island was widely challenged. Gifford thought the island mood was changing, that Vineyarders were experiencing "a kind of consciousness-raising" about the problem at hand. Soon the process of co-operative refinement, as Kennedy called it, occupied one side of an impressive, official-looking copy of S.3485. It printed everything, promised nothing.

The bill began to have a life of its own, sliding into island thinking. The County Planning Commission was spurred to renew attention to the goals for the island it had started to define several years back; it had also assembled a committee which, according to its planner Alexander Fittinghoff, would submit a bill to the Massachusetts legislature at its December 1972 session, requesting that authority be given to the Planning Commission to, in effect, govern the island. "I like the idea of people responsible to their peers," Fittinghoff said, believing that federal and state representatives should be appointed from among the people on the island: "If someone makes a decision, he better be able to look you in the eye on Main Street."

The Planning Commission with the help of Dean Swift and Shirley Frisch had enlisted some fourteen island organizations in its bid for control, insisting it would have a function whether the Kennedy bill goes through or not and, its planner said, "providing a valuable forum for discussion and agreement between people who one would not suspect could agree on anything."

The presence of the bill did not hold back plans for the lots on Menemsha Neck, which had been given Forever Wild status. The threatened building there was only briefly quiescent. By autumn, Lynn Murphy filed plans for development of his lot and celebrated Columbus' arrival in America by manning the first shovel ever to turn the sand of Menemsha Neck. McNamara's proceeding for purchase of the Lucy Vincent property was also temporarily delayed: "I'm ready to go," he said, "but first the town has to figure out what effect the bill will have on the land. It is unclear for lands in towns where the category does not match the zoning." He did not comment on the bill ("If I'm to achieve my purpose, I can't get involved in *that* controversy"), and although the admirable land plan transaction which was to have been closed five days after the bill appeared might be affected by the new concept for beaches, McNamara was as intrigued, hopeful, and enthusiastic about Lucy's land as ever, an attitude which she might well have found worthy, and the transaction was finally completed.

A year before, when Boom ⌗2 was devouring island land and the Dukes County Planning and Economic Development Commission was keeping the submitted plan under wraps, when islanders dozed through interminable meetings and off-islanders indulged in carefree vacations, no one would have imagined that there might be—by virtue of some chance turns of the wheel—a Nantucket Sound Islands Trust in one form or another in the foreseeable future.

What was happening on the island was startling. Even more

so were events in Washington which brought the island into unexpected prominence and the bill to notice beyond its own capacity.

It was given broad exposure by the Republican National Committee. Senators in both parties who might never have heard of the bill became strongly for or against it. Senator Robert Taft, Jr., Ohio Republican known to be a forthright and courageous legislator, volunteered to become a co-sponsor, telling Kennedy he thought the bill an admirable proposal. Columnists James Wechsler and James Reston both remarked on the many references to the bill and the opposition to it in *Monday*, the Republicans' weekly house organ, attacking Kennedy for "another Chappaquiddick blunder." Unpleasant as it was, this prominence also brought the unplanned result of support for the bill from the environmental lobby in the capital. To get Kennedy's interest and participation in environmental matters would strengthen the growing movement; an effective method would be to encourage Kennedy's own environmental project, S.3485, obviously important to him. "I am very hopeful of Senate action on the amended legislation either in this session or early next Congress," Kennedy commented in the summer of 1972.

A second whirl of the fortune wheel was the ensuing retirement of Hastings Keith. To end his long career as congressman for the district which includes the offshore islands, by having his name on a bill which intends to preserve them, was a prospect Keith at least toyed with in the last months of his tenure, weighing the idea against his widely advertised wish for a Nixon appointment. He hired a Vineyard high school teacher to keep him informed, unexpectedly flew into the Vineyard, stating: "One thing I'd like to see accomplished is some progress on the resolution of [the islands'] problem." He had half a year left to do it.

To schedule the necessary hearings early, there had to be a

bill in the House as well as the Senate. Keith let crucial weeks pass, backing and filling. The teacher resigned, went back to teaching. Finally, just before the House adjourned in the fall, Massachusetts Democratic Representative Edward Boland filed the bill.

A third turn of the fortune wheel delivered a complete about-face from the National Park Service. At the same time as Keith's visit, Kennedy announced that the Service's celebrated study of the islands would start early in July, "specifically focused," the senator said, "on the legislation which I have introduced. . . . I look forward to the Park Service recommendations." With the hobgoblin virtue of consistency, Shirley Frisch said she had talked to the men who were making the study and that "it had nothing to do with S.3485."

A matching bill in the House, a National Park Service study, a favorably inclined environmental lobby—add these to the rising consciousness level on the island, Kennedy's convictions, and a solidifying national move toward ecological awareness, and the bill might become a law. Equally, another turn of the wheel, a new unexpected circumstance, might set it back for years, delaying it until it is too late. There are no guarantees and the time that is left for what is a traditionally ponderous procedure is desperately short, a year or two at most.

But the events of these tumultuous months have left their certain mark in people's minds and on the land. The one sure thing is that Martha's Vineyard will never be the same again. Some new use of this island will come about and some new birds will try to adapt to it.

CHAPTER ELEVEN

The End is The Beginning

As it is the end in many places in America and abroad of a long era of land use, a time when one generation after another lived on the land in more or less the same way, so it is the end of that happy carelessness on Martha's Vineyard. The end on the island has not come quietly or without pain. Because of the nature of this place it is particularly disrupting. To everyone who valued the Vineyard as it was and counted on it to stay that way, the end of the era is an elemental dislocation.

It is also a beginning.

The Vineyard, "this precious stone set in a silver sea," as Shakespeare said about his sceptred isle, has a future. This is the precise moment and ours is the generation to decide what that future will be, at once a compelling and an awesome assignment. What happens to this island in the first years of the 1970s sets its course until the rising seas engulf it in the millennia beyond the horizons of time. This is the beginning of a conscious creation.

Shall the island become a version of Anyplace, U.S.A. (summer resort division), or a place where man can fit himself into nature's form? There are cogent arguments for the Vineyard's growth and development and there is persuasive discourse for its preservation and conservation. To decide which way to go is the immediate, pressing dilemma.

The issue was not quite clear in the 1960s. There was conformity to the past, the wish that the good old days would continue, and the hope that their institutions would keep them intact—the old way of gathering shellfish, the old loyalty to town government, the old-fashioned private generosity to save special parts of the island for conservation. There was compromise for the future—a road built through the renowned wetland but with limited access, a regional plan made but not released to public view. Compromise developed a stunningly suitable idea for one piece of island land, then enveloped it with surburban zoning cut to fit the mainland pattern.

Each decision took an inordinate amount of time and energy, satisfied no one completely, and, as things have worked out, proved that it is as impossible to be a little developed as a little pregnant. Once started, both conditions, barring accident or forced interruption, proceed to the anticipated conclusion.

By the 1970s, decisions became more difficult than ever, views more divergent than ever, because it was clear to see where the course of conformity and compromise was leading. There was less and less hope that opposing ideas could merge. All that could happen, as someone said, was that one would win out over the other, leaving inevitable bitterness to deter future effort. With such antagonisms rampaging through down-island streets and up-island hills, along beaches and front porches and on the pages of island newspapers, emotion blurs intelligence and personal loyalties overcome logic.

It is almost impossible for this small island alone to resist the assumption that Growth is Good, that zoning is an all-American land commandment, that recreation, wherever, whenever, and in whatever form it is wanted, is included in the Bill of Rights. It is hard not to believe that the four-wheeled gasoline-powered invention from Detroit and the jet-driven aluminum

skybird are the Master Planners, so that we must obediently
black-top acres next to beaches for them to be parked, or a once-
fragrant heath for them to set down. It is difficult to know
what to do, here on this small island, about the conflict between use and preservation that has yet to be resolved by the
National Park Service, or about the availability of beaches. It is
painful to struggle over permitting or forbidding night clubs or
trailer camps to penetrate this island fastness; it is agonizing
to deprive an entrepreneur of an opportunity long sought, a
neighbor of a chance to make his fortune. There is no time to
make more studies to back up the best guess of town selectmen
and county commissioners (some of whom, being contractors,
surveyors, or in the real estate business, might suffer a conflict
of interest), or to beg or buy wisdom from somebody who,
magically, knows what is right.

Look at Martha's Vineyard from within its own boundaries
and its problems appear insoluble. Open it to everyone who
wants to come—the developers, builders, trippers, campers,
pizza-parlor operators—and bring their civilization with them,
and you win the contest of everything-for-everybody . . . and
lose the island. Keep it pure and you frustrate the people business and, worse, appear to be unacceptably undemocratic. The
view from within leads to compromise . . . and destruction of
the island's special character so that visitors will have a hard
time knowing where they are when they arrive here; like the
traveler in the long-remembered cartoon, they will have to look
at their itinerary and say, "This must be Martha's Vineyard because it's Tuesday."

Martha's Vineyard looks quite different when you see it as
one of several offshore islands. From Nantucket it appears a
lost cause; most people on that island think the Vineyard has
already surrendered to the Cape Cod syndrome, while from the
Cape it looks empty, undeveloped and available to the burgeoning overflow. The Commonwealth regards it as a resource

which should be protected, its tourism potential kept strictly a quality experience; the way to achieve that goal is still undefined.

Adjust the scope to focus from the larger megalopolis of the eastern seaboard, and the island's character looks different again. And from the great land mass that is the United States, it becomes a tiny dot, a microscopic replica of the present land-use enigma everywhere.

The growing consciousness about land planning in this country has resulted in a fundamental change in our approach to its problems—from the individual to local, to regional, to national. Many communities which have undertaken the struggle of what to do about land conclude that local decisions are not valid in this new era. More and more people find comfortable reassurance in the large view, the over-all need, the long-range vision. The new national policy gives money and power to the states to plan the lands within their boundaries. States which have embarked on this contemporary adventure are beginning to refine it, developing regional plans and ways to co-ordinate them. Where there are specially valuable resources which enrich the nation, the federal presence, through one mechanism or another, becomes an active partner.

By enlarging his ability to think big, man finds a way to control his greed. Because of large-scale planning, the great San Francisco Bay was not narrowed to a sluggish shallow river; Bolinas Lagoon did not become another commercial parking place for boats. Citizens in Boulder, Colorado, can look out at its unspoiled foothills; Vermont keeps some of its green mountains green.

Just before the offshore islands in Nantucket Sound were about to be forced to contribute their tiny tithe to development of quarter-acre housing, waterside recreation, and the accouterments of civilization, to lose their special qualities in order to add a drop to the bucket of insatiable mainland needs, an energetic senator applied the modern land ethic to these low-lying lands. Kennedy's proposal was a stalwart effort to bring the Vineyard—torn asunder as it was by confusion and violent contention—into the new era of land-use planning.

The plan which the senator devised takes the responsibility for this national treasure out of the hands of the few and puts it into the hands of the many, placing it before the elected representatives of the citizens of the United States. It employs the ultimate democracy to decide the island's future.

The Nantucket Sound Islands Trust looks at Martha's Vineyard as a region in relation to other islands and to other regions on the mainland and provides it with an ongoing regional governing body. It makes a start at a regional land plan, asks for the federal presence on the island and federal funds to make this possible. It is a beginning—a compromise. Perhaps it had to be. As fogbound as a Vineyard dawn is the basic issue of preserving such a natural resource just as it is, letting those who would change it into a different environment go where that already exists. The senator left the issue of preservation vs. use open for the nation to decide. He presented the people with the grave question of quantity vs. quality, of what in essence shall happen to this island—one of the nation's more blessed outposts—which now awaits judgment.

Uneven lengths of driftwood make horizontal silver streaks across a red clay bank above the sea, holding the roots of wild beach roses, beach grass, pepperbush, and one twisted pine, planted there to protect the bank from battering hurricanes and the endless action of water and sand. Great pale morainal boulders are embedded in the upper earth. No one is afraid that they will suddenly roll down, flattening whatever might be in their path; they have always been poised in that bank, it seems, left motionless by the ending of the glacier. It is a quiet beach which these banks shelter, too stony and too far from the road to attract the crowds. There are a few naked children splashing along the water's edge in the sunshine, a few gulls, a few boulders. Can America afford this place or will it, with a man-made glacier, push the boulders down?

Interviews

Alley, James: Founder, Concerned Citizens of Martha's Vineyard; Postmaster, West Tisbury.

Alley, John: First President, Concerned Citizens of Martha's Vineyard; Recording Secretary, Vineyarders to Amend the Bill; West Tisbury.

Beinecke, Walter, Jr.: Developer; Nantucket summer resident.

Brown, Richard E.: Gay Head landowner.

Brownell, Arthur W.: Commissioner, Massachusetts Department of Natural Resources.

Burpee, William: Assistant to Congressman Hastings Keith.

Carson, David: Landscape architect; Nantucket.

Cook, Calvin H.: Land planner; Manchester.

Davis, Arthur A.: Vice President of Operations, the Conservation Foundation, Washington, D.C.

Engley, Roger: Builder; West Tisbury.

Fittinghoff, Alexander: Planning Director, Dukes County Planning and Economic Development Commission.

Flanders, Leslie (deceased): First Vice President, Martha's Vineyard National Bank; executor, Lucy Vincent estate.

Foster, Charles H. W.: Secretary, Executive Office of Environmental Affairs, Massachusetts.

Freydberg, Nicholas: Chilmark resident.

Frisch, Shirley: County Commissioner, Dukes County, Massachusetts; Vineyard Haven.

Gaines, Alice: Chairman, Advisory Committee, Dukes County Conservation Council; Edgartown.

Gifford, K. Dun: Former legislative assistant to Senator Edward M. Kennedy; assistant to the president, Cabot, Cabot & Forbes Co., Boston; Nantucket summer resident.

Gilmour, Faye Neumann: Heir of Lucy Vincent.

Gordon, Milton: Lambert's Cove summer resident.

Greer, Howard: Engineer; consultant to U. S. Corps of Engineers, Gay Head Cliffs Study; Oak Bluffs summer resident.

Gutheim, Frederick: Land planner; Washington, D.C.

Haar, Charles M.: Professor, Harvard Law School.

Hale, Anne: President, Felix Neck Wildlife Trust; Executive Director, Dukes County Planning and Economic Development Commission; first Executive Secretary, Vineyard Open Land Foundation; Vineyard Haven.

Hale, Richard W., Jr.: Acting Chairman, Massachusetts Historical Commission.

Hartzog, George B., Jr.: The former Director, National Park Service, U. S. Department of the Interior.

Hornbeck, Peter L.: Associate Professor of Landscape Architecture, Harvard Graduate School of Design.

Hough, Henry Beetle: Editor, *Vineyard Gazette*; Edgartown.

Howell, Nell: Member, Dukes County Planning and Economic Development Commission; real estate broker; Gay Head.

Hughes, John: Director, State Lobster Hatchery and Research Station, Oak Bluffs.

Ingham, Merdith: New Area Studies, National Park Service, U. S. Department of the Interior.

Jaffe, Louis: Professor, Harvard Law School; Chilmark summer resident.

Joske, Pierre: Director, Department of Parks and Recreation, Marin County, California.

Keith, Hon. Hastings: U. S. Congressman for the 12th District, Massachusetts.

Kelly, Gerald: Editor, *Grapevine*; founder, Concerned Citizens of Martha's Vineyard; West Tisbury.

Kennedy, Hon. Edward M.: U. S. Senator from Massachusetts.

King, Lewis: Selectman, Chilmark.

Kraetzer, Juliet: Chairman, Trees and Roadsides Committee, Martha's Vineyard Garden Club; West Tisbury.

Larsen, Roy M.: Vice Chairman of the Board, *Time* Inc.; Nantucket summer resident.

Lee, Henry: Staff Assistant to Governor Francis W. Sargent.

Lentowski, James: Executive Director, Nantucket Conservation Foundation.

Leventritt, Frances: West Tisbury summer resident.

Linden, Richard: Aide to Governor Francis W. Sargent.

Logue, Edward: President and Chief Executive Officer, New York State Urban Development Corporation; Chilmark summer resident.

Maciel, Manuel M.: Former President, Dukes County All-Island Selectmen's Association; Selectman, Tisbury.

Madison, Luther: Selectman, Gay Head.

Matthiessen, George C.: Marine Research, Inc., Wareham.

Mayhew, Gregory: Representative for Martha's Vineyard, Massachusetts legislature.

McClintock, Morris: Executive Director, Conservation Law Foundation of New England, Boston.

McNamara, Robert S.: President, International Bank for Reconstruction and Development, Washington, D.C.

Michelman, Frank: Professor, Harvard Law School.

Morton, Ben: Former Executive Secretary, Martha's Vineyard Chamber of Commerce; member, Dukes County Planning and Economic Development Commission; Vineyard Haven.

Murtagh, Mary: Massachusetts Desk, Office of Senator Edward M. Kennedy.

Norton, Bayes, Jr.: Member, Tisbury Planning Board; Vineyard Haven.

Oakes, John B.: Editor, Editorial Page, New York *Times*; Chilmark summer resident.

Pangburn, Katharine: Member, Martha's Vineyard Garden Club; Vineyard Haven.

Parker, Carleton: President, Concerned Citizens of Martha's Vineyard; West Tisbury.

Paul, Robert M.: Program Evaluation and Development, U. S. Department of Housing and Urban Development.

Pough, Richard H.: President, Natural Area Council; Chilmark summer resident.

Prada, Maurita: Member, Edgartown Planning Board.

Reston, James: Vice President, New York *Times*; Publisher, *Vineyard Gazette*; Edgartown summer resident.

Robinson, Horace B. B.: Chairman, Chilmark Community Center; Attorney, Dewey, Ballantine, Bushby, Palmer & Wood, N.Y.C.; Chilmark summer resident.

Sargent, Hon. Francis W.: Governor of Massachusetts.

Schell, Orville: Director, Public Utilities District, Bolinas, California.

Seward, Barbara: Chilmark resident.

Silva, Beatrice: President, Martha's Vineyard Garden Club; Vineyard Haven.

Strock, Dr. Alvin: Developer; Vineyard Haven.

Swift, Dean: First Chairman, Dukes County Planning and Economic Development Commission; Vineyard Haven.

Udall, Hon. Stewart L.: Former U. S. Secretary of the Interior; Chairman of the Board, Overview, Washington, D.C.

Underhill, A. Heaton: Assistant Director for State Grants and Resource Studies, Bureau of Outdoor Recreation, U. S. Department of the Interior.

Vigil, Terry Ann: Office of Regional Affairs, Massachusetts Department of Community Affairs.

Warnke, Paul: Attorney, Clifford, Warnke, Glass, McIlwain & Finney, Washington, D.C.

Weisberg, Thelma: Selectwoman, Gay Head.

Welch, John: Former Executive, Sherbourne Associates, Nantucket.

Whipple, Charles: Editor, Editorial Page, Boston *Globe*.

Whiting, John: Department of Anthropology, Harvard University; Chilmark summer resident.

Winge, Edwin N.: Director, Office of Information, National Park Service, U. S. Department of the Interior.

Woodruff, Robert E.: Executive Director, Vineyard Conservation Society; West Tisbury.

Bibliography

(The *Vineyard Gazette* and to a lesser degree the *Grapevine* are extensively quoted throughout. Owing to space considerations, references from these newspapers are listed only when it is particularly important for one reason or another. However, every quote, whether it be from a news story, editorial, or letter to the editor, has been validated and can be found in the newspapers' files.)

CHAPTER ONE

Banks, Charles Edward, M.D. *The History of Martha's Vineyard, Dukes County, Massachusetts.* 3 vols. Vol. I. Edgartown, Mass.: Dukes County Historical Society, 1966.

Burgess, Edward S. "The Old South Road of Gay Head." *Dukes County Intelligencer.* Vol. 12, No. 1. August 1970.

Chamberlain, Barbara Blau. *These Fragile Outposts: A Geological Look at Cape Cod, Martha's Vineyard and Nantucket.* Garden City, N.Y.: The Natural History Press, 1964.

Eisenstaedt, Alfred, and Hough, Henry Beetle. *Martha's Vineyard.* New York: Viking Press, 1970.

Grau, Shirley Ann. "The Vineyard Is 'The Place to Go.'" *New York Times Magazine,* August 15, 1965.

Hough, Henry Beetle. "Escape in August to Martha's Vineyard." *Town & Country,* August 1971.

Kennedy, Senator Edward M. "S.2605, Introduction of Legislation to provide for a study of the possible extension of the Cape Cod National Seashore to include Nantucket Island, Tuckernuck Island, Muskeget Island, Martha's Vineyard Island, No Mans Land, the Elizabeth Islands, the Monomoy Island." *Congressional Record—Senate,* 92nd Cong., 1st sess. Washington, D.C., September 29, 1971.

Martha's Vineyard Garden Club, Inc. "History of the Martha's Vineyard Garden Club, Inc." Unpublished. 1971.

Massachusetts Department of Natural Resources. "Environmental Resource." *Newsletter.* No. 1. September–October 1971.

Méras, Phyllis: *First Spring.* Riverside, Conn.: The Chatham Press Inc., 1972.

Metcalf & Eddy, Inc. *Physical Features, Natural Resources and Open Space,* Dukes County Comprehensive Plan Preliminary Study Report No. 2. Dukes County Planning and Economic Development Commission, March 1970.

———. *Summary of the Comprehensive Plan for Dukes County, Massachusetts.* Unpublished draft. Dukes County Planning and Economic Development Commission, June 1971.

Packard, Winthrop. "The Heath Hen." Boston *Transcript,* April 26, 1913.

Reynolds, Quentin. "Going! Going! Gone!" *Colliers,* February 8, 1936.

Shakespeare, William. *The Tempest,* in *The Complete Works of William Shakespeare.* William Allan Neilson, ed. Cambridge, Mass.: Houghton Mifflin Co., 1906.

Shepard, Marshall, with Annotations by Wilson, Harold C. "Captain Gosnold and the New World." *Dukes County Intelligencer.* Vol. 13, No. 3. February 1972.

Sterling, Dorothy. *The Outer Lands.* Garden City, N.Y.: The Natural History Press, 1967.

Strahler, Arthur N. *The Environmental Impact of Ground Water Use on Cape Cod.* Orleans, Mass.: The Association for the Preservation of Cape Cod, Inc., 1972.

U. S. Army Engineer Division, North Atlantic Corps of Engineers. *National Shoreline Study,* Regional Inventory Report, North Atlantic Region. Vol. 1. New York, 1971.

CHAPTER TWO

Attaquin, Helen A. A. *A Brief History of Gay Head; or Aquinuih.* Pamphlet, 1970.

Banks, Charles Edward, M.D. *The History of Martha's Vineyard, Dukes County, Massachusetts.* 3 vols. Vols. I and II. Edgartown, Mass.: Dukes County Historical Society, 1966.

Burgess, Edward S. "The Old South Road of Gay Head." *Dukes County Intelligencer.* Vol. 12, No. 1. August 1970.

"Conservationists Suffer Setback over Martha's Vineyard Road." New York *Times,* August 14, 1965.

"Dispute over New Road in Gay Head Is Settled." New Bedford *Standard Times,* August 25, 1965.

Dukes County, County of. *Annual Reports.* Oak Bluffs, Mass.: Martha's Vineyard Printing Co., 1970.

Federal Reserve Bank of Boston. *Monthly Review,* September 1953.

Friends of the Island. Petition to Governor John A. Volpe. July, 1965. Unpublished.

"Gay Head Fights Road-Taking." New Bedford *Standard Times,* December 3, 1966.

"Gay Head Road Plan Rejected." New Bedford *Standard Times,* March 31, 1965.

"Gay Head Road Threatens War." Boston *Globe,* July 25, 1965.

"Gay Head Voters Name Committee in West Basin Road Controversy." New Bedford *Standard Times,* December 12, 1966.

Hough, Henry Beetle. *Martha's Vineyard Summer Resort 1835–1935.* Rutland, Vt.: Tuttle Publishing Co., 1936.

Huntington, E. Gale. "The Indians and the Explorers," in Mayhew, Eleanor, ed., *Martha's Vineyard: A Short History and Guide.*

Josephy, Alvin M., Jr. *The Indian Heritage of America.* New York: Alfred A. Knopf, 1968.

Mayhew, Eleanor, ed. *Martha's Vineyard: A Short History and Guide.* Edgartown, Mass.: Dukes County Historical Society, 1956.

Metcalf & Eddy, Inc. *Physical Features, Natural Resources and Open Space,* Dukes County Comprehensive Plan Preliminary Study Report No. 2. Dukes County Planning and Economic Development Commission, March 1970.

Nantucket Vacation Guide. Nantucket, Mass.: Poets Corner Press, August 9–15, 1971.

Native American Rights Fund. "Memorandum Re Gay Head Indians." Unpublished. Washington, D.C., July 17, 1972.

"Pressures Mount on Road in Dunes." New York *Times,* July 21, 1965.

"Right to Squawk about the Quawk, The," editorial. *Berkshire Eagle,* July 25, 1965.

Ritchie, William A. *The Archeology of Martha's Vineyard.* Garden City, N.Y.: The Natural History Press, 1969.

"Road OK'd—Birds KO'd?" Boston *Globe,* August 25, 1965.

Shepard, Marshall, with Annotations by Wilson, Harold C. "Captain Gosnold and the New World." *Dukes County Intelligencer.* Vol. 13, No. 3. February 1972.

"State to Take Gay Head Road." New Bedford *Standard Times,* November 18, 1966.

Tisbury Tercentenary Committee. *Tisbury 1671–1971*. Oak Bluffs, Mass.: Martha's Vineyard Printing Co., 1971.

Udall, Stewart, and Stansbury, Jeff. "Environment: The Indian Message." *Los Angeles Times* Syndicate in association with *Newsday*, February 10, 1971.

"Udall Backs Menemsha Review." Boston *Globe*, July 29, 1965.

"Vineyard Feud, The," editorial. Boston *Globe*, July 31, 1965.

CHAPTER THREE

Allen, Joseph C. *Tales and Trails of Martha's Vineyard*. Boston: Little, Brown & Co., 1949.

Banks, Charles Edward, M.D. *The History of Martha's Vineyard, Dukes County, Massachusetts*. 3 vols. Vol. I. Edgartown, Mass.: Dukes County Historical Society, 1966.

Bennett, D. W., ed. *202 Questions for the Endangered Coastal Zone*. Special Publication No. 6. American Littoral Society, Inc., 1970.

Council on Environmental Quality. *Environmental Quality: The First Annual Report of the Council on Environmental Quality*. Washington, D.C.: U. S. Government Printing Office, August 1970.

Daggett, John Tobey. *It Began with a Whale: Memories of Cedar Tree Neck, Martha's Vineyard*. Somerville, Mass.: Fleming & Son, June 1965.

Davis, Michael H., ed. "Sorry Charlie," *Island Monthly Reader*, September 1971.

Hough, Henry Beetle. "How Felix Neck Got Its Name." *Felix Neck Naturalist*, Summer 1970.

Hunt, Morton. "Letter from Long Island Sound." *The New Yorker*, August 28, 1971.

Massachusetts, Commonwealth of. "Chapter 130, As amended through 1969, General Laws Relating to Marine Fish and Fisheries, Sections 45–69." 1969.

———, Metropolitan Area Planning Council. *Massachusetts Open Space Law, Open Space and Recreation Program for Metropolitan Boston*. Vol. 4. April 1969.

Matthiessen, G. C., and Toner, R. C. *Possible Methods of Improving the Shellfish Industry of Martha's Vineyard, Dukes County, Massachusetts*. Edgartown, Mass.: Marine Research Foundation, Inc., May 1966.

Mayhew, Eleanor, ed. *Martha's Vineyard: A Short History and Guide*. Edgartown, Mass.: Dukes County Historical Society, 1956.

Mayhew, Eleanor Ransom, and West, Captain Ellsworth Luce. *Captain's Papers*. Barre, Mass.: Barre Publishers, 1965.

McKee, Alexander. *Farming the Sea*. New York: Thomas Y. Crowell Co., 1969.

Metcalf & Eddy, Inc. *Year Round Population and Economic Base*, Dukes County Comprehensive Plan Preliminary Study Report No. 3. Dukes County Planning and Economic Development Commission, May 1970.

Riggs, Dionis C. and Sidney N. "Whaling and Shipping," in Mayhew, Eleanor, ed., *Martha's Vineyard: A Short History and Guide*.

Whiting, Emma Mayhew, and Hough, Henry Beetle. *Whaling Wives*. Edgartown, Mass.: Dukes County Historical Society, 1965.

Woodruff, Robert E. *Executive Director's Report*. Vineyard Conservation Society. Unpublished. November 17, 1971.

CHAPTER FOUR

Citizens Advisory Committee on Environmental Quality. *Community Action for Environmental Quality*. Washington, D.C.: U. S. Government Printing Office, 1970.

Daggett, John Tobey. *It Began with a Whale: Memories of Cedar Tree Neck, Martha's Vineyard*. Somerville, Mass.: Fleming & Son, June 1965.

Falmouth Enterprise, editorial. January 19, 1968.

Felix Neck Wildlife Trust, Inc. *The White Trail: A self-guiding nature walk at Felix Neck*. Vineyard Haven, Mass., n.d.

Ford Foundation, The. *Letter*, January 15, 1971.

Hanley, Wayne, ed. *Conservation Services, Inc*. Massachusetts Audubon Society, n.d.

Hough, Henry Beetle. "How Felix Neck Got Its Name." *Felix Neck Naturalist*, Summer 1970.

————. *History of Sheriff's Meadow Foundation*. Unpublished, n.d.

Martha's Vineyard Garden Club, Inc. "History of the Martha's Vineyard Garden Club, Inc." Unpublished. 1971.

Massachusetts Audubon Society. "Conservation Education Research." *Newsletter*, April 28, 1971.

Massachusetts, Commonwealth of (Section 29-33, Chapter 93, General Laws) *As Amended, Rules and Regulations for the Control and Restriction of Billboards, Signs and Other Advertising Devices, etc*. Outdoor Advertising Division, Department of Public Works, August 15, 1969.

Massachusetts Roadside Council. *Sign By-Law*. 1971.

Metcalf & Eddy, Inc. *Physical Features, Natural Resources and Open Space*, Dukes County Comprehensive Plan Preliminary Study Report No. 2. Dukes County Planning and Economic Development Commission, March 1970.

Moffett, George M., Jr., ed. *Felix Neck Naturalist*. Vineyard Haven, Mass.: Felix Neck Wildlife Trust, Inc., Summer 1970.

"Roadhogs, The," editorial. New York *Times*, February 15, 1972.

Sheriff's Meadow Foundation. *Newsletter*. Edgartown, Mass., n.d.

Tocker, Philip. "Standardized Outdoor Advertising: History, Economics and Self-Regulation," in Houck, John W., ed., *Outdoor Advertizing: History and Regulation*. South Bend, Ind.: University of Notre Dame Press, 1969.

Trustees of Reservations. *Natural Areas, Historic Sites*. Milton, Mass., n.d.

———. "To Preserve and Protect." *Annual Report*. Boston, Mass., 1966.

———. *Wasque, a Rare Opportunity for Conservation*. Milton, Mass., n.d.

Vineyard Conservation Society. *Minutes, Board of Directors Meetings*, April 20, 1970; September 11, 1970; October 6, 1971. Unpublished.

"Visual Pollution," editorial. New York *Times*, April 3, 1972.

CHAPTER FIVE

Banks, Charles Edward, M.D. *The History of Martha's Vineyard, Dukes County, Massachusetts*. 3 vols. Vol. I. Edgartown, Mass.: Dukes County Historical Society, 1966.

"Fragile Outpost," editorial. New York *Times*, October 11, 1971.

Hare, Lloyd C. M. "Missionaries and Methodists," in Mayhew, Eleanor, ed., *Martha's Vineyard: A Short History and Guide*.

Harvard Law School Legislative Research Bureau. "Memorandum: The Preservation of the Unique Characteristics of Martha's Vineyard, Nantucket and Other Islands off the Coast of Cape Cod." *Congressional Record—Senate*, 92nd Cong., 1st sess. Washington, D.C., November 12, 1971.

Kennedy, Senator Edward M. "S.2605, Introduction of Legislation to provide for a study of the possible extension of the Cape Cod National Seashore to include Nantucket Island, Tuckernuck

Island, Muskeget Island, Martha's Vineyard Island, No Mans Land, the Elizabeth Islands, the Monomoy Island." *Congressional Record—Senate*, 92nd Cong., 1st sess. Washington, D.C., September 29, 1971.

Massachusetts, Commonweath of. *Comments and Questions on the Draft Summary Report of the Dukes County Comprehensive Plan for Metcalf & Eddy by D.C.A.* Unpublished. Department of Community Affairs, July 22, 1971.

Mayhew, Eleanor, ed. *Martha's Vineyard: A Short History and Guide*. Edgartown, Mass.: Dukes County Historical Society, 1956.

Metcalf & Eddy, Inc. *Dukes County Comprehensive Plan Preliminary Study Reports No. 1–6.* Dukes County Planning and Economic Development Commission, 1970–71.

———. *Summary of the Comprehensive Plan for Dukes County, Massachusetts.* Unpublished draft. Dukes County Plannomic Development Commission, 1970–71.

Oakes, John B. "A Plea to Stop, Look and Listen." *Vineyard Gazette*, August 27, 1971.

"Pentagon Papers of Martha's Vineyard, The." *Grapevine*, November 3, 1971.

Simon, Anne W. "To Save the Vineyard." *New York Times*, September 24, 1971.

Thomson, George B. "Memo: Dukes County Summary Report." Unpublished. Commonwealth of Massachusetts, Department of Community Affairs, July 22, 1971.

———. "Memorandum: DCP & EDC—M & E Summary Report." Unpublished. Commonwealth of Massachusetts, Department of Community Affairs, July 28, 1971.

CHAPTER SIX

Chilmark Community Center. *Report*. Chilmark, Mass., 1971.

Freydberg, Nicholas. "An Analysis of the Real Estate Assessment Listings for West Tisbury and Chilmark." Unpublished. 1970.

Hornbeck, Peter. "Guidelines and Restrictions for the Development of the Lucinda Vincent Property, Chilmark, Massachusetts." Unpublished draft. May 1970.

———. "A Preliminary Report on the Ecological Significance and Development Potential of the Lucy Vincent Property in Chilmark, Massachusetts." Unpublished. May 1970.

Hough, Henry Beetle. "Summer Resort," in Eleanor Mayhew, ed., *Martha's Vineyard: A Short History and Guide.*

Johnson, Richard B., Trustman, Benjamin A., and Wadsworth, Charles Y. *Town Meeting Time: A Handbook of Parliamentary Law.* Boston, Toronto: Little, Brown & Co., 1962.

"Landsaving, Lincoln-style." *Open Space Action.* Vol. 1, No. 2. December–January 1968–69.

Mayhew, Eleanor, ed. *Martha's Vineyard: A Short History and Guide.* Edgartown, Mass.: Dukes County Historical Society, 1956.

McNamara, Robert S. "Biographical Sketch." Unpublished. International Bank for Reconstruction and Development, 1972.

"Robert McNamara's Strange Encounter." New York *Post,* October 11, 1972.

Seven Gates Farm Corporation, Inc. "By Laws and Rules and Regulations." 1921.

Tisbury Tercentenary Committee. *Tisbury 1671–1971.* Oak Bluffs, Mass.: Martha's Vineyard Printing Co., 1971.

Vineyard Open Land Foundation. *Annual Report.* September 1, 1970–December 31, 1971.

———. *Policy Statement.* Unpublished. April 1972.

Woodruff, Robert E. *Executive Director's Report.* Unpublished. Vineyard Conservation Society, March 23 and April 20, 1970.

CHAPTER SEVEN

Allen, Joseph C. *Tales and Trails of Martha's Vineyard.* Boston, Mass.: Little, Brown & Co., 1949.

Denison, Rev. Frederic, A.M. *Illustrated New Bedford, Martha's Vineyard and Nantucket.* Providence, R.I.: J. A. and R. A. Reid, Printers, Publishers and Engravers, 1880.

Duarte, Manuel S. *Cranberry Acres Campsites.* Vineyard Haven, Mass., 1971.

Eldridge, George Washington. *Martha's Vineyard: Its History and Advantages as a Health and Summer Resort.* Providence, R.I.: E. L. Freeman & Son, 1889.

Hough, Henry Beetle. *Martha's Vineyard Summer Resort 1835–1935.* Rutland, Vt.: Tuttle Publishing Co., 1936.

Island Properties, Inc. *Waterview Farm.* Vineyard, Haven, Mass., 1972.

Kelly, Gerald R. "Anatomy of a Protest." Unpublished, n.d.

Martha's Vineyard Chamber of Commerce. *This Week on Martha's Vineyard.* August 15–21, 1971.

Martha's Vineyard Summer Institute. *Annual Session.* No. 7. 1884.

Metcalf & Eddy, Inc. *Report to Dukes County Planning and Economic Development Commission on Comprehensive Water and Sewerage Plan for Dukes County.* January 1972.

"Methodism." *Encyclopedia Britannica.* 14th ed., Vol. 15. New York: Encyclopedia Britannica, Inc., 1929.

"On Martha's Vineyard, a Waterfront Vista." *House Beautiful's Vacation Homes,* Spring–Summer 1969.

Reston, James B. "Sketches in the Sand." *Vineyard Gazette,* November 26, 1971.

"A Rural Problem: Will Martha Get Raped?" *Progressive Architecture,* June 1966.

Seaside Gazette, July 15, 1873.

Vineyard Conservation Society. *Vineyard Conservation News.* Winter 1972.

Woodruff, Robert E. *Director's Report.* Vineyard Conservation Society. Unpublished. December 2, 1970.

———. *Executive Director's Report.* Vineyard Conservation Society. Unpublished. February 10 and December 16, 1971.

Yudis, Anthony J. "Home Planning and Conservation Go Hand-in-Hand on Vineyard." Boston *Globe,* November 23, 1969.

CHAPTER EIGHT

Audubon Canyon Ranch: A Wildlife Sanctuary, a Center for Nature and Conservation Education on Bolinas Lagoon Near Stinson Beach, California. Unpublished, n.d.

Bosselman, Fred, and Callies, David. *Summary Report: the Quiet Revolution in Land Use Control.* Council on Environmental Quality, Washington, D.C.: U. S. Government Printing Office, 1971.

California, State of, Department of Parks and Recreation. *The California State Park System.* Sacramento, Cal., n.d.

Conservation Foundation, The. *Bolinas Lagoon.* Washington, D.C.: The Conservation Foundation, 1971.

———. *About The Conservation Foundation.* Washington, D.C.: The Conservation Foundation, n.d.

———. *CF Letter: a Report on Environmental Issues.* Washington, D.C.: The Conservation Foundation, May 1972.

Conservation Society of Southern Vermont, Newsletter. 1971.

Council on Environmental Quality. *Environmental Quality. The First Annual Report of the Council on Environmental Qual-*

ity. Washington, D.C.: U. S. Government Printing Office, August 1970.

―――――. *The President's 1971 Environmental Program*. Washington, D.C.: U. S. Government Printing Office, March 1971.

Ferber, Richard. *Exploring Coastal Marin*. Stinson Beach, Cal.: Curlew Press, 1969.

Fraser, Stephen. "A National Seashore Proves a Mixed Blessing for Its Surrounding County." *City*, January–February 1972.

Freese, Harry. *Trail Map of the Mt. Tamalpais Region*. San Francisco, Cal.: Thomas Bros. Maps, n.d.

Gilliam, Harold. "White Birds and Redwoods." *Audubon*. Vol. 74, No. 3. National Audubon Society, May 1972.

Graham, Frank, Jr. *Man's Dominion*. New York: M. Evans & Co., 1971.

Gregg, Harold. *Newsletter*. San Rafael, Cal.: Marin Conservation League, March 1972.

Johnson, Bernard D. "State Land Use Planning in Vermont." Unpublished speech. 1972.

Marin County, Department of Parks and Recreation. *Open Space Acquisition Program*. San Rafael, Cal.: March 15, 1972.

―――――. *Preliminary Bolinas Lagoon Plan*. San Rafael, Cal., 1971.

Marin County Planning Department. *Preliminary Marin Countywide Plan*. 1971.

Marin County Savings and Loan Association. *Modern Days in Marin*. Sausalito, Cal.: Aero Distributors, March 1966.

Marin Visitors Bureau. *Marin County, California*, n.d.

McPhee, John. *Encounters with the Archdruid*. New York: Farrar, Straus & Giroux, 1971.

Metropolitan Council of Twin Cities Area. *A Metropolitan Area*. St. Paul, Minn.: Metropolitan Council of Twin Cities Area, 1970.

Mill Valley Cyclery with San Francisco and Marin County Parks and Recreation Departments. *Bicycle Trips: Recommended Bicycle Routes*. Graphic Arts of Marin, Inc., August 1971.

Pratt, Helen M. "Breeding Biology of Great Blue Herons and Common Egrets in Central California." *The Condor*. Vol. 72, No. 4. October 1970.

Rowntree, Rowan, and Storm, David R. "Summary of Environmental Monitoring Study for the Bolinas Lagoon Ecosystem." Unpublished, n.d.

Saltonstall, Richard, Jr. *Your Environment and What You Can Do About It*. New York: Walker & Co., 1970.

San Francisco Bay Conservation and Development Commission.

Annual Report. San Francisco, Cal., 1970.

―――. *The Bay Commission: What It Is and What It Does.* San Francisco, Cal., n.d.

Sax, Joseph L. *Defending the Environment: A Strategy for Citizen Action.* New York: Alfred A. Knopf, 1971.

Summer, Mary. *Marin Conservation League—A Brief History of Its Work.* Unpublished. January 1970.

Takesita, Wat. "Commission Advises, and Hears the Public." *Independent Journal,* March 28, 1970.

―――. "Do You Know Our County Parks?" *Independent Journal,* March 28, 1970.

―――. "Four Where the Crowds Could Gather." *Independent Journal,* March 28, 1970.

―――. "Future Parks for Growing Marin." *Independent Journal,* March 28, 1970.

Train, Russell E. "Statement by Russell E. Train, Chairman, Council on Environmental Quality before the Senate Committee on Interior and Insular Affairs." *Congressional Record—Senate,* 92nd Cong., 1st sess. Washington, D.C., May 18, 1971.

Udall, Stewart, and Stansbury, Jeff. "Boulder Makes Open Space Pay." Los Angeles *Times,* April 5, 1971.

U. S. Congress, Senate Committee on Interior and Insular Affairs. *National Land Use Policy Act.* Washington, D.C.: U. S. Government Printing Office, 1970.

U. S. Department of the Interior, National Park Service. *Our Vanishing Shoreline.* Washington, D.C., 1955.

―――. *Point Reyes.* Washington, D.C.: U. S. Government Printing Office, 1970.

Vermont, State of. *Vermont Adopted Interim Land Capability Plan.* Montpelier, Vt.: State of Vermont, March 8, 1972.

―――. *Vermont Interim Land Capability Plan.* Montpelier, Vt.: Vermont State Planning Office, June 1971.

―――. *Vermont Municipal and Regional Planning and Development Act.* Orford, N.H.: Equity Publishing Corporation, August 1971.

―――. *Vermont Social and Economic Characteristics.* Montpelier, Vt.: Vermont State Planning Office, June 1971.

CHAPTER NINE

"Buying Up an Island for Its Own Good." *Life,* September 6, 1968.

Cahn, Robert. *Will Success Spoil the National Parks?* Boston: Christian Science Publishing Society, 1968.

"Changing the National Parks to Cope with People—and Cars." *U. S. News & World Report*, January 24, 1972.

Citizens Advisory Committee on Environmental Quality. *Community Action for Environmental Quality*. Washington, D.C.: U. S. Government Printing Office, 1970.

Conti, John V. "A Quiet Revolution: With Little Fanfare, States Are Broadening Control Over Land Use." *Wall Street Journal*, June 28, 1972.

Damore, Leo. *The Cape Cod Years of John Fitzgerald Kennedy*. Englewood Cliffs, N.J.: Prentice-Hall, 1967.

Eighty-ninth Congress. S.3035. *Public Law 89–665*. Washington, D.C.: U. S. Government Printing Office, October 15, 1966.

Eighty-seventh Congress. S.857. *Public Law 87–126 Cape Cod National Seashore*. Washington, D.C.: U. S. Government Printing Office, August 7, 1961.

"Fragile Outpost," editorial. New York *Times*, October 11, 1971.

Frankel, Moses M., LL.B. *Law of Seashore, Waters and Water Courses; Maine and Massachusetts*. Forge Village, Mass.: The Murray Printing Company, 1969.

Harvard Law School Legislative Research Bureau. "Memorandum: The Preservation of the Unique Characteristics of Martha's Vineyard, Nantucket and Other Islands off the Coast of Cape Cod." *Congressional Record—Senate*, 92nd Cong., 1st sess. Washington, D.C., November 12, 1971.

Herr, Philip B., & Associates, Planning Consultants. *Cape Cod National Seashore Economic Impact Study—1969*. Washington, D.C.: U. S. Department of the Interior, National Park Service, September 1969.

Hill, Gladwin. "Pristine Preserves or Popcorn Playgrounds?" *Saturday Review*, January 1, 1972.

Honan, William H. "Will He Say: 'Help Me Finish What My Brothers Began'?" New York *Times Magazine*. November 28, 1971.

Kennedy, Senator Edward M. "S.2605, Introduction of Legislation to provide for a study of the possible extension of the Cape Cod National Seashore to include Nantucket Island, Tuckernuck Island, Muskeget Island, Martha's Vineyard Island, No Mans Land, the Elizabeth Islands, the Monomoy Island." *Congressional Record—Senate*, 92nd Cong., 1st sess. Washington, D.C., September 29, 1971.

———. *Statement by Senator Edward M. Kennedy on the Revised Master Plan for Cape Cod National Seashore*. September 9, 1970.

Massachusetts, Commonwealth of. *Appendix A: Guidelines for Preliminary Reports (Historic Districts)*. Unpublished. 1971.

―――. "Chap. 359. An Act Further Regulating the Law Establishing Historic Districts." *1971 Acts and Resolves.* June 3, 1971.

―――. *Manual for the Establishment of Historic Districts—Draft II.* Unpublished, 1971.

Massachusetts Historical Commission. *Guide to Inventory Techniques.* Published by John F. X. Davoren, Secretary of the Commonwealth, Chairman, Massachusetts Historical Commission, 1970.

McPhee, John. "George Hartzog—Ranger." *The New Yorker,* September 11, 1971.

Nantucket Conservation Foundation, Inc. *Nantucket Conservation Foundation, Inc.* Bethlehem, Pa.: Laros Printing Company, 1970.

Nantucket Historical Trust. *Jared Coffin House.* Nantuckct, Mass., n.d.

"Nantucket Is Alive and Well, Thank You." *AIA Journal,* August 1970.

Nantucket Island Chamber of Commerce. *Nantucket for the Year of 1971.* Nantucket, Mass., 1971.

Nantucket Vacation Guide. Nantucket, Mass.: Poets Corner Press, August 9–15, 1971.

Natural Resources Council of Maine. *Maine Environment.* December 1971.

"Senator Kennedy's Proposal," editorial. *Vineyard Gazette,* October 8, 1971.

Udall, Stewart L. *Remarks of Secretary of the Interior Stewart L. Udall at Dedication of Cape Cod National Seashore. Cape Cod, Massachusetts.* U. S. Department of the Interior, May 30, 1966.

U. S. Congress, Senate subcommittee on Public Lands of the Committee on Interior and Insular Affairs. *Hearings on S.2636, a Bill to Provide for the Establishment of Cape Cod National Seashore Park.* 86th Cong., 1st and 2nd sess.; 87th Cong., 1st sess. Washington, D.C.: U. S. Government Printing Office, 1960, 1961.

U. S. Department of the Interior, Bureau of Outdoor Recreation. *Islands of America.* Washington, D.C.: U. S. Government Printing Office, 1970.

―, National Park Service. *Areas Administered by the National Park Service.* Washington, D.C., December 31, 1971.

―――. *Cape Cod National Seashore, a Proposal.* Washington, D.C., 1959.

―――, *The Cape Cod Story.* Washington, D.C., n.d.

―――. *Master Plan: Cape Cod National Seashore/Massachusetts.* Washington, D.C., October 7, 1970.

―――. *nps: criteria for parklands.* Washington, D.C.: U. S. Government Printing Office, 1971.

———. *A New Park Concept*. Washington, D.C., December 8, 1970.

———. *Our Vanishing Shoreline*. Washington, D.C., 1955.

———. *Some Techniques of Environmental Protection of Federal Park and Cultural Values*. Washington, D.C., n.d.

—, Office of the Secretary. *Cape Cod National Seashore Establishment Set for May 30th*. Washington, D.C., May 5, 1966.

Woodruff, Robert E. *Executive Director's Report*. Vineyard Conservation Society. Unpublished. January 20 and March 9, 1972.

CHAPTER TEN

Cheshire, Maxine. "Chappaquiddick: A Bill to Save It." *Washington Post*, April 13, 1972.

Conservation Foundation, The. *CF Letter: A Report on Environmental Issues*. Washington, D.C.: The Conservation Foundation, December 1971.

Conti, John V. "A Quiet Revolution: With Little Fanfare, States Are Broadening Control over Land Use." *Wall Street Journal*, June 28, 1972.

Eighty-ninth Congress. *S.3035. Public Law 89–665*. Washington, D.C.: U. S. Government Printing Office, October 15, 1966.

Eighty-seventh Congress. *S.857. Public Law 87–126 Cape Cod National Seashore*. Washington, D.C.: U. S. Government Printing Office, August 7, 1961.

Hollings, Senator Ernest F., Magnuson, Senator, and others. "S.582, Introduction of the National Coastal and Estuarine Zone Management Act of 1971." *Congressional Record—Senate*, 92nd Cong., 1st sess. Washington, D.C., February 4, 1971.

Hulett, Stanley W., Associate Director, National Park Service. *Response to Senators Brooke & Kennedy, Governor Sargent & Representative Keith*. Washington, D.C.: U. S. Department of the Interior, National Park Service, March 23, 1972.

Hull, Daniel. Guest editorial, Boston *Globe*, July 10, 1972.

Jackson, Senator Henry. "S.3164, Introduction of the National Islands Conservation and Recreation Act." *Congressional Record—Senate*, 92nd Cong., 2nd sess. Washington, D.C., February 14, 1972.

Kastarlak, Bulent I. *Tourism and Its Development Potential in Massachusetts*. 5 vols. Commonwealth of Massachusetts, Department of Commerce and Development, 1970.

Kennedy, Senator Edward M. *An Act to establish the Nantucket Sound Islands Trust*. Unpublished drafts. Office of the Senator, January 3 and February 11, 1972.

————. *Memorandum: Analysis of Constructive Suggestions for Refinements in S.3485.* Office of the Senator, May 3, 1972.

————. *Open Letter from Senator Edward M. Kennedy.* Office of the Senator, May 3, 1972.

————. *Open Letter from Senator Edward M. Kennedy.* Office of the Senator, May 18, 1972.

————. "S.2605, Introduction of Legislation to provide for a study of the possible extension of the Cape Cod National Seashore to include Nantucket Island, Tuckernuck Island, Muskeget Island, Martha's Vineyard Island, No Mans Land, the Elizabeth Islands, the Monomoy Island." *Congressional Record—Senate,* 92nd Cong., 1st sess. Washington, D.C., September 29, 1971.

————. "S.3485, Introduction of a Bill to establish the Nantucket Sound Islands Trust," *Congressional Record—Senate,* 92nd Cong., 2nd sess. Washington, D.C., April 11, 1972.

————. *S.3485, Proposed Amendments.* Unpublished. Office of the Senator, May 18, 1972.

————. "S.3485, Proposed Amendments." *Congressional Record—Senate,* 92nd Cong., 2nd sess. Washington, D.C., June 20, 1972.

————. *Speech on Nantucket Sound Islands Trust Legislation.* Unpublished draft. Office of the Senator, February 29, 1972.

————. *Statement of Senator Edward M. Kennedy on Park Service Response.* Office of the Senator, March 1972.

————, with Senator Brooke, Governor Sargent, Representative Keith. *Request to George B. Hartzog, Jr., Director, National Park Service.* January 22, 1972.

"Land Use—or Giveaway?" editorial. New York *Times,* July 10, 1972.

"Notes on People: Kennedy Plea for Chappaquiddick." New York *Times,* April 14, 1972.

"An Offshore Islands Problem," editorial. Boston *Sunday Globe,* April 23, 1972.

Pollack, Bill, with Wentworth, Bernard C. "Pheasants of the Future." *Massachusetts Wildlife,* May-June 1968.

Reston, James B. "Sketches in the Sand." *Vineyard Gazette,* June 23, 1972.

Sax, Joseph L. *Defending the Environment: A Strategy for Citizen Action.* New York: Alfred A. Knopf, 1971.

Simon, Anne W. "The Future of Martha's Vineyard." Boston *Globe,* June 5, 1972.

Train, Russell E. *Statement upon Release of the Report "The Quiet Revolution in Land Use Control" by Fred Bosselman and David Callies.* Washington, D.C.: Council on Environmental Quality, January 11, 1972.

U. S. Congress, Senate Committee on Interior and Insular Affairs. *National Land Use Policy Act, Report of the Committee together with Supplementary Views to Accompany S.3354.* 90th Cong. Washington, D.C.: U. S. Government Printing Office, 1970.

————, Senate Subcommittee on Oceans and Atmosphere of the Committee on Commerce. *Coastal Zone Management, Hearings on S.582, S.632, S.638, and S.992.* 91st Cong., 1st sess. Washington, D.C.: U. S. Government Printing Office, 1971.

————, Senate Subcommittee on Public Lands of the Committee on Interior and Insular Affairs. *Hearings on S.2636, a Bill to Provide for the Establishment of Cape Cod National Seashore Park.* 86th Cong., 1st and 2nd sess. Washington, D.C.: U. S. Government Printing Office, 1960.

————. *Hearings on S.857, to Provide for the Establishment of Cape Cod National Seashore Park.* 87th Cong., 1st sess. Washington D.C.: U. S. Government Printing Office, 1961.

U. S. Department of the Interior, National Park Service. *Some Techniques of Environmental Protection of Federal Park and Cultural Values.* Washington, D.C., n.d.

Vineyard Conservation Society. *Minutes, Board of Directors Meeting.* Unpublished. March 24, 1971.

————. *Special Meeting Minutes.* Unpublished. April 18 and May 4, 1972.

Vineyard Open Land Foundation. *Statement.* Unpublished. June 2, 1972.

Wechsler, James A. "GOP Kennedy-Watchers." New York *Post*, April 20, 1972.

Woodruff, Robert E. *Executive Director's Report.* Vineyard Conservation Society. Unpublished. November 11, 1971.

(continued from front flap)

acclaimed, are about to be destroyed.

Anne Simon demonstrates that time is running out for Martha's Vineyard—for all of us. While this book focuses on one small island, it pinpoints the pressing question facing the United States; What use shall we make of our land?

Against a background of insular New England tradition, Indian settlement, and whaling history, the issue is fiercely debated by islanders, off-islanders and, because of the Vineyard's renown, the national press. By describing what has happened to bring the island to the edge of disaster, the author makes a major national dilemma an intimate, understandable, and often shocking story. Its conclusion has far-reaching implications.

The author, a devoted Vineyarder, graduated from Smith College, received a Master's Degree from Columbia University's School of Social Work, was a TV critic for *The Nation* and later for *McCalls*. She has travelled widely abroad and at home on journalistic assignments; articles by Mrs. Simon have appeared in *Saturday Review, Good Housekeeping,* the New York *Times* OpEd page and other periodicals. Her two previous books are *Stepchild in the Family* and *The New Years: A New Middle Age*. She has four children, three grandchildren, all Vineyarders.

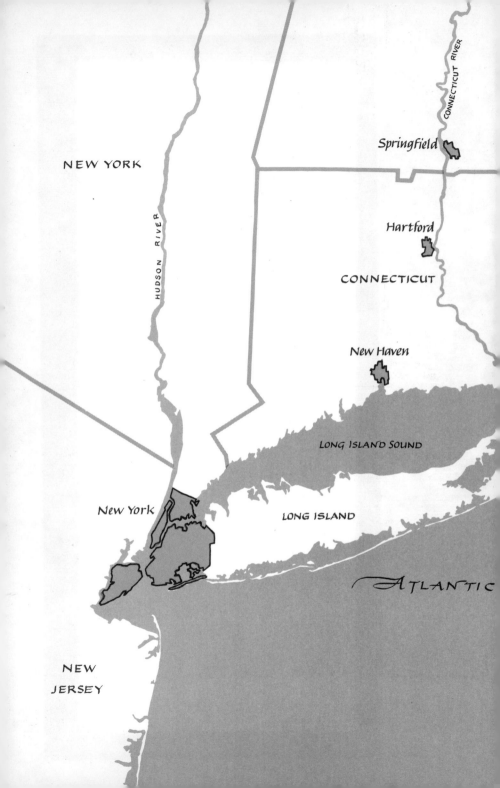